THE BEST OF
VEGETARIAN
CUISINE

THE BEST OF VEGETARIAN CUISINE

by Sarah Brown

RANDOM HOUSE
NEW YORK

Library of Congress cataloging in publication data
Brown, Sarah
   The best of vegetarian cuisine.

   Includes index.
   1. Vegetarian cookery. I. Title
   TX837.B875   1985   641.5'636   84-18294
   ISBN 0-394-54374-2

Printed in Italy by Arnoldo Mondadori, Verona

Contents

The KITCHEN PANTRY

The RECIPES

MENU AND MEAL PLANNER

Introduction

A vegetarian does not eat fish, meat or poultry and may or may not eat dairy products and eggs. People adopt this way of life for various reasons, of which the main ones are usually humanitarian or to do with ecology or health. Those who do so on humanitarian grounds have a basic respect for life in all its forms and will avoid not only meat but any product obtained by exploiting animals. Some vegetarians extend this to include all dairy products and eggs, however humanely they may be produced, and may also avoid honey. Concern for ecology leads many to prefer plant protein, which is far more economical to produce than animal protein. From the health point of view, the case for vegetarianism is a strong one. Most of the so-called diseases of civilization, including heart disease, high blood pressure, strokes, diabetes, obesity and diverticulitis, are linked with, if not directly attributable to, the conventional Western diet, which is high in animal fats, salt and sugar but low in fiber. A vegetarian diet not only replaces animal fats with vegetable ones but often cuts down on the total fat intake, since in the average diet a third of the fats come from meat and another third from dairy products. Eating cereals, legumes, fruits and vegetables will ensure adequate fiber intake. Many vegetarians eat whole foods, avoiding the high levels of added salt and sugar in many processed foods.

All the recipes in this book are vegetarian, and dairy produce and eggs are used, although in some recipes an alternative has been suggested. Whole, unrefined foods are invariably used in preference to processed.

Whatever your basic reasons for being interested in vegetarianism, it is a good idea to analyze your existing diet so that you are aware of the changes that need to be made. You may want to cut out animal products completely or perhaps you'd like to have vegetarian food as an occasional alternative to meat. If you want to give up animal products, your body will adjust better if you don't make too violent a change. Start by eating less meat than you have been used to; or give up red meat first, then chicken and fish. Get into the habit of cooking a different type of legume or grain once or twice a week. Whether your emphasis is vegetarian or on whole foods, don't throw out all your existing stores and restock with new ones. Gradually substitute vegetable oils for animal cooking fats and vegetable stock for meat stock; try small amounts of brown rice and whole-wheat pasta and flour. You could try having one or two vegetarian days a week, building up to more gradually. Eating out and traveling need forethought. If you are invited out for a meal, make sure that your friends know in advance exactly what you can and cannot eat. When making hotel reservations, state clearly your needs as a vegetarian and make sure they can be catered to. I find it a good idea to travel with some "emergency" rations, such as dried fruit and nuts, to tide me over if necessary. There are vegetarian societies in both the United States and Great Britain whose purpose is to provide information and guidance. I hope that this book and the recipes in it will help you to appreciate and enjoy vegetarianism.

The
KITCHEN PANTRY

One of the joys of trying out a different style of cookery is undoubtedly discovering a fresh range of dishes with new combinations of tastes and textures. Based as it is on the cuisines of many different countries, vegetarian cookery draws on a wide variety of ingredients, some of which will be familiar, while others, such as sea vegetables and soybean products, less so. This section is intended as a guide to those products that play a central part in vegetarian cookery and that are featured in the recipes in this book, from staples such as cereals and legumes to seasonings and flavorings.
Naturally, there's no need to buy every type of bean or cereal product shown here—you can gradually add to your stock as you try out different recipes.
Illustrated, too, is a selection of fresh foods, including less common vegetables and whole-food or vegetarian substitutes for animal products. For further information on buying, storing, preparation and cooking, turn to pages 204-223.

Grains

Center: **Whole-wheat flour** (*left*)**, whole wheat berries** (*center*)**, Couscous** (*right*)

Wheat flakes   **Bulgur wheat**   **Cracked wheat**   **Wheat germ**

Semolina   **Unbleached white flour**   **Bran**   **Wheatmeal flour**

WHEAT (*Triticum vulgare*) is grown over more of the earth's surface than any other grain and is available in a wide variety of forms. The **whole wheat grain** or **berry** is the most nutritious form, with none of the germ or outer layers removed; when cooked, it is chewy and substantial.

Cracked wheat is produced by cracking whole wheat berries between rollers so that they will cook more quickly, in only 20 minutes. If they are then hulled, steamed and roasted, they are known as **bulgur wheat** and need little or no cooking. **Wheat flakes** are similar, but rolled flatter and often toasted to a golden brown.

All of the above are variants of the whole wheat grain, which is often subjected to further milling to produce lighter, more widely desirable results. In the process two very valuable constituents are lost: **wheat germ** and bran. Wheat germ is the heart of the wheat and contains most of the nutrients. Bran is the outer covering of the grain and is valued particularly for its high fiber content. Both wheat germ and bran can be bought separately and added to breakfast cereals, breads and cakes or used as toppings.

Whole-wheat flour, made from the whole grain, is available stone-ground or, more commonly, roller-milled.

Wheatmeal flour retains a lot of the nutrients, but has 15-19 percent wheat (in practice, the germ and most of the bran) removed to make it lighter. White flour has had all the bran and germ removed; **unbleached white flour** is preferable as it has not been chemically treated.

Semolina is produced from the starchy part of the grain, the endosperm. It is available as medium or coarse meal and used for puddings or gnocchi. Semolina from durum wheat is used for making pasta commercially. Fine semolina grains coated with flour are known as **couscous,** the basis of the North African dish.

Oats (*Avena sativa*) The whole oat grain is known as a groat. It is not often seen in this form since although it can be used—for instance for making breakfast cereal—it takes time to cook.

Oatmeal is now generally available in three grades—**coarse, medium** and **fine**—but used to be available in far more. A little added to wheat flour gives taste to bread.

Millet (*Panicum miliaceum*) is prolific and easy to grow but has only recently been considered in the West although it has long been an important crop in Africa and Asia, especially Northern China. It is

Rolled oats are produced from groats that have been broken down by rolling. Heat can also be applied to prevent the oil from becoming rancid and thus improve shelf life.

Jumbo oat flakes are similar to rolled oats but, as their name implies, larger. They can also be heat-treated.

related to sorghum, an important crop in Africa, and is the staple food of the Hunzas, the Himalayan people famous for their longevity. **Millet flakes** can be used like other flakes in cereals and as toppings.

Grains

RICE (*Oryza sativa*) Brown rice is, like the wheat berry, the whole natural grain, unprocessed. The type most commonly found is **long-grain,** or *indica,* rice much grown in India.

Short-grain or *japonica* rice is, as its name indicates, popular in Japan as well as in parts of China. Another type of short-grain rice is grown in Italy and used for risottos.

Basmati rice has the finest flavor of any easily available white rice, although like all white rices it has had a high proportion of nutrients removed by milling.

Rice flakes are processed to be quick-cooking, in about 10 minutes, and can be used to thicken soups and casseroles.

Rice flour is usually made from white rice. Because of its lack of gluten, it is useful for those on low-gluten diets.

WILD RICE (*Zizania aquatica*) is not a rice although it looks like one. Its grains are longer and more slender, dark brown when raw, slightly purplish when cooked. Native to North America.

BUCKWHEAT (*Fagopyrum esculentum*) Also sometimes called Saracen corn or wheat (it was supposed to have been introduced to Europe by the Crusaders).

Roasted buckwheat grains are popular for their flavor—roasting is the usual way of preparing the grains for cooking.

Buckwheat flour is strong and savory, and is often mixed with wheat flour. It is good in pancakes and is used in Japan to make noodles called soba.

Coarse cornmeal   **Fine cornmeal**

CORN (*Zea mays*) Known as maize in Europe, this originated in Central America. **Popcorn** is a variety with a very hard endosperm, which explodes when heated.

Another variety is used to produce **cornmeal,** both **coarse** and **fine;** this is sometimes sieved, which removes the bran and some of the fiber but makes little difference nutritionally.

Barley flakes   **Barley flour**

BARLEY (*Hordeum vulgare*) Still important for food in some parts of the world, particularly Japan, although elsewhere it has been superseded as a food crop and is used mainly for brewing. It compares well with other grains nutritionally and is particularly high in niacin.

Like other cereals, it is available in flakes and as flour. The inclusion of a little flour adds a distinctive sweet taste to bread. It is one of the oldest food crops and was known to the Hebrews, Greeks and Romans, as well as in Tibet.

Rye flakes   **Rye flour**

RYE (*Secale cereale*) Popular in Northern and Eastern Europe, and parts of Russia, where its distinctive sour taste is much appreciated, particularly in bread. The groats can be made into dark rye flour, or they can be

partially husked and made into light flour. Although rye contains gluten, it is not the same sort as that in wheat and will not leaven bread, so that most rye bread is in fact made from a mixture of rye and wheat.

Beans, peas and lentils

Lima beans

Butter beans

Lima beans and Butter beans (*Phaseolus lunatus*) Originating from tropical America, these are very similar, but lima beans tend to be smaller and sweeter and are an ingredient of the traditional American Indian dish succotash.

Black beans (*Phaseolus vulgaris*) The shiny black outside contrasts with the white inside. Popular in Latin America. Not the same as the black bean used in China, which is a type of soybean, fermented, salted and used as flavoring.

Aduki beans (*Phaseolus angularis*) Tiny, round, hard, dark-red beans, also known as adzuki beans; very popular in the Far East, especially Japan. Rich in protein, they can also be made into flour.

Red kidney beans (*Phaseolus vulgaris*) Like all kidney beans, these are native to the New World. This variety is particularly popular in Mexican cookery. Also called chili bean.

Haricot beans (*Phaseolus vulgaris*) One of the best known varieties, also known as white haricots, navy beans or Great Northern beans. The original bean used in Boston baked beans.

Ful medames (*Lathyrus sativus*) These small dark-brown beans are especially popular in Egypt, where they are combined with hard-boiled eggs to make what is almost the Egyptian national dish.

Pinto beans (*Phaseolus vulgaris*) Another variety of haricot bean, not unlike the speckled Italian borlotti beans. The name means "colored". They turn pink when cooked.

Flageolet beans (*Phaseolus vulgaris*) Very popular in both France and Italy, with an unusually delicate, subtle taste and an attractive pale green color.

Cannellini (*Phaseolus vulgaris*) A variety of haricot or kidney bean much appreciated in Italy. A similar bean is widely grown in Argentina.

Broad or fava beans (*Vicia faba*) Once important in Europe, but yielded popularity to the various kidney beans, possibly because broad beans contain substances that, if eaten in quantity, can cause a blood disease known as favism.

Whole mung beans

Split mung beans

Mung beans (*Phaseolus aureus*) Native to tropical Asia and still one of the most widely grown legumes. The seeds are mainly used as a vegetable but are also popular, especially in China and the U.S., as an important source of bean sprouts.

Black-eyed peas (*Vigna unguiculata*) Also known as cowpeas and native to Central Africa; taken to the New World in the 16th century. Not only the seeds are eaten: the immature pods can be cooked and the young shoots and leaves can be boiled like spinach or eaten raw in salads.

Soybeans (*Glycine max*) The most nutritious bean of all, containing all the essential amino acids. Originally from China, where their value has been recognized for nearly 5,000 years. Can be made into curd, paste or sauce.

Chick peas (*Cicer arietinum*) Highly popular all over the Mediterranean and the Middle East, as well as in India where they are known as Bengal gram (the Indian word *gram* means "legume"). They are also known as garbanzos. High in protein, they are very nutritious and can be ground into flour.

Split green peas

Continental lentils

Brown lentils

Whole green peas

Split yellow peas

Split red lentils

Peas (*Pisum sativum*) Common peas are now mostly eaten fresh, in which form they can be canned or frozen, but were formerly valuable as a dried vegetable. They are available split or whole.

Lentils (*Lens esculenta*) One of the oldest crops, cultivated since prehistoric times; originally from the eastern Mediterranean, now found all over the Middle East and India. Available whole or split and in a variety of colors.

Nuts and seeds

Whole almond

Shelled almond   **Blanched almond**   **Slivered almonds**

Almonds (*Prunus amygdalus*) The most popular nut of all. The sweet variety is the kind normally used; bitter almonds are toxic, but the unpleasant taste is a deterrent. Almonds have the highest protein content of any nut and are also rich in minerals, especially calcium.

Ground almonds

Whole hazelnuts   **Shelled hazelnuts**

Hazelnuts, cobnuts, filberts (*Corylus avellana; C. maxima*) Widely grown in Italy, France and Turkey, they are low in fat and high in vitamins B and E.

Cashews (*Anacardium occidentale*) The unusual fruit looks like an apple with the kidney-shaped nut hanging beneath it. The nutshell contains an acid and is removed before the nuts are sold.

Whole walnut   **Shelled walnuts**

Walnuts (*Juglans regia; J. nigra*) Good sources of protein, vitamins, minerals and unsaturated fats, especially the black, or American, walnut. Green or unripe walnuts are rich in vitamin C; they are delicious pickled.

Brazil nuts (*Bertholletia excelsa*) From the Amazon basin, the nuts cluster like orange segments inside a woody fruit. They have the highest fat content of any nut and are also rich in minerals.

Whole Brazil nut   **Shelled Brazil nut**

Whole pecans

Shelled pecans

Pecans (*Carya illinoensis*) Related to walnuts, but richer, milder and subtler in flavor. They are much appreciated in their native North America. Hickory and bitternut are also related.

Whole chestnut   **Shelled chestnut**   **Shelled and peeled chestnut**

Sweet chestnuts (*Castanea sativa*) Native to Southern Europe and unlike most other nuts in that they are very starchy and low in protein. Both the hard shell and the thin inner skin need to be removed. Often also available dried.

Whole pistachios

Shelled pistachios

Pine nuts (*Pinus pinea*) The seeds of various pines, chiefly the stone pine of the Mediterranean, and also known as pignolias.

Pistachios (*Pistacia vera*) Native to the Mediterranean and Middle East, where they are eaten as a snack. Prized for their bright green color.

Sunflower seeds (*Helianthus annuus*) Rich in proteins and minerals and containing 40 percent unsaturated oil, they make an excellent snack.

Whole (unshelled) peanuts

Shelled peanuts, with and without skin

Chinese water chestnuts (*Eleocharis tuberosa*) are not true nuts, but tubers of a sedge, although with their crisp texture they can be used as nuts.

Peanuts (*Arachis hypogaea*) Sometimes called groundnuts, these are not true nuts but underground legumes.

Pumpkin seeds (*Cucurbita maxima*) Good source of proteins, fats and minerals, especially zinc.

Fresh coconut

Desiccated coconut

Coconut (*Cocos nucifera*) The coconut palm is a source of fiber, soap and animal fodder, as well as oil and other edible products. The dried flesh may be compressed into blocks or sold as flakes or powder.

Creamed coconut

Sesame seeds (*Sesamum indicum*) Of African origin, now an important crop in the Middle and Far East, as well as in Mexico. Excellent source of oil.

Linseeds (*Linum usitatissimum*) The seeds of the flax plant. The Greeks and Romans used them as food.

15

Dried fruit

Dried peach

Dried nectarine

Whole sulfured apricot

Hunza apricot

Half sun-dried apricot

Half unsulfured apricot

Peaches and Nectarines (*Prunus persica*) come mainly from Australia, China and California. Some Chinese varieties are preserved in sugar; this will be stated on the box or package.

Dried apple ring

Apricots (*Prunus armeniaca*) Mainly grown in the Far East, North Africa and California. Some dried apricots come from Turkey and Australia. The best of all are considered to be the wild, or Hunza, apricots from the Himalayas. Apricots contain more protein than other dried fruits.

Apples (*Malus communis*) are usually peeled, cored and cut into rings; occasionally they are cut into segments. The whiter the apple, the more sulfur has been used to preserve it.

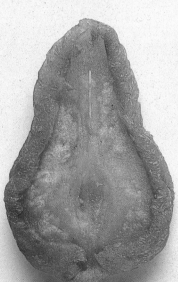

Pears (*Pyrus communis*) are not peeled before drying. Some Chinese varieties are preserved, like peaches, in sugar or glucose syrup to retain their moisture content.

Bananas (*Musa spp.*) dry most successfully when fully ripe with a high sugar content; they may be dried in pieces or slices. Do not confuse with banana chips, thin slices of unripe banana that have been deep-fried.

Figs (*Ficus carica*) are valued according to size, and should be rich brown with a thin skin. The thinner the skin, the more likelihood of sugaring on the surface; this therefore indicates quality. Lerida figs (above) are best.

Dates (*Phoenix dactylifera*) are very high in sugar (66 percent) and also contain vitamin A and some B vitamins. Dessert dates (above) are sold unpitted; the best variety is Deglet Noor. Dried dates for cooking are sold in blocks.

Prunes (*Prunus domestica*) The type of plum grown for drying is usually late-ripening and black-skinned. Prunes are sold pitted or unpitted. "Tenderized," or partially cooked, prunes need only 8 minutes further cooking.

Thompson seedless raisins

Golden Raisins (*Vitis vinifera*) come from seedless white grapes. Unlike currants, they are often treated chemically—sulfured to preserve color and sprayed to give them an attractive gloss.

Muscat raisins

Lexia raisins

Raisins (*Vitis vinifera*) are not chemically treated and darken naturally in the sun. Dessert raisins (the best known variety is the Lexia raisin from Australia) are larger and juicier.

Currants (*Vitis vinifera*) come from small black seedless grapes grown near Corinth (hence their name) and other parts of Greece. They are not chemically treated. Vostizza is considered the best variety.

Seasonings and flavorings

Shoyu

Tamari

Naturally fermented soy sauce, made from soybeans with barley or wheat, is known as **shoyu** or **tamari**, and should not be confused with the manufactured soy sauce, which is not the same and usually contain sugar and other additives. True tamari, a liquid from the manufacture of miso, contains no wheat and is therefore suitable for gluten-free diets, but is very difficult to find.

Dried mushrooms are available in several varieties, from the strongly flavored cep (*Boletus edulis*) to the ordinary cultivated mushroom (*Agaricus bisporus*) shown above. Even this kind makes a valuable contribution of flavor.

Mugi miso

Hatcho miso

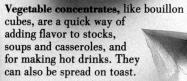

Vegetable concentrates, like bouillon cubes, are a quick way of adding flavor to stocks, soups and casseroles, and for making hot drinks. They can also be spread on toast.

Vegetable bouillon cubes are quite widely available, but make sure they contain no artificial additives. They should be a concentration of vegetables, yeast and vitamins.

Genmai miso

Grated horseradish, when fresh, is very pungent, and much liked in Germany and Scandinavia as well as Britain. It can be used rather in the same way as mustard.

Miso, like shoyu and tamari, is a product of the fermented soybean, a little like peanut butter in texture. All misos have quite a high salt content, although lighter colored miso has slightly less.

Yeast extracts are made from a mixture of brewer's yeast and salt, which produces a highly flavored brown residue, full of protein, iron, potassium and B vitamins, some with added B_{12}.

Brewer's yeast is exceptionally high in protein, as well as in calcium, iron and B vitamins. It can be sprinkled over cereals or used as part of a topping; it adds an interesting flavor as well as nourishment.

Japanese gomashio, or sesame salt, is available in health-food stores, but it is easy to make your own by grinding 4-5 parts roasted sesame seeds with one part salt. Keep in an airtight container and use instead of salt, not in addition to it.

Mustard powder is made mainly from black mustard seeds. Its clean, sharp taste makes it ideal for flavoring sauces, dressings and dips.

Whole-grain mustard, usually from France, contains the whole mustard seed and is often flavored with herbs such as tarragon. It is used as a relish.

Peanut butter is not only a nutritious spread but can be adapted to other uses, particularly as a flavoring for sauces and dressings.

Rock salt

Salt substitute

Sea salt

Salt (*sodium chloride*) comes from the sea, either as sea salt or as bay salt, which is directly evaporated from sea water, or as rock salt, which is usually found as deposits left by vanished prehistoric seas. Salt substitutes, for those who wish to cut down on sodium, are also available.

Tahini is sesame seed paste, widely used in the Middle East. Strong and nutty, it can be used as a dip on its own or to flavor other dips and sauces.

Sea vegetables

Carrageen (*Chondrus crispus*), also called Irish moss, is still eaten in Ireland, and used to be valued as a cure for bronchial diseases and tuberculosis.

Arame (*Eisenia bicyclis*) has a mild taste that blends well with other flavors, and is a good introduction to sea vegetables. It is rich in iron.

Nori (*Porphyra spp.*) is intensively grown in Japan, where it is usually sold in sheets, which can be wrapped around rice. Laver, still used in Wales, is similar.

Dulse (*Rhodymenia palmata*) grows in the North Atlantic and is eaten in Ireland and New England, as well as Iceland and parts of Canada.

Kombu (*Laminaria spp.*) is much cultivated in Japan and considered suitable for offering as a gift.

Wakame (*Undaria pinnatifida*) is another Japanese favorite. Softer than kombu, it can be used in many of the same ways, particularly in soup.

Agar flakes

Agar powder

Agar (or agar-agar, from a Malay word meaning "jelly") is obtained from several different species of sea vegetables. It is used as a substitute for animal gelatine.

Sweeteners

Muscovado sugar is a dark, moist, partly refined sugar with a strong distinctive flavor.

Demerara sugar is a granulated brown sugar but it can be white sugar dyed with caramel. If the country of origin is stated on the package, it is less likely to be dyed.

Light brown sugar As with demerara, check the package for the country of origin.

Carob powder Carob pods, the size of a banana, but flat and dark brown, contain small black seeds, so uniform in size that the word "carat" as a measure of weight derives from them.

Apple juice concentrate This and other concentrated fruit juices are useful flavorings for fruit salads, sauces and cereals.

Corn syrup is made by heating cornstarch and water with a little sulfuric or hydrochloric acid.

Molasses is the residue left when cane sugar is refined. It has some vitamins and minerals.

Maple syrup comes from the sugar maple and black maple. It takes 50 gallons of sap to make one gallon of syrup, so it is a very concentrated form of sweetener.

Malt extract, sometimes also called barley syrup, is not as sweet as sugar; it is used to flavor drinks and malted breads and cakes.

Spices

Capers (*Capparis spinosa*)
The buds of a small Mediterranean
bush, these are usually sold pickled in
vinegar and should not be allowed
to dry out. Used mostly in sauces
and salads.

Cloves (*Eugenia caryophyllata*)
Buds of an evergreen tree, widely used
in curries, marinades, mincemeat,
fruit dishes and mulled wine. Use
sparingly as the flavor is strong.

Nutmeg (*Myristica fragrans*)
Always buy whole and grate as
required. Ground nutmeg quickly
loses it aroma. Sometimes nutmeg
is sold coated with lime to repel
insects; this is harmless.

Cardamom (*Elettaria
cardamomum*) The flavorless
pod encloses black aromatic
seeds which are used in curries
and pastries and to flavor
drinks, including coffee.

Ginger (*Zingiber officinale*)
Fresh gingerroot is firm and juicy. It
needs peeling before being grated or
chopped for use in curries or puddings.

Saffron (*Crocus sativus*)
Always buy the stigmas, or
threads, of this extremely
expensive spice, as the
powder is very easy to
adulterate.

Juniper (*Juniperus communis*)
The berries have a pungent, slightly
resinous flavor. They go well
with cabbage and add a light touch to
oily or heavy dishes.

Cinnamon
(*Cinnamomum
zeylanicum*)
The sticks of dried bark
can flavor drinks and
syrups; ground cinnamon is
widely used in breads
and sweet dishes.

Mace (*Myristica fragrans*)
The dried outer membrane of nutmeg,
which it resembles in taste, it is sold
both in "blades" and ground, as
it is difficult to grind at home.

Vanilla (*Vanilla planifolia*)
The fruit of an orchid plant
from Mexico, traditionally
used to flavor chocolate.
It is expensive, but good in
many sweet dishes.

Allspice (*Pimenta officinalis*) Also called Jamaica pepper; the taste combines cloves, cinnamon and nutmeg.

Aniseed (*Pimpinella anisum*) Popular in Mexico and all over the Mediterranean for its licorice flavor.

Celery (*Apium graveolens*) The slightly bitter taste of celery seeds goes well in bread, egg dishes and salads.

Chili (*Capsicum frutescens*) Ripe chili peppers dry and keep well. Chili powder often includes other spices.

Dill (*Anethum graveolens*) Popular in Eastern and Northern Europe, dill seed is much used in pickles.

Fennel (*Foeniculum vulgare*) Like the bulb, fennel seeds have a slight aniseed flavor. Good with fruit and salads.

Paprika (*Capsicum annuum*) Made from very mild, sweet peppers, popular in Hungary and Spain. Use generously.

Pepper (*Piper nigrum*) Unripe whole peppercorns are green. When dried, they turn brown-black.

Caraway (*Carum carvi*) Looks like cumin seed and often confused with it, but the taste is quite different.

Cayenne (*Capsicum frutescens*) A very hot, pungent red chili sold ready-ground. Use sparingly.

Coriander (*Coriandrum sativum*) Mild but aromatic, coriander seed is important in Arab and Eastern food.

Cumin (*Cuminum cyminum*) The pungent seed is often combined with coriander as a basic curry mixture.

Fenugreek (*Trigonella foenum-graecum*) Produces spicy sprouts. Use the ground seed sparingly.

Mustard (*Brassica alba; B. nigra*) The white (or yellow) seed is milder than the black (or brown) seed.

Poppy seed (*Papaver rhoeas; P. somniferum*) White poppy seed is much used in curries, and blue in pastries.

Turmeric (*Curcuma longa*) Always sold ground. Do not confuse with saffron. The taste is mustier.

Herbs

Chives (*Allium schoenoprasum*)
Mostly eaten raw, this herb is
also good in omelettes. It is
widely used from China
and Japan to Europe
and America.

Basil (*Ocimum basilicum*) If you
cannot find fresh, do not use dried;
substitute another herb. A pot of basil
in the kitchen will keep flies away.

Lemon balm (*Melissa officinalis*) The
crushed leaves give off a wonderful
lemony scent. They can be used
generously in salads.

Bay leaf (*Laurus nobilis*) This herb is
good in milk puddings, as well as in
savory stews and sauces. A leaf kept
in a package of grains will give
them a delicate taste.

Coriander (*Coriandrum sativum*) Also
known as Chinese or Japanese parsley,
it is used lavishly in the East in the
same way as parsley.

Marjoram (*Origanum majorana*) Sweet
marjoram, native to the Mediterranean,
is very fragrant and can be dried
successfully.

Chevril (*Anthriscus
cerefolium*) Very popular in France it
can be used like parsley but has a
more delicate taste with a hint of anise.

Dill (*Anethum graveolens*)
The leaves are known as dill
weed, one of the most popular
herbs in Scandinavia.

Mint (*Mentha spp.*) There are many
species of this popular herb, from
spearmint to the fresh-tasting
peppermint used for teas.

Oregano (*Origanum vulgare*) This is wild marjoram, which for the best flavor must be grown in strong sun. Luckily it keeps all its aroma when it is dried.

Winter savory (*Satureja montana*) Its German name means "bean-herb," which indicates its traditional use. Summer savory (*S. hortensis*) is similar and even more aromatic.

Rosemary (*Rosmarinus officinalis*) A wonderfully aromatic herb with a strong camphor-like flavor. The spiky needles can be a menace when dried.

Parsley (*Petroselinum crispum*) Available curled (above) or flat (below), parsley is a good source of both vitamin C and iron.

Tarragon (*Artemisia dracunculus*) If possible, make sure that you are getting French tarragon not Russian, which is far less aromatic.

Flat-leaf parsley is generally grown in Europe and it is thought to have a finer taste than curled parsley.

Sage (*Salvia officinalis*) There are many varieties. It dries well, but can become musty if kept too long.

Thyme (*Thymus vulgaris*) This popular herb contains an essential oil, thymol, which helps to digest fatty foods.

Vegetables

Bok choy
(*Brassica chinensis*)

Spinach beet
(*Beta vulgaris*)

Less well known than some other leaf vegetables, **bok choy,**
or Chinese cabbage, is crisp and delicate-tasting and needs
little or no cooking. **Chard** (Swiss chard) and **spinach
beet** are the same species; they resemble spinach, but
lack its distinctive flavor. The central spines of **chard** are
often cut out and cooked separately.

Chard (*Beta vulgaris*)

Batavian endive (escarole)
(*Cichorium endivia*)

Chicory (curly endive)
(*Cichorium endivia*)

Belgian endive
(*Cichorium intybus*)

Radicchio
(*Cichorium endivia*)

Batavian endive (or escarole), chicory (or curly endive) and **Belgian endive** all have a similar slightly bitter taste. They are usually blanched by the grower to reduce this bitterness to an acceptable level. The Belgian endive can be eaten raw, braised or stir-fried. Chicory (the French *frisée*), the more wavy Batavian endive, and the crisp **radicchio** from Treviso in Northern Italy and are eaten raw.

Salad greens and sprouts

Lamb's lettuce (*Valerianella olitoria*) Also known as corn salad and (in France) as *mâche*, this is a very useful winter salad.

Sorrel (*Rumex acetosa*) is high in oxalic acid. This gives it its fresh, sharp taste but also impedes assimilation of minerals, notably calcium and iron. Garden sorrel (*Rumex scutatus*) is less acid.

Dandelion (*Taraxacum officinale*) Dandelion leaves offered for sale have been blanched (like celery and chicory) to reduce their bitterness. If you want to use wild dandelions, pick the young leaves.

Arugula (*Eruca sativa*) is deservedly popular in Italy and parts of France. The young, tender leaves (above) become toothed and taste peppery.

Lovage (*Levisticum officinale*) The young, reddish leaves (above) are good in salads; the older leaves (left) and the stems make powerful flavorings.

Mung beans (*Phaseolus aureus*)   **Alfalfa** (*Medicago sativa*)   **Wheat** (*Triticum vulgare*)

Garden cress (*Lepidium sativum*)   **Mustard** (*Sinapis alba*)

Aduki beans (*Phaseolus angularis*)   **Fenugreek** (*Trigonella foenum-graecum*)   **Lentils** (*Lens esculenta*)

Sprouts from **wheat** (and other grains such as rye) and from **lentils** are best when grown to about the length of the seeds. **Aduki bean** sprouts should be about ½ inch long; **mung beans** can be grown to 1 inch. **Mustard** and **garden cress** are eaten at the two-leaf stage, when 1-1½ inches long; so are **alfalfa** sprouts, which take 5-6 days. **Fenugreek** sprouts are best when not more than 2-3 times the length of the seed, which takes 3-6 days.

Vegetables

Okra (*Hibiscus esculentus*), also known as lady's finger and gumbo. The edible part is the pod, picked and eaten while still unripe, since when fully ripe it becomes fibrous and indigestible. It is very mucilaginous and when added to soups and casseroles gives them a rich, thick consistency.

Fennel (*Foeniculum vulgare var. dulce*), often known as Florence fennel. The "bulb" is the swollen leaf-base and has a pronounced anise flavor. Usually served raw in salads.

Kohlrabi (*Brassica oleracea*) A variety of cabbage, also called turnip cabbage, although the apparent root is actually the swollen stem. Both green and purple varieties are good when young, crisp and tender: they can then be eaten raw and have a delicate, slightly turnip-like flavor. Pound for pound they have more vitamin C than oranges.

Daikon (*Raphanus sativus*) A large winter radish, also known as Japanese radish. It has a crisp texture and a milder flavor than ordinary radishes. It is used like them, in salads and stir-fried dishes. All winter radishes have slightly more nutritional value than spring ones.

Winter radish (*Raphanus sativus*) A useful vegetable for winter salads, much grown in China and Japan. The large roots are crisp, but not quite so tender as spring radishes. Excellent in stir-fried dishes.

Salsify (*Tragopogon porrifolius*) Also called oyster plant, as its subtle taste is supposed to resemble that of oysters. Black salsify is the related scorzonera, similar in appearance but black-skinned.

Sweet potato (*Ipomoea batatas*) This name is also sometimes given to the brown-skinned yam, which is similar in taste but has little nutritive value.

Jerusalem artichoke (*Helianthus tuberosus*) No relation to globe artichokes, but a cousin of the sunflower, it has a sweet, nutty flavor.

Cheeses

All the cheeses on these two pages are made without animal rennet (see page 221). On this page, from top left, clockwise: **Double Gloucester;** **Botton** (an English farmhouse cheese from Yorkshire) made with chives; **farmhouse** cheese made with celery seeds; **hard goat's** cheese; and **Cheddar.** Other hard cheeses available include Gouda and Munster.

Geska is a Swiss whey cheese, also known as Sapsago and Schabzieger. It can replace Parmesan. The greenish color comes from a specially grown variety of clover.

Cream cheese is made, as the name indicates, from cream and therefore has a very high fat content. It is valued for its smooth, rich taste and texture.

Chèvre, or French goat's cheese, is a traditional soft cheese with a distinctive taste. It is usually found in the shape shown here or as a small cylinder.

Feta is the best known Greek cheese; with tomato and cucumber, it becomes "Greek salad." Traditionally made from sheep or goat's milk, it is curdled naturally without the addition of rennet.

Coulommiers is a mild French cheese, similar to Brie (it is also called Brie de Coulommiers). Usually eaten unripened, it is often sprinkled with paprika or herbs.

Cottage cheese is a type of low-fat curd cheese made from cooked skimmed cow's milk. It is drained, washed and coated with thin cream and has a granular appearance.

Curd cheese is soft cheese made from whole cow's milk, usually set without using rennet, and sometimes known as lactic curd cheese.

Ricotta is a very low-fat cheese made from whey, not from pressed curds. Sometimes available in mature hard form for grating.

Dairy products and alternatives

Soy milk can be used as a substitute for dairy milk (for how to make it yourself, see page 220). Commercial soy milk sometimes has added sugar, so do read the package carefully.

Vegetable shortening is the only vegetarian alternative to lard or suet. Vegetable oils are hydrogenated to make them solid at room temperature (see page 219).

Buttermilk is the liquid remaining after fresh cream has been churned to make butter. Much of the buttermilk sold today is cultured and soured by adding bacteria to form lactic acid.

Silken tofu

Firm tofu

Yogurt, one of the most popular fermented milk products, is a natural antibiotic, the acid in it killing almost all harmful organisms. It is easily digested, especially goat's milk yogurt (above).

Soft tofu

Tofu, a product of the soybean, is generally available as silken tofu, made from lightly pressed soybean curd, and firm tofu, which is more heavily pressed. Soft or regular tofu has a texture in between the two.

Ghee generally denotes clarified butter but a vegetable version (above) made from hydrogenated vegetable oils is also available.

Strained yogurt, popular in Greece, is much smoother, creamier and sweeter than ordinary yogurt, not unlike the French *crème fraîche*. It is an excellent substitute for cream.

The
RECIPES

★ *indicates that the dish is suitable for freezing*

APPETIZERS

Whether you eat a formal meal with separate courses, or whether you follow the example of many vegetarians and combine several dishes at the same time, something to start with is always welcome. This can be simple, perhaps eaten with a drink before the meal—pâté spread on little biscuits, raw vegetables with various dips—or more elaborate, such as a mousse or a savory water ice.

Vegetarian food lends itself admirably to the occasion and offers endless possibilities. In addition to the recipes given here, you will find many dishes in other sections of the book that can be scaled down to make ideal first courses. Soufflés, quiches or stuffed vegetables are always welcome. For a substantial start to a meal, try pasta, pancakes, risottos or polenta, while for a lighter one, salads are perfect.

Photograph
page 39

Ingredients
¾ pound button mushrooms
Marinade
4 tablespoons sherry
1 tablespoon shoyu
½ teaspoon honey
1 teaspoon grated gingerroot
1 clove garlic, crushed
Batter
1 egg white
2 tablespoons whole-wheat flour
3-4 tablespoons water

oil for deep frying
For serving
Chinese celery cabbage, shredded
sprigs of fresh watercress

Serves 4

Tempura mushrooms

Tempura, the technique of cooking vegetables quickly in a light crispy batter, originated in the Far East.

1 Remove the stalks from the mushrooms and chop them finely. Mix with the marinade ingredients; pour this mixture over the mushroom caps and leave for 3-4 hours.

2 Prepare the batter by beating together the egg white and flour, then adding the water gradually, still beating, until the batter has the consistency of heavy cream.

3 Heat 1 inch oil in a deep skillet. Drain the mushrooms, dip them in batter and deep fry, about 6 at a time, for 2-3 minutes. Drain on paper towel and keep warm while cooking the remaining mushrooms. Serve immediately on a bed of shredded Chinese celery cabbage garnished with watercress.

Artichokes with lemon sauce

A more elaborate variation is to prepare the artichokes as for stuffed artichokes on page 63 and partly fill them with sauce.

1 Wash the artichokes thoroughly. Remove the stalks and trim the bases so that the artichokes will sit flat. Trim the points off the leaves with scissors.

2 Bring a large kettle of water to the boil and cook the artichokes, covered, for 30-40 minutes, or until a leaf pulls out easily.

3 Meanwhile, melt half the butter in a saucepan. Add the flour and cook, stirring, over gentle heat for 2-3 minutes. Pour in the boiling water, stirring vigorously, and as soon as the mixture is smooth, beat in the remaining butter. Stir in the lemon juice, grated lemon rind and garlic. Season to taste. Keep warm, stirring from time to time, over very low heat.

4 Drain the artichokes as soon as they are cooked and arrange them on a serving dish or on individual plates. Pour the sauce into a heated gravy boat and sprinkle it with chives.

Ingredients
4 globe artichokes
6 tablespoons butter
1 tablespoon wheatmeal flour *or*
   ½ tablespoon each of whole-wheat flour and all-purpose white flour mixed
1¼ cups boiling water
2 teaspoons lemon juice
grated rind of ½ lemon
3 cloves garlic, crushed
salt and pepper
1 tablespoon snipped chives

Serves 4

Photograph
pages 186-187

Spinach gnocchi

Leftover baked potatoes can be successfully used for this.

1 Put the potatoes on to boil. When they are cooked, peel and mash them without adding any more liquid.

2 Meanwhile, wash the spinach and cook it without adding any extra water. Drain, squeezing out as much liquid as possible, and chop finely.

3 Mix the potatoes and spinach with all the other ingredients except for 1 tablespoon of the Parmesan and half the butter. Be generous with the pepper. Chill for 45 minutes.

4 Preheat the oven to 400°F and bring a large kettle of salted water to the boil.

5 To cook the gnocchi, drop teaspoonsful of the mixture into the kettle, a few at a time. Keep the water boiling. The gnocchi are done when they rise to the surface, after only a couple of minutes. Remove them with a slotted spoon to an ovenproof dish and repeat the process until all the gnocchi are cooked.

6 Melt the remaining butter and pour it over the gnocchi. Sprinkle the rest of the Parmesan over the top and bake for about 10 minutes, or until well browned. Serve very hot.

Ingredients
1 pound potatoes
1 pound fresh spinach
2 eggs
8 ounces ricotta *or* cream cheese
½ cup butter
2 tablespoons freshly grated Parmesan
salt and pepper
¼ teaspoon grated nutmeg
4-5 tablespoons semolina

Serves 6-8

Photograph
page 39

★

Ingredients
2 ounces dried chestnuts
2 tablespoons butter
1 small onion, finely chopped
1 clove garlic, crushed
¼ pound mushrooms, chopped
1 teaspoon paprika
1 tablespoon whole-wheat flour
6 tablespoons red wine
6 ounces ground walnuts
⅔-1⅓ cups fresh breadcrumbs
2 celery ribs, very finely diced
2 teaspoons shoyu
salt and pepper

Serves 6-8

Chestnut pâté

This is a rich but not too heavy pâté that makes a splendid start to a dinner party. It can be served warm or cold.

1 Bring a large kettle of water to the boil. Put in the chestnuts, remove from the heat and leave them to soak for 1 hour.

2 Return them to the boil in the same water and cook, covered, until tender. This takes 50-60 minutes. Drain, reserving the liquid. Grind or finely chop the chestnuts.

3 Preheat the oven to 375°F.

4 Melt the butter in a small skillet and gently fry the onion and garlic for 3-4 minutes, until translucent. Stir in the mushrooms and paprika, cover and continue cooking for 5-8 minutes.

5 Sprinkle with the flour, stir it in and cook for another 2-3 minutes. Pour in 6 tablespoons of the chestnut stock and the wine. Stir well, bring to the boil and simmer for another 3 minutes. The sauce should be quite thick.

6 Mix together the walnuts, ⅔ cup breadcrumbs, the celery and cooked chestnuts in a large bowl. Add the sauce and season with the shoyu, salt and pepper. Mix very thoroughly. The mixture should be soft but not too wet. Add a few more breadcrumbs if it is too moist.

7 Press into a 1 quart loaf pan lined with oiled wax paper. Cover with foil and bake for 50-60 minutes.

★

Photograph
pages
44-45

Ingredients
½ cup whole lentils, green or
    brown
1 medium eggplant
3 tablespoons olive oil
¼ pound mushrooms, chopped
2 cloves garlic, crushed
1 teaspoon ground coriander
2 tablespoons chopped mint
juice of ½ lemon
salt and pepper

Serves 4-6

Lentil and eggplant pâté

The texture of lentils is perfect for pâté. Here their earthy flavor marries well with the eggplant and mushrooms. An effective way of serving the pâté is in individual ramekins, with melba toast.

1 Preheat the oven to 350°F.

2 Bring the lentils to the boil in a large kettle of water. Skim off any foam, cover and simmer until soft—about 45 minutes. Let cool for 5-10 minutes.

3 Meanwhile, split the eggplant in half lengthwise, brush the cut surfaces with oil and bake the halves for 20 minutes or until soft. Scrape out all the pulp and chop finely.
Continued

Clockwise from top: **Tempura mushrooms** (*see p. 36*); **Chestnut pâté**; **Spinach gnocchi** (*see p. 37*)

*Lentil and eggplant
pâté continued*

4 Gently heat 2 tablespoons olive oil and sauté the mushrooms and garlic over low heat for 5-6 minutes or until they are soft and well browned.

5 Separately, fry the ground coriander in 1 teaspoon oil over moderate heat for 3-4 minutes to bring out the aroma.

6 Mix together the lentils, eggplant pulp, mushrooms and garlic. Stir in the coriander, mint, lemon juice and seasoning; and blend until smooth. Serve at room temperature.

★

Photograph
*pages
44-45*

Ingredients
1 tablespoon olive oil
1 bunch scallions, finely
    chopped
2 cloves garlic, crushed
6 ounces tomato, peeled and
    chopped
4 ounces pitted black olives,
    minced
¼ teaspoon celery seeds
salt
¾ cup red wine

Serves 4

Wine and black olive pâté

This pâté is quite rich, and a little of it goes a long way.

1 Heat the oil and gently fry the scallions and garlic for 3-4 minutes, or until soft.

2 Add the tomato, olives and celery seeds, sprinkle with a little salt. Cook very gently, covered, for 10 minutes.

3 Pour in the red wine, bring to the boil and simmer for another 20 minutes, uncovered.

4 Turn up the heat and stir vigorously for 2-3 minutes, or until the mixture has reduced to the consistency of a soft pâté.

5 Turn out into a serving dish and allow to cool. This is good with crackers or rye bread, or with blinis and sour cream.

★

Photograph
*pages
136-137*

Soaking
overnight

Ingredients
¼ cup wheat berries, soaked
    overnight
4 ounces cashew nuts, finely
    ground
1 ounce sunflower seeds
2 tablespoons oil, preferably
    sunflower
¼ pound carrots, grated
1 small onion, minced or grated
1 tablespoon finely chopped
    parsley
2-3 tablespoons vegetable stock
    (see p. 151)
dash of shoyu
salt and pepper
1 egg, beaten
1 cup fine oatmeal
oil for shallow-frying

Makes 12 small patties

Cashew patties

1 Drain the wheat berries. Put them in a saucepan with enough water to cover them by at least 1 inch. Bring to the boil and simmer for 1 hour, or until the grains burst; add more water if they dry out.

2 Mix together the ground cashews, sunflower seeds and wheat berries. Add the oil and work it evenly into the mixture.

3 Mix in the carrots, onion and parsley, and enough stock to moisten and bind the mixture.

4 Season with shoyu, salt and pepper. Divide into 12 pieces and shape each one into a patty about 2 inches across. Dip into beaten egg and then into oatmeal.

5 Shallow fry for 5-6 minutes over gentle heat, until well browned. Serve hot or cold.

Cucumber mousse

A low-fat combination of tofu and curd cheese that has a lovely creamy consistency and a delicate color and flavor.

1 Blend together the tofu and curd cheese until smooth.

2 Gently heat the water and agar in a small saucepan until the agar has dissolved and the water boils. Pour this quickly over the tofu mixture and blend again so that the agar is well distributed.

3 Stir in the diced cucumber, scallions and tarragon and season well.

4 Beat the egg whites until stiff. Fold 1 tablespoon of egg white into the tofu mixture, then very carefully fold in the remaining egg white.

5 Pile the mixture into individual ramekins and chill for 3-4 hours before serving.

Ingredients
1 cake silken tofu—approx. 11 ounces
8 ounces curd cheese *or* cream cheese
½ cup water
1 tablespoon agar powder
½ large cucumber, very finely diced
3 scallions, finely chopped
1 tablespoon finely chopped tarragon
salt and pepper
2 egg whites

Serves 4

Foreground: **Red pepper ice** (*see p. 42*); behind: **Cucumber mousse**

★

Photograph
page 41

Red pepper ice

Ingredients
4 red peppers
½ small onion, very finely
    chopped
1-1½ teaspoons salt
1 teaspoon grated gingerroot
2 egg yolks
2 tablespoons sunflower oil
1 tablespoon brandy
1-2 teaspoons honey

Serves 4

1 Preheat the oven to 400°F.

2 Roast the peppers in the oven until the skins are blistered all over. Rub off the skins, cut the peppers in half and remove the seeds and white pith.

3 Put the peppers with all the other ingredients in a blender and blend until smooth. Adjust the seasoning.

4 Turn out into a shallow container, cover and freeze for 1 hour. Stir, then freeze again for 2-3 hours, or until just firm. If it becomes very hard, stand it in the refrigerator for 20 minutes before serving.

Photograph
*pages
44-45*

Crudités

Belgian endives, in blades
Broccoli or cauliflower, in tiny
    flowerets
Brussels sprouts, quartered
Carrots, in julienne strips
Celeriac, in julienne strips
Celery, in whole ribs or cut on the
    diagonal
Fennel, in thin slices across
Kohlrabi, swede or turnip, in
    julienne strips
Mushrooms, wiped and sliced (or
    quartered)
Peppers, red, green or yellow, in
    rings or strips
Radish or daikon, in small chunks
Red or white cabbage, shredded
Scallions, trimmed
Zucchini or cucumbers, in strips

Crudités, or raw vegetables, are usually served as part of an hors d'oeuvre, but also make excellent food for a party. Use only top-quality fresh vegetables. Almost any that can be eaten raw are suitable; avoid ones that are too soft, like avocados, or too juicy, like tomatoes. Here are some suggestions. For a party, cut into larger strips and choose vegetables that can be easily picked up. See p. 215 for preparation of vegetables.

Arrange a selection on a serving dish, bearing in mind color, texture and taste. The vegetables can be garnished with olives, lemon wedges, cherry tomatoes or sprigs of fresh herbs. As an appetizer, allow 4-6 ounces per person. If you provide one dip, allow ¾-1¼ cups for 4-6 people. If you offer a selection, ½ cup each of two or three dips should be enough for 6-10.

Photograph
*pages
44-45*

Caper and olive dip

Ingredients
2 tablespoons fresh breadcrumbs
1 tablespoon lemon juice
2 cloves garlic, crushed
2 tablespoons finely chopped parsley
½ ounce capers
2 ounces pitted green olives
1 hard-boiled egg yolk
⅔ cup olive oil
white wine vinegar to taste

Makes ¾-1¼ cups

1 Soak the breadcrumbs in the lemon juice for 15-20 minutes.

2 Put them in a blender with all the other ingredients except the oil and vinegar and blend until smooth.

3 Add the olive oil, a teaspoon at a time, until 2 tablespoons have been added; then pour in the remainder in a thin stream, blending constantly.

4 Thin down the sauce with a little vinegar, turn out into a small bowl or gravy boat and serve with crudités.

Almond dip

1 Preheat the oven to 350°F.

2 Put the almonds on a cookie sheet and toast them in the center of the oven for about 7-10 minutes, until lightly browned.

3 Put them in a blender with the garlic, cayenne, salt, tomatoes and vinegar and blend to a smooth paste.

4 Now blend in the olive oil, a teaspoon at a time, making sure each teaspoonful is absorbed before adding any more. When about half the oil has been added, pour in the remaining oil in a slow thin stream, beating constantly, until the sauce becomes thick and creamy.

5 Pour into a small bowl gravy boat and serve with crudités.

Ingredients
1½ ounces blanched slivered almonds (see p. 209)
1 clove garlic, crushed
¼-½ teaspoon cayenne
1 teaspoon salt
2 small tomatoes, peeled and finely chopped
3 tablespoons red wine vinegar
⅔-¾ cup olive oil

Makes ¾-1¼ cups

Photograph *pages 44-45*

Tofu dip

Blend all the ingredients together until smooth, adding salt and pepper only if you feel it needs it. This gives a light creamy dip. For a peppery version, omit the oil and garlic and add half a teaspoon each of finely ground yellow mustard seeds and black peppercorns with 2 teaspoons shoyu.

Ingredients
1 cake silken tofu—approx. 11 ounces
2 tablespoons lemon juice
1-2 tablespoons sunflower oil
1 clove garlic, crushed

Makes ¾-1¼ cups

Photograph *pages 44-45*

Hummus

This version uses less olive oil than the classic recipe.

1 Drain and rinse the chick peas. Put them in a large kettle with plenty of fresh water, bring to the boil and boil fiercely for 10 minutes. Reduce the heat, skim off any foam, and simmer, covered, until soft—about 60-90 minutes, depending on the age of the peas.

2 Drain them thoroughly, reserving the liquid, and grind to a fine powder, using the knife blade of a food processor or a coffee grinder.

3 Add ⅔ cup of the reserved stock and blend to a stiff paste. You may need to add more stock. Add all the other ingredients, mix thoroughly, and leave to stand for at least 2 hours for the flavors to develop. Taste, and add more seasoning and lemon juice if necessary.

4 Turn out the hummus into a shallow dish. Just before serving, garnish it with a trickle of oil, lemon slices and parsley. It is traditionally served with pita bread, but whole-wheat bread or toast also goes well.

Ingredients
1 cup chick peas, soaked overnight
4-5 tablespoons tahini
juice of 1½ lemons
2 tablespoons olive oil
2-3 cloves garlic, crushed
¼ teaspoon paprika
½ teaspoon salt
black pepper
Garnish
extra olive oil *or* sesame oil
lemon slices
sprigs of fresh parsley

Makes about 3 cups

★

Photograph *pages 44-45*

· Soaking *overnight*

Cocktails and buffets

Vegetables, cheese and eggs can form the basis for a variety of delicious, easy-to-eat mouthfuls, suitable for parties or light buffets.

Quiches and other pastry dishes offer plenty of scope, as well as the ones shown here. Try the festive pie (page 84) or the flamiche (page 85), cut into small squares or triangles, or serve miniature pizzas or tortillas. Raw vegetables, cut into chunks or slices, go well with savory dips. As well as olives, nuts and vegetarian cheeses cut into cubes, you could serve little nut patties (page 40) or bean croquettes (page 96), savory spreads on biscuits, or spicy stuffed vine leaves (page 67). Fill celery and hollowed-out cucumbers with ricotta and chopped walnuts sprinkled with paprika, or with cream cheese mixed with chopped watercress and toasted sunflower seeds.

Kiwi fruit juice with mineral water or carrot and orange are healthy non-alcoholic drinks.

1 Kiwi fruit drink 2 Carrot and orange juice 3 & 10 Lentil and eggplant pâté (*p. 38*) on cheese water biscuits cut into crescents and stars (*p. 135*); wine and olive pâté (*p. 40*) on round oatcakes (*p. 173*) 4 & 6 Tartlets with various fillings: asparagus (*p. 130*), lentil (*p. 92*) and tomato (the pizza topping on *p. 120*); quiche with vegetables (*p. 130*) 5 Peppers with caper and olive, almond and tofu dips (*pp. 42-43*) 7 Cheese puffs with avocado filling (*pp. 134-135*) 8 Cheese dip (*p. 135*) with crudités (*p. 42*) 9 Cucumber and celery "boats" (*see above*); cheese shortbread "straws" (*p. 135*) 11 Hummus (*p. 43*) with crudités.

SOUPS

A pot of lentils or beans, pasta or rice, onions, celery or tomatoes, all simmered in a savory broth made from fresh vegetables and seasoned with shoyu, herbs and spices—this is more than a welcome hot soup: it is a meal itself, rich in protein, full of flavor, and with a nutritious balance of beans, grains and vegetables. For summer evenings, light purées of green vegetables such as fresh peas or watercress, or chilled fruit soups make tempting first courses.

It needs no special skill to produce a splendid homemade soup, nor, in most of these recipes, does it require much preparation. The bulk of the work, including presoaking peas and beans, can often be done well in advance; indeed, many of the soups benefit from being made the day before and given time to rest and develop their flavor.

★

Soaking
overnight

Flageolet with juniper

The light, delicate flavor of flageolets combines well with the pungency of the juniper berries and leeks.

Ingredients
¾ cup flageolet beans, soaked
   overnight
½ pound leeks, thinly sliced
2 bay leaves
5 juniper berries
2 cloves
1 tablespoon olive oil
2½-3 cups water
salt and pepper
1 tablespoon finely chopped
   parsley

Serves 4-6

1 Drain the flageolets and put them in a large kettle together with the leeks, bay leaves, juniper berries and cloves.

2 Add the oil and water, bring to the boil and simmer, covered, for 1 hour. Remove the bay leaves, juniper berries and cloves and allow to cool for a few minutes.

3 Place two-thirds of the soup in a blender and blend, adding a little extra water if it seems too thick, and season to taste.

4 Return all the soup to the kettle and reheat gently. Sprinkle with parsley just before serving.

From top: **Cream of split pea** (*see p. 48*); **Flageolet with juniper;**
Spiced lentil with coconut (*see p. 48*)

★
Photograph
page 47

Ingredients
½ cup yellow split peas
1 medium onion, finely chopped
1 clove garlic, crushed
1 tablespoon sunflower oil
1 large potato, diced
2 celery ribs, diced
1 teaspoon caraway seed
¼ teaspoon ground mace
1 bay leaf
3-3⅔ cups light
   vegetable stock (see p. 151)
   or water
salt and pepper

Serves 4-6

Cream of split pea

Yellow split peas give this soup a particularly attractive color, but green split peas or red lentils could be used instead.

1 Soak the split peas in hot water for an hour and drain.

2 In a large, heavy-bottomed saucepan, fry the onion and garlic gently in the oil for 3-4 minutes.

3 Add the potato, celery, split peas, caraway and mace. Cook for another 5-6 minutes, stirring occasionally.

4 Put in the bay leaf and most of the stock. Bring to the boil and simmer, covered, for 40 minutes. Remove the bay leaf and let soup cool for a few minutes.

5 Purée in a blender, adding more stock if soup is too thick. Season generously, reheat and serve.

Photograph
page 47

Ingredients
½ cup red split lentils
1 tablespoon peanut oil
1 medium onion, finely chopped
½ teaspoon chili powder
½ teaspoon grated gingerroot
¼ teaspoon grated nutmeg
1 medium red pepper, seeded and
   diced
1 medium green pepper, seeded
   and diced
1¼ cups vegetable stock
   (see p. 151) *or* water
2½ cups coconut milk
   (see p. 209)
salt and pepper

Serves 4-6

Spiced lentil with coconut

1 Soak the red lentils in hot water for 10 minutes and drain.

2 Heat the oil in a large, heavy-bottomed saucepan and gently fry the onion and spices for 3-4 minutes.

3 Add the peppers and lentils and continue frying for 4-5 minutes, stirring to distribute the spices evenly among the vegetables.

4 Pour in the stock, bring to the boil and simmer gently, covered, for 10 minutes.

5 Stir in the coconut milk and continue to simmer, covered, for 35-40 minutes. Let soup cool for a few minutes.

6 Purée in a blender until completely smooth, season to taste and reheat gently before serving.

Photograph
pages
86-87

Ingredients
3-3⅔ cups water
1 small cauliflower, divided into tiny
   flowerets
1 medium onion, finely chopped
4 ounces blanched almonds,
   chopped (see p. 209)
2 celery ribs, chopped
2 tablespoons sunflower oil
salt and pepper
grated nutmeg

Serves 4-6

Cream of cauliflower and almond

A subtle and rich soup, made with almonds that have been gently fried to bring out their flavor. It can be prepared a day or so in advance and served hot or chilled, but is not suitable for freezing.

1 Bring the water to the boil and poach the cauliflower in it for 5 minutes, or until just tender. Drain, reserving the stock.

2 In a large, heavy-bottomed saucepan, fry the onion, almonds and celery in the oil for 5-6 minutes, until the almonds are fairly well browned.

3 Add the cauliflower stock, bring to the boil and simmer for 5 minutes. Let cool slightly.

4 Purée in a blender until completely smooth—this will take several minutes. Season to taste, add the flowerets and reheat gently in a clean saucepan.

5 Sprinkle with grated nutmeg and serve.

Red bean and vegetable

This can be prepared ahead of time up to the point of cooking the kidney beans. Once the fresh vegetables and pasta have been added, however, it should not be reheated.

1 In a large, heavy-bottomed saucepan, cook the onions and garlic for 3-4 minutes in the oil until soft.

2 Add the stock and the drained beans, bring to the boil and boil rapidly for 10 minutes, then simmer, covered for 20 minutes. Add the zucchini, snap beans and tomatoes, stir in the tomato paste and simmer for another 20 minutes.

3 Season well. Add the basil, 2 tablespoons parsley and the macaroni and cook for a further 15 minutes. Serve hot, sprinkled with the remaining parsley.

Ingredients
1 bunch scallions, diced
1 medium onion, diced
2 cloves garlic, crushed
2 tablespoons olive oil
2½ cups light vegetable stock
 (see p. 151)
⅔ cup red kidney beans,
 soaked overnight and drained
3 ounces zucchini, sliced
3 ounces snap beans, sliced
¼ pound tomatoes, peeled
 and chopped
1 tablespoon tomato paste
salt and pepper
2 tablespoons finely chopped basil
3 tablespoons finely chopped parsley
1 ounce whole-wheat elbow
 macaroni

Serves 4-6

★
Photograph *page 50*

Soaking *overnight*

Cream of broccoli

Sour cream gives the needed touch of sharpness to this rich, green soup. It is thinned with light cream to make it easier to pour; the exact proportions are a matter of taste.

1 In a large, heavy-bottomed saucepan sauté the onion and garlic in the oil with the bay leaf until soft—3-4 minutes.

2 Add the broccoli and stock, bring to the boil and simmer gently, covered, for 10 minutes, when the broccoli should be tender but still bright green. Remove the bay leaf and let the soup cool a little.

3 Purée in a blender until completely smooth. Season to taste, add the lemon juice and reheat gently in a clean pan.

4 Meanwhile, steam the broccoli flowerets until tender—about 8-10 minutes. Scatter them over the soup and stir in the cream just before serving.

Ingredients
1 medium onion, chopped
1 clove garlic, crushed
1 tablespoon sunflower oil
1 bay leaf
1 pound green broccoli, chopped
2½ cups light vegetable
 stock (see p. 151)
salt and pepper
juice of ½ lemon
Garnish
¼ pound broccoli flowerets
4 tablespoons mixed sour cream
 and light cream

Serves 4-6

★
Photograph *page 50*

Carrot and coriander

These quantities give a very pronounced spicy flavor. You may prefer to use half the amount of coriander and cumin.

1 Melt the butter in a large, heavy-bottomed saucepan but do not let it brown. Sauté the carrots and celery in it over gentle heat for a minute or two, stirring and turning to coat them with butter.

2 Add the ground coriander and cumin, turn the heat up a little and fry for another 3-4 minutes, stirring fairly vigorously.

3 Pour in the stock, bring to the boil and simmer, covered, for 30 minutes. Let cool a little.

4 Put through a blender and return to a clean saucepan. Season to taste and reheat gently. Add the chopped coriander leaves and serve hot, garnished with a few whole coriander leaves and lemon croûtes.

Lemon croûtes

1 Trim the crusts from the bread and cut into triangles.

2 Heat a little oil (or oil and butter mixed) in a skillet until it sizzles. Fry the triangles quickly until crisp and brown on both sides. Sprinkle with lemon juice and serve immediately.

Ingredients
3 tablespoons butter
12 ounces carrots, diced
3 celery ribs, diced
2 teaspoons ground coriander
1 teaspoon ground cumin
3-3⅔ cups light
   vegetable stock (see p. 151)
salt and pepper
1 tablespoon finely chopped
   coriander leaves
Garnish
fresh coriander leaves
lemon croûtes (*see below*)
Lemon croûtes
4-6 slices stale bread
oil for frying
lemon juice

Serves 4-6

Country vegetable broth

If you do not have the individual grains, peas and lentils readily at hand, a "soup mix," available in many health-food stores, makes an ideal base.

1 Soak the grains, peas and lentils in hot water for an hour and drain.

2 Gently soften the vegetables in the oil for 10 minutes in a large, heavy-bottomed saucepan with a lid. Add the grains, peas and lentils and fry gently for a further 5 minutes, stirring occasionally.

3 Add the stock and shoyu, bring to the boil and simmer, covered, for 50-60 minutes.

4 Stir in the herbs and season to taste. You can serve the soup immediately, just as it is, or blend it briefly in a blender if you prefer a smoother texture, but do not purée it completely or it will lose its character.

Ingredients
2 tablespoons whole barley
2 tablespoons wheat berries
2 tablespoons green split peas
2 tablespoons red lentils
1 medium onion, finely chopped
1 medium parsnip, diced
1 medium turnip, diced
1 medium potato, diced
2 tablespoons sunflower oil
3-3⅔ cups vegetable
   stock (see p. 151) *or* water
1 tablespoon shoyu
2 teaspoons finely chopped rosemary
1 teaspoon finely chopped thyme
salt and pepper

Serves 4-6

★
Photograph
page 52

From top: **Carrot and coriander; Cream of broccoli** (*see p. 49*);
Red bean and vegetable (*see p. 49*)

Onion soup

A vegetarian adaptation of the traditional French onion soup that makes a welcome start to a winter meal.

1 Heat the oil in a large, heavy-bottomed saucepan and add the onions, garlic, carrot and turnip. Cover the saucepan and cook the vegetables for 15-20 minutes over very gentle heat. Sprinkle with a little salt to bring out extra juices.

2 Add the bay leaf, celery seeds, mustard powder, stock and shoyu. Stir well, bring to the boil and simmer, covered, for 20 minutes. Remove the bay leaf and carrot (unless you prefer to leave the pieces of carrot in for extra color).

3 Blend the miso with 1 tablespoon of the soup in a small bowl. Stir it back into the soup, mixing well, and season to taste.

4 Simmer gently for another 5 minutes and serve sprinkled with the chopped parsley or chervil and the sesame seeds.

Ingredients
1½ tablespoons sunflower oil
1 pound onions, finely chopped
1-2 cloves garlic, crushed
1 medium carrot, coarsely chopped
1 small white turnip, grated
1 bay leaf
1 teaspoon celery seeds
¼ teaspoon mustard powder
2½ cups dark vegetable
   stock (see p. 152)
2 teaspoons shoyu
1 teaspoon miso
salt and pepper
Garnish
2 tablespoons finely chopped
   parsley *or* chervil
1 tablespoon sesame seeds

Serves 4-6

★

Miso julienne

With its strong, salty flavor, miso makes an excellent warming basis for a clear stock. This recipe includes a julienne of carrots and daikon, the subtly flavored Japanese white radish. The sea vegetable arame contributes a rich mineral content.

1 Soak the arame in hot water for 10 minutes and drain. Either chop it finely or, if you prefer, leave it in strips.

2 In a large, heavy-bottomed saucepan fry the ginger in the peanut oil for 2-3 minutes over medium heat.

3 Add the sesame oil, carrots, daikon and arame and continue to cook, covered, over gentle heat for 15 minutes.

4 Add the stock and stir in the shoyu and miso. Bring to the boil and simmer, covered, for a further 10 minutes. Serve immediately.

Ingredients
¼ ounce arame
½ teaspoon sliced gingerroot
1 tablespoon peanut oil
2 teaspoons sesame oil
½ pound carrots, cut into
   julienne strips (see p. 222)
½ pound daikon, cut into
   julienne strips
2½ cups dark vegetable
   stock (see p. 152)
2 tablespoons shoyu
1 tablespoon miso, preferably
   mugi

Serves 4-6

★

Thanksgiving

Vegetables are the *raison d'être* of a harvest festival and really come into their own for a Thanksgiving dinner. Here a whole pumpkin takes pride of place, acting as a tureen for its own soup, made with spices and sour cream.

For the main course, serve a raised pie made in an ornamental hinged pie mold, filled with layers of mushrooms, tomatoes, fennel and eggplant and accompanied by a well-flavored tomato and orange sauce. More vegetables appear in the two salads—one light, one more substantial—and there are simple baked potatoes to contrast with the more elaborate dishes. Corn, a traditional American harvest symbol, is represented in the golden cornbread.

Cranberries flavor the light, airy pudding made with egg whites and set with agar. The yolks are used for the sauce, supplying the protein needed to balance a mainly vegetable-based menu, but one that reflects the original purpose of Thanksgiving: to appreciate and give thanks for the home-grown, carefully cultivated, simple but nourishing fruits of the earth.

1 Spiced cranberry soufflé (*p. 160*)
2 Pumpkin soup (*p. 56*) 3 Baked potatoes
4 Belgian endive, orange and watercress salad in yogurt and cream cheese dressing (*p. 144*)
5 Raised pie (*p. 89*) 6 Spinach, apple and cauliflower salad in vinaigrette dressing (*p. 142*)
7 Tomato and orange sauce (*p. 154*)
8 Cornbread (*p. 179*)

Photograph
pages
54-55

Ingredients

1 tablespoon sunflower oil
1 teaspoon grated gingerroot
1 teaspoon grated nutmeg
½ teaspoon ground coriander
1 small onion, chopped
1 medium carrot, chopped
1 medium potato, chopped
2 celery ribs, chopped
1½-2 pounds pumpkin meat,
    chopped
1¼-2 cups light
    vegetable stock (see p.151)
salt and pepper
lemon juice *or* apple juice
    concentrate, to taste
sour cream (optional) to taste

Serves 4

Pumpkin soup

For Halloween this is made with a traditional bright orange pumpkin. When this is not available, any well-flavored squash with orange or yellow pulp can be substituted.

1 Heat the oil in a large, heavy-bottomed saucepan and fry the ginger, nutmeg and coriander over medium heat for 4-5 minutes. Add the chopped vegetables and cook, covered, over low heat for 20 minutes or until the pumpkin flesh is meltingly soft.

2 Add 1¼ cups stock, season with salt, pepper and lemon juice (or apple juice concentrate) and stir well. Bring to the boil and simmer, covered, for another 20 minutes. Allow to cool a little.

3 Put through a blender adding more stock if necessary. Check the seasoning and reheat gently in a clean pan. If using sour cream, stir it in just before serving.

For a really spectacular party dish, use a whole pumpkin and serve the soup in its shell.

Prepare the pumpkin as shown. Dice the meat, removing the seeds, and weigh it. Adjust the quantities of the other ingredients accordingly. Fry the spices and then the vegetables, add the stock and seasonings and put through a blender. Pour into the pumpkin and replace its "lid."

Stand the pumpkin on a flan ring or on an ovenproof dish on which it can be brought to the table and bake at 375°F for 45 minutes or until the pumpkin meat is completely tender. As you serve the soup, scoop out a few chunks of meat from the sides of the pumpkin into each bowl.

PREPARING THE PUMPKIN

1 *Slice off the top of the pumpkin about one-third of the way down, making a V-shaped nick to ensure that it can be replaced correctly.*

2 *Scoop out the inside, leaving a thickness of about 1 inch of meat in the shell. Season this with a little oil and salt.*

Mushroom with herbs

For extra flavor you can include some dried mushrooms and use their soaking water in the vegetable stock.

1 Heat the oil in a large, heavy-bottomed saucepan and sauté the onion and herbs gently for about 5 minutes.

2 Add the mushrooms and cook for another 5 minutes or until they are well browned.

3 Stir in the stock, wine, tomato paste and parsley. Bring to the boil, cover and simmer for 30-45 minutes.

4 Remove the bay leaves, season to taste and serve hot. Croutons or crackers go well with this soup.

Ingredients
3 tablespoons sunflower oil
1 medium onion, finely chopped
2 bay leaves
1 teaspoon chopped marjoram
1 teaspoon chopped tarragon
½ pound mushrooms, chopped
2 cups dark vegetable
   stock (see p. 152)
4 tablespoons red wine
2 tablespoons tomato paste
2 tablespoons chopped parsley

Serves 4

★
Photograph
*pages
188-189*

Gumbo

An easy-to-make adaptation of the Creole dish, characterized by the velvety texture of the okra.

1 In a heavy-bottomed saucepan sauté the onion and garlic gently in the oil until soft—about 3-4 minutes.

2 Add the pepper and okra and fry for another 5 minutes. stirring occasionally.

3 Stir in the tomatoes and tomato paste and add the stock. Bring to the boil, cover and simmer for 20-25 minutes, stirring occasionally. Season to taste and serve immediately.

Ingredients
1 medium onion, finely chopped
1 clove garlic, crushed
1 tablespoon sunflower oil
1 medium green pepper, seeded
   and diced
½ pound okra, trimmed and
   chopped
1 pound tomatoes, peeled
   and chopped
1 tablespoon tomato paste
1¼ cups dark vegetable
   stock (see p. 152)
salt and pepper

Serves 4-6

★
Photograph
page 58

Avgolemono

A refreshing lemony soup, this is usually made in the Greek way with white rice. Bulgur wheat makes a nutritious alternative.

1 In a large, heavy-bottomed saucepan, sauté the onion gently in the oil for 3-4 minutes.

2 Stir in the celery, carrot and spices. Add the lemon juice and water, bring to the boil, cover and simmer for 40 minutes.

3 Strain the stock. Return it to a clean pan and mix in the bulgur wheat. Reheat gently for 5 minutes but do not let it boil.

4 Beat the egg yolks and juice of 1 lemon together in a bowl and mix in a tablespoon or two of the stock. Gradually add this mixture to the pan, heating gently until the soup thickens. It should be the consistency of light cream. Season to taste and serve immediately.

Ingredients
1 medium onion, finely chopped
2 tablespoons olive oil
3 celery ribs, diced
1 small carrot, diced
8 coriander seeds, lightly crushed
12 peppercorns
½ teaspoon aniseeds
½ cup lemon juice
4¼ cups water
⅓ cup bulgur wheat
3 egg yolks
juice of 1 lemon
salt and pepper

Serves 4-6

Photograph
page 58

Cold beet rassolnik

The name rassolnik *comes from the Russian for "brine" or "pickle" and is given to fish or meat soups containing pickled cucumber. Here the idea is combined with another Russian specialty,* borshch *or beet soup.*

1 Put the beets in a kettle with the water and apple juice concentrate. Bring to the boil, cover and simmer for 20 minutes. Let cool.

2 Put through a blender, add the dill weed, and season.

3 Pour into a tureen and stir in the minced pickle, the diced fresh cucumber and all except a tablespoon or two of the sour cream. Chill thoroughly and garnish with the remaining sour cream just before serving.

Ingredients
¾ pound raw beets, peeled and thinly sliced
2 cups water
1 tablespoon apple juice concentrate
1 teaspoon dried dill weed
salt and pepper
4 ounces dill pickle, minced
2 inches cucumber, peeled and diced
⅔ cup sour cream

Serves 4-6

Fresh pea with mint

This makes a lovely chilled summer soup, but is equally good served hot.

1 Melt the butter in a large, heavy-bottomed saucepan over gentle heat. Add the Chinese celery cabbage and peas and braise them for 10 minutes with the lid on.

2 Add the stock or water. Bring to the boil, stirring occasionally, and simmer gently, covered, for 20 minutes. Allow to cool a little.

3 Purée in a blender until completely smooth. Stir in the mint and season to taste.

4 To serve hot, reheat gently, garnish with the cream and sprigs of mint and serve immediately. To serve cold, chill for an hour or two and garnish just before serving.

Ingredients
4 tablespoons butter
½ pound Chinese celery cabbage, sliced
2½ cups shelled fresh peas
2½ cups light vegetable stock (see p. 151) *or* water
1-2 tablespoons finely chopped mint
salt and pepper
Garnish
3-4 tablespoons light cream (optional)
sprigs of fresh mint

Serves 4-6

★
Photograph
page 61

Watercress

In contrast to many recipes that use onion and stock to soften the taste of watercress, here yogurt and lemon juice are used to bring out its natural sharpness.

1 Chop the watercress finely. Melt the butter and soften the watercress in it for 10 minutes, covered, over gentle heat. Let cool.

2 Purée in a blender with the lemon juice and yogurt. Season to taste and chill thoroughly before serving.

Ingredients
½ pound cleaned watercress (approx. 4 bunches)
6 tablespoons butter
2 tablespoons lemon juice
2½ cups yogurt
salt and pepper

Serves 4

Photograph
page 61

From top: **Cold beet rassolnik**; **Avgolemono** (*see p. 57*); **Gumbo** (*see p. 57*)

★

Ingredients
½ small cucumber, peeled and
   coarsely chopped
1 pound tomatoes, peeled and
   coarsely chopped
2 ounces scallions, diced
1 small green pepper, seeded
   and diced
2 cloves garlic, crushed
⅔ cup fresh breadcrumbs
1 tablespoon red wine vinegar
1 teaspoon salt
1 tablespoon olive oil
1 tablespoon tomato paste
Garnish
1 large scallion, finely chopped
1 ounce chopped peeled cucumber
1 small green pepper, seeded
   and finely chopped

Serves 4-6

Gazpacho

This version uses no water and has a substantial, satisfying consistency. It is worth making an effort to find really well-flavored ripe tomatoes as they make all the difference to the taste and appearance.

1 Put the cucumber, tomatoes, scallions, green pepper, garlic and breadcrumbs into a bowl and mix thoroughly. Stir in the vinegar, salt, olive oil and tomato paste.

2 Blend in a blender for about 1 minute, or until you have a smooth purée. Adjust the seasoning and chill the soup thoroughly before serving.

The garnishes can be sprinkled on the soup, or handed round with it, each in a separate bowl.

★

Ingredients
1 tablespoon sunflower oil
1 medium onion, finely chopped
2 medium-sized crisp eating apples,
   peeled, cored and chopped
1 large potato, chopped
½ pound leeks, sliced
2½-3 cups light vegetable stock
   (see p. 151) *or* water
⅔ cup yogurt (optional)
salt and pepper
1 tablespoon snipped chives

Serves 4-6

Vichyssoise with apple

The unexpected flavor of apple blends very well with the traditional leek and potato Vichyssoise.

1 Heat the oil in a large, heavy-bottomed saucepan and cook, covered, the onion, apples, potato and leeks for 7-10 minutes over low heat.

2 Add the stock or water, bring to the boil and simmer gently, covered, for 20 minutes. Let cool.

3 Purée in a blender until completely smooth, adding a little extra liquid if you think it is too thick.

4 When quite cold, stir or blend in the yogurt and season to taste. Serve chilled, sprinkled with the chives.

★

Photograph
page 62

Ingredients
4 ounces dried apricots, washed
   and diced
4 oranges, peeled and sliced
2½ cups water
6 cloves
1¼ cups white wine
Garnish
1 orange, peeled and thinly sliced
1 tablespoon chopped blanched
   almonds and/or cashews
   (see p. 209)
Serves 4-6

Chilled apricot and orange

Fresh apricots can be used, but dried ones give more flavor.

1 Put the apricots and oranges in a large saucepan with the water. Add the cloves, bring to the boil and simmer, covered, for 30 minutes. Let cool a little.

2 Remove the cloves. Add the white wine and purée in a blender. Chill thoroughly. Garnish just before serving with the orange slices and chopped nuts.

From top: **Watercress** (*see p. 59*); **Vichyssoise with apple; Fresh pea with mint** (*see p. 59*); **Gazpacho**

Ingredients
1 pint strawberries
2½ cups water
2 tablespoons dried hibiscus flowers
2 teaspoons arrowroot
1-2 tablespoons maple syrup
¼ cup rosé wine
Garnish
4 tablespoons sour cream
1 tablespoon slivered almonds

Serves 4-6

Strawberry and hibiscus

Fruit soups are popular in Scandinavia. Hibiscus flowers can be found in some health-food stores, but you could substitute one tea bag of rose hip and hibiscus tea.

1 Slice the strawberries very thinly, reserving 4-6 whole ones for the garnish.

2 Put the sliced strawberries, water and hibiscus flowers into a saucepan. Bring to the boil and simmer, covered, for 20 minutes, or until the strawberries have lost most of their color. Remove the sachet, if you have used one, and let stand for several hours or overnight.

3 Strain the stock and return it to a clean saucepan. Make a paste with the arrowroot and 1 tablespoon of the strained stock. Add this and the maple syrup to the pan and blend well. Bring to the boil and simmer for 5 minutes.

4 Toast the almonds under the broiler for 1-2 minutes on each side, or until lightly browned.

5 Stir the wine into the soup. Allow to cool and serve slightly warm, garnished with the sour cream, toasted almonds and reserved strawberries.

Left: **Chilled apricot and orange** (*see p. 60*); **Strawberry and hibiscus**

VEGETABLES

Vegetable dishes are very versatile. They can form the centerpiece of a meal or act as a side dish to complement a substantial main course. A recipe for one can usually be adapted for another; for example, the vine leaf stuffing given here also goes well with peppers or zucchini. A simple preparation can be made more elaborate by adding pastry, or a topping of cornbread or nut crumble.

A meal of vegetables alone will be low in protein, so try to have a dish based on grains or beans as well. Some of the recipes here already include high-protein ingredients; for example, the nuts in the hazelnut and zucchini bake or the broccoli and walnut pie. Whole-wheat flour is a nutritious ingredient in a vegetable tart, pie or brioche, all of which are suitable main dishes for a dinner party.

It is difficult to be precise about servings. Most of these recipes serve 4 or 4-6, depending on what else is served.

Stuffed artichokes

Either the lemon sauce on page 37 or one of the tofu dips on page 43 can accompany these artichokes stuffed with a purée of beans and mushrooms.

1 Wash the artichokes thoroughly. Trim the bases so that the artichokes will sit flat, and cut off the sharp tips of the leaves as shown on page 64.

2 Rinse the artichokes and cook them in plenty of boiling water for 35-40 minutes.

3 Simmer the fava beans in plenty of water for about 10 minutes, or until quite soft.

Continued

Ingredients
4 globe artichokes
10 ounces fresh fava beans
2 tablespoons olive oil
3 cloves garlic, crushed
1 bunch scallions, chopped
¾ pound mushrooms, diced
2 teaspoons dried dill weed
2 tablespoons lemon juice
salt and pepper

Serves 4

★ (*filling*)
Photograph
page 65

Stuffed artichokes continued

4 Heat the oil and gently sauté the garlic, scallions and mushrooms until soft. Leave to cool a little.

5 Preheat the oven to 325°F.

6 Drain the artichokes. Remove the center leaves and use a teaspoon, as shown, to take out the inedible choke.

7 Purée the mushroom mixture with the cooked beans, dill weed and lemon juice to make a stiff paste. Season well and divide this among the artichokes.

8 Arrange them in a shallow baking dish, cover loosely with foil and bake for 30 minutes. Serve hot.

PREPARING THE ARTICHOKES

1 Cut off the stalks of the artichokes and use scissors to trim the leaves.

2 When the artichokes are cooked and cool enough to handle, pull out the soft inner leaves.

3 Carefully scoop out all the fibrous choke with a teaspoon.

★

Ingredients
2 large eggplants
1 tablespoon olive oil
3 medium onions, chopped
3 cloves garlic, crushed
6 ounces mushrooms, diced
6 ounces cashew nuts, finely
  ground
1 tablespoon tomato paste
1 tablespoon finely chopped parsley
salt and pepper
1 bay leaf
1¼ pounds tomatoes, peeled and
  chopped
3 tablespoons red wine

Serves 4

Mushroom-stuffed eggplants

These are served with a rich sauce of tomatoes and red wine. If you cannot get good-quality ripe tomatoes, use canned ones.

1 Bring a large pan of water to the boil and simmer the eggplants, whole, for 10 minutes. Drain, slice them in half lengthwise and let them cool completely.

2 Scoop out the centers, leaving the shell intact, and chop the pulp finely.

3 Heat the oil in a skillet and gently sauté the onions for 3-4 minutes. Add the garlic and mushrooms, cover the pan and cook for a further 10 minutes.

4 Put two-thirds of this mixture into a bowl for the filling. Mix in the chopped eggplant pulp, ground cashews, tomato paste, parsley, salt and pepper.

Continued on page 66

Clockwise from top: **Baked cabbage with chestnuts** (*see p. 66*); **Mushroom-stuffed eggplants**; **Stuffed artichokes** (*see p. 63*)

*Mushroom-stuffed eggplants
continued*

5 To the remaining mixture in the pan add the bay leaf, tomatoes and red wine. Cover and continue cooking for another 20 minutes, stirring from time to time, until you have a thick, smooth sauce. While the sauce is cooking, preheat the oven to 350°F.

6 Arrange the eggplant shells in a shallow ovenproof dish and divide the filling between them. Remove the bay leaf from the sauce and pour this over the stuffed eggplants. Bake, covered, for 15 minutes, then remove the lid and bake for a further 5 minutes. Serve hot.

★ *(filling)*

Photograph
page 65

Ingredients
4 ounces dried chestnuts
1 small cabbage
2 tablespoons butter
1 clove garlic, crushed
¼ pound leeks, sliced
¼ pound mushrooms, diced
2 teaspoons lemon juice
2 teaspoons paprika
2 teaspoons dried dill weed
1 egg
salt and pepper

Serves 4-6

Baked cabbage with chestnuts

A loosely packed cabbage, such as a Savoy, is good for this dish. Although fresh chestnuts could be used, dried ones are much easier to handle and have a richer flavor.

1 Soak the chestnuts in hot water for an hour. Cook them in their soaking water for 40 minutes, or until soft. Drain and chop finely.

2 While the chestnuts are cooking, detach 8 leaves from the outside of the cabbage, cut out the center rib of each leaf with a sharp knife and blanch the leaves for 2 minutes in boiling water. Chop the rest of the cabbage finely.

3 Preheat the oven to 325°F.

4 Melt the butter in a skillet and cook the garlic, leeks, mushrooms and chopped cabbage over low heat for 7-10 minutes, or until well softened. Add the chestnuts, lemon juice, paprika and dill weed. Allow to cool a little, then beat in the egg and season well.

5 Line a greased, ovenproof 5-cup mold with some of the blanched cabbage leaves, making sure there are no gaps. Spoon in the filling and cover with the remaining leaves. Put a plate on top to weight the mixture down and bake for an hour. Turn out before serving. A tomato or a creamy sauce goes well with this.

Spinach darioles

*Delicious with most egg dishes, the spinach also complements
bakes, roasts or pilafs such as the hazelnut and zucchini
bake on page 73 or the kasha ring on page 110. This dish looks
particularly attractive in the individual molds.*

1 Preheat the oven to 350°F and bring a large saucepan
of water to the boil.

2 Blanch the spinach for a minute in the boiling water so
that it becomes slightly wilted. Drain, refresh under cold
running water and remove any coarse stems.

3 Lightly grease 8 dariole molds or a 9-inch flan dish.
Line with a little over half the spinach leaves, allowing them
to overlap the top.

4 Fill with layers of tomato slices, sprinkling each layer with
basil, scallions and pepper. Fold the edges of the spinach
over the top and cover with the remaining spinach.

5 Put a small ovenproof plate or weight on top, brush
any exposed leaves with a little vegetable oil, and bake for 35-40
minutes. Turn out and serve immediately.

Ingredients
10 ounces spinach
10 ounces tomatoes, peeled and
  sliced
4-5 teaspoons chopped basil
3-4 scallions, finely chopped
pepper
a little oil

Serves 4

Photograph
*pages
188-189*

Stuffed vine leaves

*A classic Middle Eastern dish that can be eaten hot or cold.
Cabbage leaves make an excellent substitute for vine leaves.*

1 Heat the oil in a large skillet and gently fry the onion
and garam masala in it over low heat for 5-7 minutes.

2 Add the rice and stir gently for 2-3 minutes, or until the
grains are lightly fried, then pour in the boiling water
and add the saffron, pine nuts and raisins.

3 Bring back to the boil, cover and simmer for about 25-30
minutes, or until the rice is tender. Season to taste and stir
in the mint and lemon juice. Preheat the oven to 350°F.

4 Meanwhile, prepare the vine or cabbage leaves. If using
fresh leaves, blanch them, a few at a time, for a minute or
two in boiling water; if using vine leaves from a package,
rinse them thoroughly in hot water. For cabbage leaves, trim
the center rib of each leaf as shown on page 68.

Continued

Ingredients
2-3 tablespoons sunflower oil
1 onion, finely chopped
1 teaspoon garam masala
  (see p. 214)
½ cup long-grain brown rice,
  washed and drained
1¼ cups boiling water
large pinch of saffron
2 ounces pine nuts
2 ounces dark seedless raisins
salt and pepper
2 tablespoons finely chopped mint
juice of ½ lemon
24 vine leaves *or* 12 cabbage leaves
⅔ cup vegetable stock
  (see p. 151)
1 bay leaf
Garnish
slices of lemon
chopped mint

Serves 4

★

Photograph
page 69

Stuffed vine leaves continued

5 Fill each leaf as shown below and arrange them, seam side down, in a lightly greased ovenproof dish. Pour in the stock, add the bay leaf, cover with a lid or foil and bake for 45 minutes. Remove the bay leaf. Serve garnished.

FILLING THE LEAVES

1 *Remove the stalk by making straight cuts on either side of the base. If the central vein is very thick, remove it as shown for a cabbage leaf, right.*

2 *To prepare a cabbage leaf, carefully remove the thickest part of the central vein by cutting along either side with a sharp knife.*

3 *Put 2 heaping teaspoonful of filling on the center of each leaf.*

4 *Starting from the left side of the leaf, fold the base up over the filling.*

5 *Still working on the same part of the leaf, fold the side of the leaf over the filling. Fold in the other side of the leaf.*

6 *Working slowly and carefully, roll the leaf away from you to form a neat cylindrical shape.*

★

Ingredients
4 large zucchini
3 tablespoons oil, preferably olive
1 medium onion, finely chopped
2 cloves garlic, crushed
1⅓ cups bulgur wheat, washed
 and drained
2 red peppers, seeded and diced
1 teaspoon ground allspice
salt and pepper
up to 1¼ cups vegetable stock
 (see p. 151)

Continued

Stuffed zucchini with walnut sauce

Bulgur wheat, a light-textured, partially cooked wheat, provides the perfect base for the different vegetables and spices used in this stuffing.

1 Blanch the zucchini for 3-4 minutes in boiling water. Cut them in half lengthwise, scoop out the centers and chop the pulp roughly.

2 Heat 2 tablespoons of the oil in a large pan and sauté the onion and garlic gently for 3-4 minutes until transparent.

3 Put in the bulgur wheat, diced red peppers, chopped zucchini and allspice and season well. Add some stock if the mixture seems too dry and cook for 10 minutes over gentle heat, stirring constantly. Preheat the oven to 350°F.

4 Fill the zucchini shells with the mixture. Arrange them in a lightly oiled ovenproof dish, brush with the remaining oil, cover with a lid or foil and bake for 25 minutes. (Excess filling can be reserved for some other use, or cooked with the stuffed zucchini and presented on a serving dish as a bed for them.) Serve with the walnut and garlic sauce.

Sauce

Put all the ingredients into a blender and blend until smooth. Use ⅔ cup water to start with and add more if your prefer not too thick a sauce. Let stand for 1 hour. Blend again just before serving and garnish.

Sauce
4 ounces shelled walnuts, ground
4 cloves garlic, crushed
2 tablespoons fresh breadcrumbs
1 teaspoon salt
2 tablespoons olive oil
juice of 1 lemon
water
Garnish
1½ ounces finely chopped walnuts

Serves 4

Left: **Stuffed zucchini with walnut sauce**; right: **Stuffed vine leaves** (*see p. 67*)

Neapolitan peppers

The area around Naples is famous for its mild, sweet yellow peppers. This vegetarian version of a traditional dish includes raisins, hard-boiled eggs and tomato sauce.

1 Make the tomato sauce first. Gently sauté the onion and garlic for 3-4 minutes in the oil until soft. Add the tomatoes and tomato paste and simmer gently, uncovered, for 10-15 minutes, stirring from time to time, until it has reduced to a rich sauce. Season well.

2 Preheat the oven to 350°F, and bring a large saucepan of water to the boil.

3 Blanch the peppers in the boiling water for 5 minutes. Drain them and run cold water over them until they are cool enough to handle. Slice a "lid" off the top of each and reserve. With a teaspoon remove the seeds and any white pith or ribs from the inside, taking care not to puncture the skin.

4 Mix 6 tablespoons of olive oil with the breadcrumbs, raisins, olives, eggs, herbs and capers. Season well, adding more oil if the mixture seems a little dry. Stuff the peppers and arrange them in a deep baking dish.

5 Put 2 tablespoons of sauce on top of each pepper and cover with its "lid." Cover the dish and bake for 50-60 minutes. Serve hot, accompanied by the remaining sauce.

Ingredients
Tomato Sauce
1 small onion, finely chopped
2 cloves garlic, chopped
1 tablespoon olive oil
1 pound tomatoes, peeled
  and chopped
1 tablespoon tomato paste
salt and pepper

4 large peppers, yellow or red
6-8 tablespoons olive oil
8 tablespoons fresh breadcrumbs
1 ounce raisins
12 black olives, pitted and sliced
2 hard-boiled eggs, chopped
2 teaspoons dried oregano
2 tablespoons finely chopped parsley
2 tablespoons capers
salt and pepper

Serves 4

★

Broccoli and walnut bake

1 Scrub the potatoes and cook them in their skins until tender in plenty of boiling water. Peel them, mash them with the milk and season to taste.

2 Meanwhile, fry the onion and garlic gently in the oil for 3-4 minutes until soft. Add the broccoli and walnuts, cover the pan and continue cooking for 5 minutes over low heat.

3 Preheat the oven to 350°F.

4 In another saucepan, melt the butter and fry the mushrooms gently for 5 minutes. Sprinkle with the flour and cook for another 2-3 minutes, stirring.

5 Meanwhile, heat the milk to just below boiling point. Pour two-thirds of it over the mushrooms, turn up the heat and bring to the boil, stirring. Reduce the heat and simmer for 2-3 minutes. Season well.
Continued

Ingredients
1½ pounds potatoes
6 tablespoons milk
salt and pepper
1 small onion, very finely chopped
1 clove garlic, crushed
2 tablespoons oil, preferably
  sunflower
½ pound broccoli flowerets
4 ounces shelled walnuts, chopped
Sauce
4 tablespoons butter
½ pound mushrooms, chopped
⅓ cup whole-wheat flour
2 cups milk *or* milk
  and water mixed
salt and pepper

Serves 4

★

 (see p. 72)（see p. 80)

71

Broccoli and walnut bake continued

6 Put half the mashed potato in a lightly greased ovenproof dish. Cover with the walnut and broccoli mixture and pour in half the mushroom mixture. Top with the rest of the mashed potato and bake for 35 minutes or until the potatoes are just browned.

Serve with the remaining mushroom mixture, thinned to a pouring consistency by the rest of the milk and reheated gently.

★

Photograph
page 70

Ingredients
Tomato sauce
1 pound tomatoes, skinned
  and coarsely chopped
2 celery ribs, finely chopped
1 medium onion, finely chopped
2 cloves garlic, crushed
1 teaspoon chopped marjoram
1 tablespoon tomato paste

1¼ cups milk
1 medium cauliflower, divided
  into flowerets
salt and pepper

Cheese sauce
3 tablespoons butter
2 tablespoons whole-wheat flour
2 eggs
½ cup grated cheese
  (Cheddar, Gruyère or a mixture)

olive oil for frying
¾ pound eggplants, thickly
  sliced

Serves 4

Cauliflower moussaka

It is difficult to give an exact quantity of oil, since the amount eggplants soak up varies. Start with 2 tablespoons and add more as necessary. Olive oil is recommended, but it could be combined with peanut or other oils.

1 Start by preparing the tomato sauce. Put all the ingredients into a pan, cover and simmer over gentle heat for at least 15 minutes, or until you have a thick sauce. Stir occasionally. It can cook for 30 minutes or more without coming to harm.

2 Bring the milk to boiling point and poach the cauliflower in it for 5 minutes. Drain, reserving the milk. Add enough water to make it up to 1¼ cups. Chop the cauliflower finely and season well.

3 Heat the butter until it foams. Sprinkle with the flour, stir it in and cook over gentle heat for 2-3 minutes. Add the reserved cauliflower milk gradually, stirring well until thoroughly mixed. Let this simmer gently for 5 minutes.

4 Allow to cool a little, then beat in the eggs and cheese and season well. Preheat the oven to 350°F.

5 Meanwhile, heat 2 tablespoons oil in a large skillet and lightly brown the eggplant slices on both sides. Remove and drain on paper towels. Only do a few at a time, so that the oil remains hot and less of it is absorbed by the eggplants. When adding more oil, make sure it is well heated before you put in the eggplant.

6 Mix half the cheese sauce with the cauliflower. Lightly grease a 1½-quart overproof dish. Put in a layer of eggplant, then one of cauliflower mixture, and cover with tomato sauce. Continue in this order until you have used all the ingredients, finishing with a layer of eggplant. Cover with the rest of the cheese sauce and bake for 30 minutes. Serve hot.

Baked potatoes with almonds

An easy way to turn a simple baked potato into a special dish.

1 Preheat the oven to 375°F.

2 Scrub the potatoes, prick their skins and bake for 1 hour. Cut them in half and remove some of the insides, leaving enough for a good shell.

3 Mix together the garlic, almonds and lemon juice. Gradually stir in the olive oil by degrees until the mixture has a creamy consistency. Mash in the potato. Add the mushrooms and grated carrots and season well. Pile the mixture generously into the potato skins and bake for 30 minutes.

4 Meanwhile, prepare the sauce. Heat the oil and gently fry the onion and garlic for 3-4 minutes, until soft. Add the spices and bay leaf and fry for another 2 minutes. Add the remaining ingredients, bring to the boil and simmer for 30 minutes. Remove the bay leaf. If the sauce still has a grainy appearance, put it through a blender before serving.

Ingredients
4 good-sized potatoes
1-2 cloves garlic, crushed
2 ounces ground almonds
1-2 tablespoons lemon juice
3 tablespoons olive oil
¼ pound mushrooms, chopped
½ pound carrots, grated
salt and pepper
Sauce
1 tablespoon oil, preferably sunflower
1 medium onion, finely chopped
2 cloves garlic, crushed
½ tablespoon paprika
¼ teaspoon cayenne
1 bay leaf
1 tablespoon cider vinegar
3 ounces ground almonds
2 cups water
1 teaspoon honey
1 teaspoon shoyu

Serves 4

★
Photograph
page 74

Hazelnut and zucchini bake

A nutritious combination of nuts, vegetables and oatmeal, this makes a loaf that is satisfying yet not at all heavy.

1 In a large skillet gently sauté the onion for 3-4 minutes in 2 tablespoons oil. Add the hazelnuts and zucchini and cook them over moderate heat for about 10 minutes, until the nuts have browned lightly and the zucchini are soft. You may find you need to add a little extra oil, because although nuts are rich in oil themselves they tend to absorb oil while frying, especially if finely chopped.

2 Preheat the oven to 350°F.

3 Heat 2 teaspoons of oil in a small, heavy-bottomed saucepan. Mix the sesame, cumin, turmeric and ginger and fry over medium heat, stirring, for 2-3 minutes, or until they darken.

4 Away from the heat, mix the hazelnuts and zucchini with the spices, oatmeal, ground nuts, coconut and cayenne and work everything together thoroughly. Season well and stir in the puréed tomatoes.

5 Grease a 1-quart loaf pan or deep pâté dish and press the mixture in well. Bake for 35-40 minutes, or until the top is well browned and firm to the touch. Serve hot.

Ingredients
1 medium onion, finely chopped
3-4 tablespoons oil, preferably sunflower
4 ounces shelled hazelnuts, roughly chopped
1¼ pounds zucchini, diced
½ tablespoon sesame seeds
½ tablespoon cumin seeds
½ teaspoon turmeric
¼ teaspoon grated gingerroot
¾ cup medium oatmeal *or* rolled oats
3 ounces ground nuts (peanuts, cashews or almonds)
2 ounces creamed coconut, grated
pinch of cayenne
salt and pepper
5 ounces canned tomatoes, puréed

Serves 4

★
Photograph
page 74

Casserole amandine

Small new potatoes look best in this robust casserole. It takes its name from the ground almonds, which give a subtle flavor to the sauce.

1 In a large, heavy pan, ideally one with a matching lid, cook the onions gently in the oil for 3-4 minutes, stirring frequently, until they are soft and transparent but not brown.

2 Add the potatoes and carrots, cover and cook for a further 5 minutes.

3 Add the parsley, garlic, white wine and water and season well. Cover and continue cooking for another 10 minutes.

4 Meanwhile, mash the ground almonds, egg yolks and turmeric to a smooth paste, using a mortar and pestle or a wooden spoon and a bowl. Thin with 3 tablespoons of the cooking liquid and stir this mixture gradually back into the pan until thoroughly mixed.

5 Add the peas, cover, and simmer for a further 10 minutes, or until the vegetables are tender. Adjust the seasoning and serve hot, sprinkled with parsley and the finely chopped egg white.

Ingredients
2 large onions, finely chopped
1½ tablespoons olive oil
1 pound new potatoes, scrubbed
1 pound carrots, diced
2 tablespoons finely chopped parsley
6 cloves garlic, peeled and left whole
¾ cup white wine
1¼ cups water
salt and pepper
3 ounces ground almonds
2 hard-boiled egg yolks
½ teaspoon turmeric
¼ pound peas
Garnish
extra chopped parsley
hard-boiled egg white

Serves 4

Vegetable cobbler

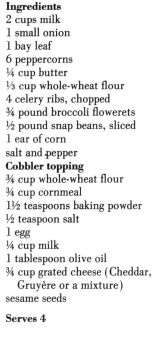

Photograph
page 77

Broccoli and corn make a simple yet effective color combination, but almost any vegetables could be used. If you want to cut down the fat content, use half milk and half vegetable stock.

1 Put the milk in a pan with the onion, bay leaf and peppercorns. Bring slowly to boiling point, turn off the heat, cover and let steep for 10 minutes. Strain.

2 Melt the butter, stir in the flour and cook for 2-3 minutes over gentle heat. Gradually add the milk, stirring constantly. Bring to the boil and simmer for 4 minutes.

3 While the milk is steeping, prepare the vegetables, starting with the celery. Put it in a large steamer over boiling water and cook for 2-3 minutes. Add the broccoli and beans and continue steaming for another 8 minutes.

4 Cook the corn in boiling water for 4-8 minutes. (The fresher it is, the less time it will take to cook.) Drain it and use a very sharp knife to scrape off the kernels.
Continued

Ingredients
2 cups milk
1 small onion
1 bay leaf
6 peppercorns
¼ cup butter
⅓ cup whole-wheat flour
4 celery ribs, chopped
¾ pound broccoli flowerets
½ pound snap beans, sliced
1 ear of corn
salt and pepper
Cobbler topping
¾ cup whole-wheat flour
¾ cup cornmeal
1½ teaspoons baking powder
½ teaspoon salt
1 egg
¼ cup milk
1 tablespoon olive oil
¾ cup grated cheese (Cheddar, Gruyère or a mixture)
sesame seeds

Serves 4

From top: **Casserole amandine; Baked potatoes with almonds** (*see p. 73*);
Hazelnut and zucchini bake (*see p. 73*)

Vegetable cobbler continued

5 Mix the vegetables with the white sauce and season well. Preheat the oven to 400°F.

6 To make the topping, mix the flour, cornmeal, baking powder and salt together in a bowl. In another bowl, beat the egg thoroughly and stir in the milk and olive oil. Beat again, pour this over the flour mixture and stir gently, adding a little extra milk if necessary, until you have a mixture stiff enough to pat out.

7 Mix in the grated cheese and roll the dough out to ½-inch thickness on a lightly floured board. Cut the dough into 1½-inch circles.

8 Pour the sauce and vegetables into a greased dish and arrange the dough circles in an attractive pattern on top. Sprinkle with sesame seeds and bake for 25 minutes, or until the top is golden brown. Serve immediately.

★

Ingredients
1 tablespoon olive oil
2 medium onions, chopped
3 cloves garlic, crushed
1 teaspoon dried thyme
1 teaspoon dried marjoram
½ teaspoon chopped fresh rosemary
2 carrots, diced
½ pound potatoes, diced
6 ounces rutabaga or kohlrabi, diced
6 ounces mushrooms, sliced
6 ounces leeks, sliced
1 pound tomatoes, peeled and chopped
1 tablespoon tomato paste
2 bay leaves
⅔ cup red wine
salt and pepper
Crumble topping
6 tablespoons butter
¾ cup whole-wheat flour
¾ cup flakes—oats, wheat, rye or barley
2 tablespoons sunflower *or* sesame seeds (optional)
salt and pepper

Serves 4

Winter hotpot

A crunchy, savory crumble topping transforms this simple stew into a substantial main dish.

1 Heat the oil in a heavy saucepan and gently fry the onion and garlic for 3-4 minutes until soft.

2 Add the herbs, carrots, potatoes, rutabaga, mushrooms and leeks, cover the pan and cook over low heat for another 3-4 minutes

3 Now add the tomatoes, tomato paste, bay leaves and red wine. Simmer, covered, for 40 minutes. Season to taste.

4 Preheat the oven to 350°F.

5 To make the crumble topping, rub the butter into the flour until the mixture resembles coarse breadcrumbs. Mix in the flakes and seeds (if used) and season well. Sprinkle this over the vegetables and bake for 25-30 minutes.

Clockwise from top: **Vegetable cobbler** (*see p. 75*); **Winter hotpot; Samosas** (*see p. 81*); **Broccoli and mushroom gratin** (*see p. 79*); **Peas and bok choy au gratin** (*see p. 78*)

SIDE VEGETABLES

If you are serving vegetables as an accompaniment, a simple presentation is often the best. Cook them lightly and serve immediately to preserve as much goodness as possible.

For most vegetables, allow ¼-½ pound per person. Almost all are suitable for boiling or steaming, except some of the fruit vegetables; eggplants benefit from being lightly fried, and tomatoes can be grilled. Carrots, parsnips, potatoes and sweet potatoes are suitable for baking. Braising is a good method for coarse leaves, such as kale, Swiss chard or red cabbage, as well as for celery and fennel. Zucchini, squashes and pumpkins can be roasted. Stir-frying is suitable for nearly all vegetables, except potatoes and woody root vegetables, such as parsnips.

Even with a simple presentation, it is worth sparing a moment or two to make it look attractive. Sprinkle with fresh herbs, chopped toasted nuts or grated orange and lemon rind. For extra flavor, toss the cooked vegetables in a little fruit juice or shoyu, or a mixture of shoyu and tahini.

Two rather more elaborate methods of preparing vegetables are cooking them *au gratin* and stir-frying. These can be served either as a main course or as an accompaniment to a substantial dish of grains or beans.

Photograph
page 77

Ingredients
1 pound shelled fresh peas
1 pound bok choy, shredded
3 tablespoons butter
2 tablespoons whole-wheat flour
1 cup Cheddar, grated
Topping
½ cup Cheddar, grated *or*
    2 tablespoons fresh
    breadcrumbs

Serves 4-6

Peas and bok choy au gratin

Gratins do not necessarily involve cheese. Gratin is a term used when a crust forms on a dish during cooking. Breadcrumbs can be used, or a mixture of breadcrumbs and cheese. A secret of success is to undercook the vegetables. Steam green vegetables until barely tender; boil root vegetables in water or milk. Use the steaming or boiling liquid as stock for the sauce. More elaborate versions can be made with two or three different vegetables, perhaps steaming one and lightly sautéing another for a contrast of texture.

1 Steam the vegetables together for 5-7 minutes, until just tender. Measure out 2½ cups of the steaming water.

2 Melt the butter. Add the flour and stir until smooth. Add the water, which should be hot but not boiling, return to a low heat and stir until thoroughly blended. Simmer for 5-6 minutes.

3 Beat the cheese into the sauce. Mix the sauce with the vegetables, turn out into a lightly greased gratin dish, sprinkle with the topping and put under a hot broiler for 3-4 minutes, until brown. Serve hot.

Broccoli and mushroom gratin

As in the previous recipe, the vegetables should be undercooked. This is a lighter dish, made by baking them in an egg custard. Other possible combinations are: steamed leek with sliced tomato, seasoned with basil; blanched fennel and celery; boiled potato and shredded cabbage sautéed and flavored with garlic and caraway.

1 Preheat the oven to 400°F.

2 Steam the broccoli for 5-7 minutes until barely tender.

3 Heat the oil and gently sauté the garlic and mushrooms for 5 minutes. Mix together the broccoli and mushrooms and turn out into a lightly greased ovenproof dish.

4 Beat the eggs thoroughly and stir in the milk. Season well and pour over the vegetables. Sprinkle with the cheese and bake for 40-45 minutes or until the custard has set.

Ingredients
1 pound broccoli flowerets
1 tablespoon olive oil
1 clove garlic, chopped
½ pound mushrooms, diced
4 eggs
2½ cups milk *or* 1¼ cups each milk and water mixed
salt and pepper
½-⅔ cup grated Cheddar

Serves 4-6

Photograph
page 77

STIR-FRYING

This is a method of frying vegetables rapidly, using a minimum amount of oil, so that they retain all their flavor and freshness and the texture is light and crisp. To achieve this, the oil must be very hot and the vegetables cut into similarly sized small pieces so that they cook as quickly and evenly as possible.

The traditional cooking vessel is a wok. It is usually made of thin metal, so the oil heats up quickly, and its rounded shape with high flaring sides means far less oil is needed than in conventional Western frying while still providing a large area for cooking.

Peanut oil is the most popular, since it can be heated to high temperatures without any loss of flavor. Sunflower oil and soybean oil are also widely used. All vegetables must be prepared beforehand, as once you start frying there is no time to do anything else.

Continued

Stir-frying continued

The basic process is as follows: spices, often garlic and ginger, are fried over medium heat to flavor the oil. Then the vegetable pieces are put in, those that will take longer to cook going first, and stirred over high heat. Finally any liquid—for example, shoyu or sherry—is added and cooked a little longer to reduce and concentrate the flavoring.

You need roughly 2-2½ pounds of vegetables to serve 4-6 people, depending on what else you are having.

Photograph
page 70

Ingredients
Marinade
1 small onion, very finely chopped
4 tablespoons peanut oil
4 tablespoons lemon juice
3 tablespoons shoyu *TAmari*
2 tablespoons dry sherry
2 teaspoons honey
1 tablespoons grated gingerroot
3 cloves garlic, crushed

8 ounces firm tofu
1 tablespoon peanut oil
1 teaspoon grated gingerroot
6 ounces bean sprouts
1 bunch scallions, chopped
6 ounces green pepper, diced
6 ounces mushrooms, sliced
6 ounces Chinese celery cabbage, shredded

Serves 4-6

Stir-fried vegetables with tofu

1 Mix all the marinade ingredients together. Cut the tofu into small chunks, pour the marinade over and leave for several hours.

2 Drain the tofu, straining the marinade into a small saucepan. Set this to heat gently while you stir-fry the tofu and vegetables as shown. Serve immediately, with the rest of the marinade passed round separately.

STIR-FRYING IN A WOK

1 *Heat the oil until it begins to smoke. Add ginger and fry, stirring, over medium heat for a minute or two.*

2 *Turn the heat up, put in the tofu chunks and stir-fry for 2-3 minutes until just beginning to brown.*

3 *Move the tofu to the side of the wok, add all the prepared vegetables and fry, stirring constantly, for 2-3 minutes, keeping the heat high.*

4 *Add 2 tablespoons of the warmed marinade and continue cooking for another 3 minutes.*

Stir-fried Chinese celery cabbage with green beans

1 Mix together the miso, hot water and shoyu. Blend the sherry and arrowroot and stir them into the miso stock.

2 Heat the oil in a wok and stir-fry the scallions, garlic, ginger and aniseeds for 1 minute over medium-high heat.

3 Put in the green beans and Chinese celery cabbage, turn the heat up high and fry for a further minute.

4 Pour the stock over the vegetables. Add the bean sprouts and continue to stir-fry for 3-4 minutes or until the liquid has evaporated. Serve immediately, sprinkled with a little sesame oil.

Ingredients
2 teaspoons miso
6 tablespoons hot water
4 tablespoons shoyu
4 tablespoons dry sherry
4 teaspoons arrowroot
4 tablespoons peanut oil
8 scallions, chopped
4 cloves garlic, finely chopped
1 inch gingerroot, diced
1 teaspoon aniseeds
½ pound green beans, sliced into 1-inch lengths
1 pound Chinese celery cabbage, sliced
½ pound bean sprouts
a few drops sesame oil

Serves 4-6

Photograph
page 83

Samosas

Traditional Indian savory snacks, with a spicy filling of potatoes and mung beans.

1 Sift the flour and salt into a bowl. Add the oil and work it in with your fingers until the mixture resembles coarse breadcrumbs. Gradually add about 4 tablespoons water and gather the dough into a stiff ball.

2 Turn the dough out onto a clean surface and knead for 3-4 minutes, or until it is quite smooth. Rub the surface lightly with a little oil, cover it with plastic wrap and let rest for 30 minutes.

3 Drain the mung beans and bring them to the boil in a saucepan of fresh water. Boil rapidly for 10 minutes, then reduce the heat and simmer, covered, for 20-30 minutes until soft.

4 Meanwhile, boil the potatoes until they are just cooked. When they are cool enough to handle dice them.

5 Heat the oil in a heavy-bottomed saucepan. Put in the spices and fry over medium-high heat until the seeds start to pop. Reduce the heat, add the onion and garlic and continue cooking over medium heat for 3-4 minutes until the onion just begins to turn brown.

6 Add the mung beans, potatoes and lemon juice. Cook over low heat for 4-5 minutes, stirring gently. Add salt to taste and let the mixture cool.

Continued

Ingredients
Pastry
2 cups whole-wheat pastry flour
½ teaspoon salt
4 tablespoons oil, preferably sunflower
4 tablespoons water
a little extra oil
Stuffing
2 ounces mung beans, soaked overnight
½ pound potatoes, peeled
1 tablespoon soya oil
¼ teaspoon turmeric
½ teaspoon ground cumin
½ teaspoon cumin seeds
1½ teaspoons coriander seeds
½ teaspoon mustard seeds
pinch of cayenne
¼ teaspoon grated gingerroot
1 small onion, finely chopped
1 clove garlic, crushed
juice of ½ lemon
salt

oil for deep-frying

Makes 16 samosas

★

Photograph
page 77

Soaking
overnight

Samosas continued

7 Knead the dough again and divide it into 8 balls. Roll each one into a 5-inch round. Cut each round in half, shape it into a cone and fill it as shown.

FILLING THE DOUGH

1 *Coil each half-circle around your thumb to shape it into a cone. Wet the edges and pinch them together to seal.*

2 *Fill each cone with a tablespoon or so of the bean and potato mixture. Do not fill it too full.*

3 *Fold the free end up over the stuffing, moisten it and press together to close firmly.*

8 Heat 2-inches oil in a deep pan over medium heat and deep fry the samosas, a few at a time. Fry slowly for 4-5 minutes, turning frequently, until they are crisp and golden brown. Drain on paper towel. They are best eaten hot or warm.

Ingredients
Choux pastry
⅔ cup water
4 tablespoons butter
⅓ cup wheatmeal flour *or*
    2½ tablespoons each whole-wheat
    flour and all-purpose white flour
    mixed
2 eggs
½ cup grated Gruyère cheese
pinch of mustard powder
pepper
Filling
1 medium onion, finely chopped
2 tablespoons butter
2 cloves garlic, crushed
1 green pepper, seeded and diced
1 pound zucchini, diced
3 teaspoons whole-wheat flour
⅔ cup milk
½ teaspoon grated nutmeg
1 teaspoon dried oregano
salt and pepper
¼ cup grated Gruyère cheese

Serves 4

Gougère with zucchini

In its native Burgundy, a gougère is served on its own, without embellishment, and can be eaten hot or cold. It also goes very well with vegetables; apart from zucchini, try cauliflower or broccoli, Brussels sprouts, mushrooms or a mixture of carrots and celery.

1 Preheat the oven to 425°F.

2 Bring the water and butter to the boil in a heavy pan.

3 Sieve the flour. When the water and butter are boiling, take the pan off the heat, add the flour all at once and beat very well until glossy.

4 Add one of the eggs, beating thoroughly until well blended. There should be no trace of egg left. Repeat with the second egg.

5 Stir in the grated cheese, mustard and pepper. Spoon the mixture round the sides of a lightly greased 9-inch flan ring or tart pan to form a ring.

6 Bake for 20 minutes. Reduce the oven to 375°F and bake for a further 10 minutes.
Continued on page 84

Top left: **Gougère with zucchini**; bottom right: **Festive pie** (*see p. 84*); top right and bottom left: **Stir-fried Chinese celery cabbage with green beans** (*see p. 81*)

Gougère with zucchini continued

7 Meanwhile, prepare the filling. Sauté the onion in the butter for 3-4 minutes. Add the garlic, green pepper and zucchini and continue cooking for another 3-4 minutes.

8 Sprinkle in the flour, stirring well, and cook for a further 3 minutes over gentle heat.

9 Stir in the milk. Bring to the boil and simmer, stirring occasionally, for 2-3 minutes. Add the nutmeg and oregano and season well.

10 When the gougère is cooked, spoon the filling into the middle, sprinkle with the grated cheese and put under a hot broiler for 3-4 minutes, or until the cheese melts and browns lightly. Serve hot.

★
Photograph
page 83

Ingredients
Flaky pastry
1⅓ cups wheatmeal flour *or* half whole-wheat flour and all-purpose white flour mixed
¼ cup rye flour
½ teaspoon salt
¾ cup vegetable shortening
squeeze of lemon juice
up to ⅔ cup ice-cold water
Filling
1 pound spinach
grated nutmeg
salt and pepper
1 pound carrots, chopped
rind and juice of ½ orange
2 tablespoons butter
3 tablespoons whole-wheat flour
2 ounces ground walnuts

Serves 4

Festive pie

Put the shortening in the freezer for at least 1 hour before beginning this recipe.

1 Mix together the two flours and the salt. Grate in the shortening. Add the lemon juice and just enough water to bind the mixture to a dough and chill for at least 4 hours. (You can make this pastry 2-3 days beforehand and keep it in the refrigerator.)

2 Wash the spinach and cook it in its own juices for 6-8 minutes, using a heavy-bottomed saucepan. Purée it with nutmeg and season to taste.

3 Cook the carrots in a little boiling water until completely soft. Drain, reserving the stock, and purée them with the orange rind and juice. Season to taste.

4 Melt the butter in a small saucepan. Add the flour and stir over gentle heat for a minute or two. Add ⅔ cup of the carrot stock, bring to the boil and simmer for 2 minutes. Remove from the heat and stir in the ground walnuts.

5 Preheat the oven to 425°F.

6 Roll out and fold the pastry as shown opposite. Use two-thirds of it to line the base and sides of a 9-inch pie plate. Layer with the carrot purée, then the walnut sauce, and finally the spinach purée.

7 Roll out the remaining pastry and cut it into strips. Use these to make a lattice top. Bake for 25-30 minutes, or until the pastry is well cooked.

Flamiche

1 Make the pastry as in the preceding recipe for festive pie. Put the shortening in the freezer for at least 1 hour before use.

2 Heat the oil or butter and gently cook the leeks and garlic for 10-15 minutes in a covered pan.

3 Sprinkle with the soy flour and mix well. Add the stock and bring to the boil, stirring. Reduce the heat and simmer for 5 minutes. Season well and let cool.

4 Roll out and fold the pastry as shown below. Preheat the oven to 425°F.

5 Roll out two-thirds of the pastry and line a 9-inch pie plate with it. Fill with the cooled leek mixture.

6 Roll out the rest of the pastry, cut it into strips and arrange them in a lattice topping. Brush with a little beaten egg and salt and bake for 20-25 minutes.

Ingredients

Flaky pastry
1⅓ cups wheatmeal flour *or* half whole-wheat flour and all-purpose white flour mixed
¼ cup rye flour
½ teaspoon salt
¾ cup vegetable shortening
squeeze of lemon juice
up to ⅔ cup ice-cold water

Filling
4 tablespoons sunflower oil *or* 4 tablespoons butter
2 pounds leeks, chopped
3 cloves garlic, crushed
½ cup soy flour
1¼ cups light vegetable stock (see p. 151)
salt and pepper

Glaze
1 egg beaten with a little salt

Serves 4

★

Photograph pages 136-137

ROLLING AND FOLDING FLAKY PASTRY

1 *Take the pastry out of the refrigerator and roll it out into a rectangle.*

2 *Mark this rectangle into thirds and fold the bottom third (the one nearest you) over the center third.*

3 *Fold over the top third and press the edges to seal them. Give the pastry a quarter turn (through 90 degrees).*

4 *Repeat the rolling and folding 3 more times, giving the pastry a quarter turn each time. Be patient if you find it a little tricky the first time.*

Christmas

A Christmas meal to please all but the most die-hard traditionalist, with a magnificent mushroom brioche as the centerpiece. It is preceded by a smooth cream of cauliflower soup flavored with sautéed almonds, and is accompanied by Brussels sprouts with chestnuts, glazed carrots and paprika rice. A thick cashew sauce adds richness, balanced by a simple salad based on salad greens in season.

The Christmas pudding, cake and mincemeat in the mince pies are all made without sugar. A persimmon sorbet offers a refreshing contrast. For a low-fat alternative to brandy butter, blend 1 cake (11 ounces) silken tofu with 1-2 tablespoons maple syrup.

Protein is provided by the rice, nuts and brioche, complemented by a variety of vegetables, both cooked and raw. The rich pudding and pies are followed by fresh fruit and nuts. The result: a festive meal proving that a sense of occasion is compatible with a healthy, balanced diet.

See pages 193-4 for a countdown of the work required, and for details on preparing the sprouts with chestnuts and the glazed carrots.

1 Mince pies (*p. 173*) **2** Rich fruit cake (*p. 167*) **3** Brandy butter **4** Rich fruit pudding (*p. 158*) **5** Persimmon and claret water ice (*p. 163*) **6** Brussels sprouts with chestnuts (*p. 194*) glazed carrots (*see p. 194*) **7** Paprika rice (*p. 100*) **8** Cashew sauce (*p. 153*) **9** Mushroom brioche (*p. 88*) **10** Green salad (*see above*) **11** Cream of cauliflower and almond soup (*p. 48*)

★

Photograph
*pages
86-87*

Ingredients
Brioche dough
½ ounce compressed yeast
1 teaspoon brown sugar
3 tablespoons lukewarm milk
1-1¼ cups wheatmeal flour *or* half
   each of whole-wheat and all-purpose
   white flour mixed
1 teaspoon salt
2 eggs
6 tablespoons butter
Filling
3 tablespoons olive oil
3 tablespoons butter
2 pounds mushrooms, chopped
2 cloves garlic
2 celery ribs, chopped
1 crisp eating apple, diced
2 tablespoons finely chopped
   parsley
1 teaspoon finely chopped marjoram
2 cups fresh breadcrumbs
2 teaspoons miso
salt and pepper

Serves 8

Mushroom brioche

An impressive party dish, with the golden crust of the brioche surrounding a dark mushroom filling. The filling and the main preparation of the dough can be done ahead of time.

1 Mix the yeast, sugar and milk together thoroughly until smooth and creamy.

2 Mix 1 cup flour with the salt in a warm bowl. Make a well in the flour and pour in the yeast mixture. Break in the eggs and stir together to make a paste.

3 In a separate bowl, beat the butter until soft, then beat it into the paste. The dough will be soft and shiny. If it is too slack, add a little extra flour. Turn it out into a clean bowl, cover with a cloth and let rise for 1-1½ hours in a warm place.

4 Punch down the dough. Knead for 2-3 minutes, place in a floured bowl, cover and leave in a cold place overnight.

5 For the filling, heat the oil and butter and gently sauté the mushrooms, garlic, celery and apple for 3-4 minutes. Cover the pan and cook over low heat for 10-15 minutes. Mix in the parsley, marjoram and breadcrumbs, beat in the miso and season to taste.

6 Preheat the oven to 400°F.

7 Roll out the brioche dough and stuff it as shown, using either a greased cookie sheet or a greased 2-quart loaf pan. If you have made the filling in advance, reheat it gently before using or it will come away from the crust.

PREPARING THE BRIOCHE

1 *Roll the dough out into a large oblong. If you are using a cookie sheet, lay the dough on it and heap up the mushroom filling down the center.*

2 *Fold up first one side and then the other so that they meet in the center.*

3 *Moisten all the edges and press them together into a neat seal. You should brush the dough with a little cream at this stage if you want to glaze it.*

4 *If you are using a loaf pan, lift the rolled-out dough with the rolling pin and ease it over the pan.*

5 *Fit the dough carefully into the pan and use a knife to trim off the excess.*

6 *Pile in the filling. Fold the sides up to meet in the center. Trim, moisten the edges and pinch together to seal.*

8 Bake for 20-25 minutes (if on a cookie sheet) or 30-35 minutes (if in a loaf pan).

Raised pie

Another party piece for which the filling can be made in advance. This one uses hot-water crust.

1 Heat the oil in a large skillet, add the diced eggplant and stir-fry briskly for 2-3 minutes until lightly browned.

2 Mix in the mushrooms, cover and cook over low heat for 10-15 minutes or until the vegetables are very soft. Stir occasionally. Mix in the parsley, season to taste and set aside to cool.

3 Meanwhile, in a saucepan, melt the butter and gently stew the fennel for 10 minutes.

4 Warm the brandy, pour it over the fennel and light it. When the flames have died down, put in the tomatoes, cover the pan and cook for another 10 minutes.

5 Add the bulgur wheat and cook for 10 minutes more, adding a little water if necessary. The mixture should be quite thick. Finally stir in the almonds, season and set aside to cool.

6 To make the crust, first mix together the flour and the salt.

7 Continue as shown on page 90. If the dough is a little dry, you may need to add extra boiling water.
Continued

Ingredients
Filling
3 tablespoons olive oil
1¼ pounds eggplant, diced
1¼ pounds mushrooms, diced
2 tablespoons finely chopped parsley
salt and pepper
2 tablespoons butter
1¼ pounds fennel bulbs, chopped
3 tablespoons brandy
1¼ pounds tomatoes, peeled
  and chopped
⅓ cup bulgur wheat
2 ounces blanched almonds,
  coarsely chopped (see p. 209)
Crust
3¾ cups whole-wheat flour
1 teaspoon salt
¾ cup vegetable shortening
⅔ cup water
beaten egg for glazing

Serves 6-8

★
Photograph
*pages
54-55*

Raised pie continued

8 Preheat the oven to 425°F.

9 Use two-thirds of the dough as shown to line the base and sides of a 9-inch straight-sided cake pan or hinged raised-pie mold. Put in half the mushrooms and eggplant, then all the fennel and tomato mixture, and finally the rest of the mushrooms and eggplant. Press in well.

10 Cover with the remaining dough as shown. Brush it with a little beaten egg to glaze and pierce a hole in the center so that the steam can escape.

11 Bake for 20 minutes, then reduce the oven to 375°F and bake for a further 50-60 minutes, or until the pastry is well cooked. Serve hot.

MAKING THE CRUST

1 Melt the shortening and water together, bring to a rapid boil and pour this over the flour and salt. Mix together with a wooden spoon.

2 As soon as the mixture is cool enough to handle, knead it quickly into a ball. Divide into two-thirds and one-third.

3 Work the larger piece of dough over the base and up the sides of the mold, stretching and patting it into position.

4 With your forefinger, make a channel around the base where it joins the side. This is to avoid having too solid a chunk of pastry.

5 Roll out the rest of the dough to fit the top and use the rolling pin to lay it on. Moisten the edges with water.

6 Pinch the edges to seal and make an attractive pattern. Trim off excess dough. You can use the trimmings to make decorations.

BEANS, PEAS & LENTILS

Beans, peas and lentils are far more than just a necessary source of protein. By themselves they are savory and satisfying; combined with vegetables and cereals they create a balance of complementary flavors, textures and nutrients.

Preparation is simple. You may need to pick them over first, especially lentils, for small pieces of grit, then rinse to get rid of surface dust. Whole beans and peas need preliminary soaking—see page 208 for details and cooking times.

In all these recipes, except the Mexican croustade, the bean mixture can be made in advance—in fact should be, if you have time, as the flavors improve and develop. Plainly cooked beans can be frozen, which often saves time.

Haricots Catalan

1 Drain the beans. Cover with fresh water, bring to the boil and boil rapidly for 10 minutes. Reduce the heat and simmer, covered, for 40-50 minutes, or until tender. Drain and set aside.

2 Meanwhile, parboil the snap beans in boiling water for 3-5 minutes until barely tender. Drain and set aside.

3 In a large, heavy-bottomed skillet gently sauté the garlic and onions in the oil over moderate heat for about 5 minutes or until the onion is soft and translucent.

4 Stir in the chopped tomatoes and parsley and season well with pepper. Bring to the boil and cook, uncovered, until most of the liquid has evaporated.

5 Stir in all the beans and simmer for 5-6 minutes longer or until heated through. Check the seasoning and serve hot.

Ingredients
¾ cup haricot *or* pinto beans, soaked overnight
½ pound snap beans, cut into 2-inch pieces
3-4 cloves garlic, finely chopped
¼ pound onions, finely chopped
2 tablespoons oil, preferably olive
1¼ pounds tomatoes, peeled and finely chopped
2 tablespoons finely chopped parsley
salt and pepper

Serves 4

★
Photograph
page 93

Soaking
overnight

★

Ingredients
Piecrust
¾ cup whole-wheat flour
½ teaspoon baking powder
pinch salt
2 tablespoons butter
2 tablespoons vegetable shortening
1 teaspoon brown sugar
2-3 tablespoons water
2 teaspoons oil
Filling
1 tablespoon sunflower oil
6 ounces onions, chopped
1 teaspoon ground coriander
1 teaspoon ground cumin
¾ cup red split lentils
1⅔ cups boiling water
¾ pound spinach
1 tablespoon lemon juice
salt and pepper
Garnish
2 tablespoons sesame seeds

Serves 4

Lentil and spinach quiche

Lentils are particularly suitable as fillings for quiches or pies since they cook to a purée quickly. This recipe is an excellent way of using up any leftover cooked lentils.

1 Mix the flour, baking powder and salt together in a bowl. Cut in the butter and shortening until you have a mixture resembling fine breadcrumbs.

2 Dissolve the sugar in 2 tablespoons water. Mix in the oil and add this to the flour mixture. Add a little more water if necessary to bind the mixture. The dough should be on the wettish side. Leave to rest for 30 minutes.

3 Preheat the oven to 400°F.

4 Roll out the dough to line an 8-inch flan ring. Press it in well, prick the base all over and bake for 5 minutes to set it.

5 Meanwhile, heat the oil in a large, heavy-bottomed saucepan and gently fry the onions and spices for 3-4 minutes.

6 Add the lentils to the saucepan together with the boiling water. Bring back to the boil and simmer, covered, for 10-15 minutes, until the lentils turn to a stiff purée.

7 While the lentils are cooking, wash the spinach, drain it well and cook it in its own juices in a covered pan for 6-8 minutes, until just done. Drain and chop. Mix it into the lentils with the lemon juice and seasoning.

8 Spread this filling over the prepared flan base. Cover loosely with foil and bake for 25-30 minutes until the pastry is cooked and the filling hot. Sprinkle with sesame seeds and serve hot or warm.

Variations
For an alternative, simpler filling, use 1 cup each of lentils and onions. Fry the onions in the oil, as above, using 1 teaspoon turmeric instead of the coriander and cumin. Mix this into the lentils and add about 2 teaspoons whole-grain mustard, 1 tablespoon peanut butter, and salt and pepper to taste.

This filling also lends itself to tartlets, ideal for a cocktail party or buffet (see photograph on pages 44-45). The quantities given are enough for 12 medium or 20 miniature tartlets. As a further variation, peel and roughly chop about ½ pound tomatoes. Put one or two pieces in each tartlet before covering with the lentil purée and baking.

From top: **Haricots Catalan** (*see p. 91*); **Chick pea and fennel casserole** (*see p. 94*); **Lentil and spinach quiche**

★
Photograph
page 93

Soaking
overnight

Ingredients
¾ cup chick peas, soaked
    overnight
2 tablespoons olive oil
1 clove garlic, crushed
5 celery ribs, diced
½ pound fennel bulbs, sliced
½ pound green beans, chopped
2 ounces bulgur wheat
1¼ cups cider, sweet or dry
1¼ cups light vegetable stock
    (see p. 151)
2 tablespoons finely chopped mint
salt and pepper

Serves 4

Chick pea and fennel casserole

Serve with lightly steamed green vegetables and cornbread or barley for a complete meal.

1 Drain the chick peas. Cover with fresh water, bring to the boil and boil rapidly for 10 minutes. Reduce the heat and simmer, covered, for 45-50 minutes, or until just soft. They need not be fully cooked at this stage as they will get another 20 minutes cooking. Drain and set aside.

2 Heat the oil and lightly fry the garlic for 2-3 minutes. Put in the celery, fennel and green beans and cook them over low heat, covered, for 5-6 minutes.

3 Add the chick peas and stir-fry for 2-3 minutes. Add the bulgur wheat, cider and stock, bring to the boil, cover and simmer for 20 minutes.

4 Stir in the fresh mint and season well. Cook for another 10 minutes and serve hot.

★
Soaking
overnight

Ingredients
½ cup red kidney beans, soaked
    overnight
Crust
⅔ cup fresh breadcrumbs
½ cup whole-wheat flour
½ cup wheat germ
½ cup rolled oats
8 tablespoons butter
Filling
¾ pound sweet potato, peeled
    and diced
salt and pepper
1 medium onion, diced
1⅓ tablespoons sunflower oil
½ teaspoon ground cardamom
½ teaspoon ground cinnamon
1 ripe avocado, diced
juice and grated rind of 1 orange

Serves 4

Mexican croustade

There is a strong Mexican influence in this combination of sweet potato, red kidney beans (chili beans), orange and avocado.

1 Drain the beans. Cover with fresh water, bring to the boil and boil fast for 10 minutes. Reduce the heat and simmer, covered, for 35-40 minutes or until tender. Drain and set aside.

2 Preheat the oven to 375°F.

3 To make the crust, mix together the breadcrumbs, flour, wheat germ and oats. Melt the butter and pour it over the dry ingredients. Mix thoroughly and press into a 9-inch greased flan ring. Bake for 15-20 minutes.

4 Meanwhile, cook the sweet potato in boiling water, covered, for 15-20 minutes. Drain and mash with plenty of salt and pepper.

5 Gently fry the onion in the oil for 3-4 minutes, until soft. Add the spices and continue frying over moderate heat, stirring, for a minute or two. Put in the cooked beans and the avocado and fry for a further 2-3 minutes. Add the orange juice and rind and cook for 5 minutes more.

6 Spread the sweet potato over the flan base and cover with the bean and avocado mixture. Cover loosely with foil and bake for 10-15 minutes. Serve hot or warm.

Clockwise from left: **Black-eyed pea croquettes** (*see p. 96*); **Corn and lima bean casserole** (*see p. 96*); **Mexican croustade**

★

Photograph
page 95

Soaking
overnight

Ingredients
½ cup lima beans, soaked
  overnight
½ pound fresh corn kernels
  (about 2 ears)
1 small onion, finely chopped
4 celery ribs, cut into ½-inch
  lengths
3 tablespoons sunflower oil
1 tablespoon whole-wheat flour
⅔ cup yogurt
2 tablespoons chopped parsley
salt and pepper
Topping
1½ tablespoons sesame seeds
1½ tablespoons fresh breadcrumbs
a little oil (preferably sesame)

Serves 4

Corn and lima bean casserole

1 Drain the beans. Cover with fresh water, bring to the boil and boil rapidly for 10 minutes. Reduce the heat and simmer, covered, for 50-60 minutes. Drain, reserving the stock.

2 Meanwhile, cook the corn in boiling water until tender— about 4 minutes if very fresh, another minute or two if less so.

3 In a large, heavy-bottomed saucepan, gently fry the onion and celery in the oil for 4-5 minutes until soft. Put in the cooked lima beans and corn and fry for another 2-3 minutes. Sprinkle with flour, stir well and cook for another 2-3 minutes.

4 Preheat the oven to 350°F.

5 Mix together ⅔ cup of the bean stock and the yogurt. Stir this into the vegetables and cook over gentle heat for 10-15 minutes, stirring occasionally. Mix in the parsley, season and turn out into an ovenproof dish.

6 To make the topping, mix the sesame seeds and breadcrumbs with just enough oil to moisten but not bind them. Sprinkle over the casserole and bake for 10-15 minutes or until crisp.

★

Photograph
page 95

Soaking
overnight

Ingredients
1 cup black-eyed peas,
  soaked overnight
2 cups fresh breadcrumbs
2 ounces ground Brazil nuts
1 cup grated Cheddar
1 clove garlic, crushed
1 teaspoon marjoram
1 teaspoon dried sage
salt and pepper
Coating
1 egg white, beaten
flour or breadcrumbs
salt and pepper

oil for shallow frying

Makes 8 croquettes

Black-eyed pea croquettes

For a different texture, use cooked short grain rice, millet or buckwheat instead of the breadcrumbs.

1 Drain the beans. Cover with fresh water, bring to the boil and boil rapidly for 10 minutes. Reduce the heat and simmer, covered, for 35-40 minutes or until tender.

2 Drain the beans again and mash them. Mix with all the other ingredients and season to taste. The mixture should be quite moist. Chill for an hour or two or until firm.

3 Shape into 8 croquettes about ½-inch thick. Dip first into beaten egg white and then into seasoned flour or breadcrumbs. Shallow fry for 4-5 minutes on each side.

★

Photograph
*pages
180-181*

Soaking
overnight

Ingredients
¾ cup aduki beans, soaked
  overnight
2 tablespoons olive oil
¾ pound mushrooms, chopped
1 clove garlic, crushed
Continued

Mushroom and aduki croquettes

These are also good with herbs, such as parsley or coriander, instead of spices. They can be served in a wholemeal bun.

1 Drain the beans. Cover with fresh water, bring to the boil and boil rapidly for 10 minutes. Reduce the heat and simmer, covered, for 35-40 minutes or until tender. Drain and set aside.

2 Heat the oil in a large saucepan and gently fry the mushrooms, garlic, chili peppers and cumin for 5-6 minutes, or until the mushrooms are very soft.

3 Sprinkle with the flour. Continue cooking over low heat, blending the flour well in, for 2-3 minutes. Off the heat, mix in the beans and season well. The consistency should be soft but not mushy. Chill for several hours or overnight.

4 Shape into 8 croquettes about ½-inch thick. Dip first into beaten egg and then into oatmeal. Fry in hot oil for 4-5 minutes on each side. Serve hot.

1-2 dried red chili peppers, seeded and diced
1 teaspoon ground cumin
2 tablespoons whole-wheat flour
salt and pepper
Coating
1 small egg, beaten
⅔ cup fine oatmeal

oil for shallow frying

Makes 8 croquettes

Aduki beans in wine

1 Drain the beans. Put them in a pan with fresh water to cover. Add the onion studded with cloves, the garlic, carrot, peppercorns, celery and half the olive oil. Bring to the boil and boil rapidly for 10 minutes. Reduce the heat and simmer, covered, for 35-40 minutes, or until tender.

2 Drain the beans again, reserving the stock. Discard the onion, garlic and peppercorns. Mash or purée the carrot and celery into the stock.

3 Heat the remaining oil in a large, heavy-bottomed saucepan and gently cook the onions, potatoes and zucchini for 3-4 minutes. Add the beans and cook for 5 minutes. Pour in 1¼ cups of the bean stock. Stir in the tomato paste, wine and cognac and bring to the boil. Simmer, covered, for 35 minutes, or until thick. Season well and serve hot.

Ingredients
1 cup aduki beans, soaked overnight
1 onion, peeled
2 cloves
3 cloves garlic, peeled
1 carrot, chopped into 3 pieces
8 peppercorns
2 celery ribs, cut into 1-inch pieces
2 tablespoons olive oil
½ pound small white onions, peeled
½ pound potatoes, diced
½ pound zucchini, sliced
3 tablespoons tomato paste
3 tablespoons red wine
3 tablespoons cognac
salt and pepper

Serves 4

★

Photograph
page 98

Soaking
overnight

Mung dhal with spinach

1 Wash the mung beans and soak for 2 hours. Drain.

2 Wash the spinach, drain well and cook, covered, for 5 minutes, until barely cooked. Drain and chop coarsely.

3 Heat the ghee or oil in a skillet and gently fry the onion and ginger for 2-3 minutes. Add the garlic, cumin and turmeric and fry, stirring, for another minute or two.

4 Add the drained dhal and continue frying over moderate heat for 2-3 minutes. Add 1¼ cups cold water, bring to the boil, cover and simmer for 20 minutes, or until the dhal is tender. Purée if desired.
Continued on page 99

Ingredients
1 cup split mung beans
1 pound spinach
1½ tablespoons ghee (see p. 220) *or* oil
1 medium onion, finely chopped
1 inch gingerroot, thinly sliced
2 cloves garlic, crushed
2 teaspoons ground cumin
1 teaspoon ground turmeric
1¼ cups cold water
2 ounces creamed coconut, grated
⅓ cup boiling water
salt

Serves 4

★

Photograph
page 98

5 Dissolve the creamed coconut in ⅓ cup boiling water, stirring vigorously until well blended. Add this to the dhal together with the chopped spinach. Season with salt and serve hot or warm.

Mung dhal with spinach continued

Spiced black beans

This recipe looks good served on contrastingly colored bulgur wheat, but also goes well with brown rice or couscous.

1 Drain the beans. Cover with fresh water, bring to the boil and boil rapidly for 10 minutes. Reduce the heat and simmer, covered, for 15-20 minutes. Drain, reserving the stock.

2 Meanwhile, using a heavy-bottomed saucepan, gently fry the onion and garlic in the oil for 3-4 minutes. Put in the spices and fry for another minute or two, stirring.

3 Add the drained beans, chili, green peppers, carrots, peanuts and sliced orange. Cook, covered, over gentle heat for 10 minutes, stirring occasionally.

4 Mix in the sherry, lemon juice and shoyu. Add up to 2 tablespoons bean stock if the mixture is dry, although the end result should not be watery. Cook, covered, for a further 10-15 minutes. Adjust the seasoning and serve hot, garnished with the extra orange slices.

Ingredients
½ cup black beans, soaked overnight
1 onion, finely chopped
2 cloves garlic, crushed
1-2 tablespoons olive oil
1 teaspoon grated gingerroot
½ teaspoon ground cumin
½ teaspoon ground coriander
1 small fresh green chili, finely chopped
2 green peppers, diced
½ pound carrots, diced
2 ounces roasted peanuts
1 orange, peeled and thinly sliced
1 tablespoon sherry
juice of ½ lemon
1 teaspoon shoyu
salt and pepper
Garnish
1 orange, sliced

Serves 4

Soaking
overnight

Soybean casserole

Soybeans take a long time to cook whole but are good in casseroles, especially here with the contrast of water chestnuts.

1 Drain the soybeans. Cover with plenty of fresh water, bring to the boil and boil rapidly for 1 hour. This long boiling time makes them more digestible. Reduce the heat and simmer, covered, for another hour, or until they are soft. Drain, reserving the stock, and set aside.

2 Heat the oil in a large, heavy-bottomed saucepan and briskly sauté the chili, ginger and garlic for 2-3 minutes. Add the vegetables, including the water chestnuts, and continue cooking, covered, for 10 minutes over gentle heat.

3 In a bowl, mix together the cornstarch, sherry and shoyu and blend in the stock. Add to the saucepan together with the cooked soybeans. Stir well, bring to the boil and simmer, covered, for 10 minutes. Season and serve hot.

Ingredients
½ cup soybeans, soaked overnight
1 tablespoon sunflower oil
½ teaspoon chili powder
1 teaspoon grated gingerroot
1 clove garlic, crushed
3 ounces scallions, diced
¾ pound mushrooms, sliced
4 celery ribs, cut into julienne strips (see p. 222)
¼ pound carrots, cut into julienne strips (see p. 222)
3 ounces water chestnuts, thinly sliced
3½ teaspoons cornstarch
1 tablespoon sherry
1 tablespoon shoyu
1¼ cups soybean stock
salt and pepper

Serves 4

★

Soaking
overnight

From top: **Spiced black beans; Aduki beans in wine** (*see p. 97*); **Mung dhal with spinach** (*see p. 97*); **Soybean casserole**

99

GRAINS

As with legumes, the vegetarian kitchen pantry comes into its own with grains. Apart from rice, there are many others, such as wheat, barley, millet, buckwheat and bulgur wheat, to give different textures and unexpected flavors. Cook grains as casseroles, with fresh vegetables or dried beans and lentils, or serve them as accompaniments to other dishes, perhaps with a nut or vegetable sauce. For croquettes, millet and bulgur wheat are the best, since they can be easily molded. Otherwise, most grains can be used interchangeably, although the delicate taste of wild rice is probably best appreciated when it is boiled plain.

Grain dishes are generally simple and quick to make, often using only one saucepan. Many can be cooked in advance and/or frozen. Thaw overnight in the refrigerator and reheat gently, either in the oven covered with wax paper or foil, or by steaming. There are more ideas for cold grain dishes in the Salad section.

★

Photograph
pages
86-87

Ingredients
1 tablespoon oil
1 small onion, finely chopped
2 celery ribs, diced
1 cup long-grain brown rice
1 tablespoon paprika
2 cups boiling water
1 bay leaf
2 teaspoons shoyu
salt and pepper

Serves 4

Paprika rice

An easy variation on a basic method of cooking long-grain rice. For golden rice, substitute 1-2 teaspoons turmeric (or a pinch of saffron threads) for the paprika. For a simpler version, omit the celery and paprika.

1 Heat the oil in a large, heavy-bottomed saucepan and gently sauté the onion and celery for 3-4 minutes until beginning to soften.

2 Add the rice and paprika and continue cooking for another 3-4 minutes, stirring and turning the rice to coat it thoroughly with the oil.

3 Add the boiling water and bay leaf and bring back to the boil.

4 Cover and simmer for 20-25 minutes, or until the rice is tender. Remove the bay leaf. Stir in the shoyu and season to taste. Let stand for 5-10 minutes before serving. This can be kept warm for up to 20 minutes in a warm oven— useful if you want to serve it with, say, stir-fried vegetables, which will need all your attention.

Sweet pilaf with fennel sauce

Pale golden seedless raisins look better in this than the dark ones.

1 In a large, heavy-bottomed saucepan, fry the onion gently in the oil for 3-4 minutes. Add the spices and cook for 2-3 more minutes to bring out the flavor.

2 Put in the almonds, raisins, figs or dates, and the rice. Cook for 3-4 minutes, stirring well. Add the lemon juice, then the boiling water, and simmer, covered, for about 30-35 minutes, or until the rice is tender and all the water absorbed. Season to taste. Keep hot.

3 Meanwhile, prepare the sauce. Simmer the fennel in the boiling water for 40 minutes with the lid on. Strain, discard the fennel and mix the stock with the orange juice.

4 Blend the arrowroot with the cold water. Mix it into the stock, bring to the boil and simmer for 3-4 minutes, or until the arrowroot is cooked and you have a clear, smooth sauce. Season to taste and serve with the pilaf.

Ingredients
Pilaf
1 small onion, finely chopped
1 tablespoon sunflower oil
1 teaspoon grated gingerroot
1 teaspoon coriander seeds, crushed
½ teaspoon fennel seeds
1 ounce almonds, blanched (see p. 209) and chopped
1 ounce golden seedless raisins
4 ounces dried figs *or* dates, finely chopped
¾ cup long-grain brown rice
juice of ½ lemon
2 cups boiling water
salt and pepper
Sauce
½ pound fennel, finely chopped
1¼ cups boiling water
juice of 2 oranges
1 tablespoon arrowroot
1 tablespoon cold water

Serves 4

★

Photograph
page 102

Risotto verde

This is a basic recipe for cooking short-grain rice. Unlike long-grain rice, it needs the liquid to be added a little at a time in order to cook to the right consistency. Mushrooms, fresh or dried, go well in risottos. So do fresh young peas, broccoli and zucchini. Chopped nuts make a good contrast in textures.

1 In a heavy-bottomed saucepan, cook the spinach in its own juices for about 6 minutes over moderate heat, covered. Drain and chop finely.

2 Heat the oil with half the butter and gently fry the onion for 4 minutes. Put in the rice and cook gently, stirring, for 5 minutes. It should be coated with the oil and butter but must not brown.

Continued

Ingredients
1 pound spinach, washed
1 tablespoon olive oil
4 tablespoons butter
1 onion, finely chopped
1½ cups short-grain brown rice
4¼ cups boiling vegetable stock (see p. 151)
1 clove garlic, crushed
1 teaspoon dried oregano
¾ cup grated Parmesan cheese
juice of ½ lemon
salt and pepper

Serves 4

★

Photograph
page 102

3 Add about a quarter of the stock and continue to cook over low heat, stirring occasionally, until all the stock has been absorbed. This will take from 5 to 10 minutes.

4 Add the same amount of the stock again, together with the spinach, garlic and oregano, and cook in the same way until this stock too has been absorbed.

5 Add the remaining stock gradually, stirring from time to time, until the rice is tender. You may not need quite all the stock. Just before serving, stir in the grated Parmesan, lemon juice and the rest of the butter and season to taste.

Risotto verde continued

Vegetable curry with cashews

The curried vegetables can be prepared well in advance, but the rice is best if freshly cooked, and the cashews should be added at the last minute. Plain yogurt goes well with this.

1 Heat the oil or ghee in a large, heavy-bottomed saucepan and fry the garlic and spices for 3-4 minutes over medium heat to bring out the flavor.

2 Blanch the eggplants for 4-5 minutes in boiling water. Drain and dice them.

3 Add all the vegetables, including the green chili, to the saucepan. Fry gently for 5-7 minutes, stirring to mix thoroughly with the spices.

4 Dissolve the grated coconut in the boiling water and mix with the vegetables. Add the tomatoes and cook, covered, for 20 minutes. Keep warm.

5 To cook the rice, bring 2 cups water to the boil. Put in the rice, stir once and bring back to the boil. Cover and simmer for 20-25 minutes, or until the rice is cooked. Do not salt the water but add salt to taste when the rice is cooked.

6 Toast the cashews under the broiler for 2-3 minutes, turning once. Stir them into the vegetables just before serving.

Ingredients

1 tablespoon peanut oil or ghee
  (see p. 220)
2 cloves garlic, chopped
¼ teaspoon cayenne
2 teaspoons ground coriander
1 teaspoon ground cumin
1 teaspoon turmeric
¾ inch gingerroot, sliced
2 medium eggplants
1 small cauliflower, divided into
  flowerets
2 medium potatoes, diced
4 ounces green beans, chopped
1 fresh green chili, finely chopped
2 ounces creamed coconut, grated
½ cup boiling water
1 pound tomatoes, peeled
  and chopped
1 cup long-grain brown rice
salt
4 ounces cashew nuts

Serves 4-6

Clockwise from top left: **Sweet pilaf with fennel sauce** (*see p. 101*); **Vegetable curry and yogurt**; **Risotto verde** (*see p. 101*)

103

Photograph
*pages
180-181*

Ingredients
½ cup yellow split peas
1 tablespoon sunflower oil
1 onion, finely chopped
½ teaspoon coriander seeds, crushed
½ teaspoon cumin seeds, crushed
½ inch gingerroot, chopped
1 teaspoon turmeric
¼ teaspoon cayenne
½ cup long-grain brown rice
1 fresh green chili, finely chopped
2 cups boiling water
juice of ½ lemon
2 tomatoes, peeled and chopped
salt

Serves 4

Khichhari

This is the forerunner of the modern British kedgeree. It is an ideal dish to make in advance and reheat. Lentils or mung beans, whole or split, can be used instead of the split peas.

1 Soak the split peas in boiling water for 1 hour and drain.

2 In a large, heavy-bottomed saucepan, heat the oil and fry the onions and spices for 3-4 minutes over medium heat.

3 Add the drained split peas, rice and green chili. Mix well. Add the boiling water and lemon juice. Then add the tomatoes, stir once, cover and simmer very gently for 35-40 minutes, or until the rice and peas are tender. Season with salt and serve hot or warm.

★

Photograph
page 106

Soaking
overnight

Ingredients
1 cup wheat berries, soaked
    overnight and drained
¾ pound asparagus, cleaned
4 tablespoons butter
1 large leek, diced
½ small cauliflower, divided into
⅔ tiny flowerets
3 tablespoons whole-wheat flour
    cup milk
2 tablespoons chopped chervil *or*
    parsley
juice of ½ lemon, or to taste
4 ounces sorrel *or* lovage,
    chopped
salt and pepper

Serves 4-6

Fricassée Argenteuil

This vegetable dish takes its name from Argenteuil, near Paris, famous for its asparagus. If you are using lovage, you will need more lemon juice than if you are using sorrel.

1 Put the wheat berries in a kettle with plenty of water, bring to the boil and simmer, covered, for 50-60 minutes, adding more water if they dry out. Drain.

2 Tie the asparagus into a bunch. Bring a kettle of water to the boil and cook the asparagus for 7-8 minutes, until just tender. Drain, reserving the stock. Cut off the tough woody ends of the asparagus and chop the rest into 1-inch lengths.

3 Melt the butter in a heavy-bottomed saucepan and gently cook, covered, the leek and cauliflower for 10 minutes. Sprinkle with the flour and cook for another 2-3 minutes, stirring from time to time.

4 Mix 1¼ cups of the asparagus stock with the milk. Add this to the pan and bring to the boil, stirring constantly to prevent the formation of lumps.

5 Put in the cooked wheat berries, chervil and lemon juice. Return to the boil and simmer for 2-3 minutes. Stir in the asparagus and sorrel or lovage. Season well and simmer for another 2-3 minutes for the flavors to develop. Stir and serve immediately.

Couscous

A vegetarian adaptation of the traditional North African dish. If you do not have a proper couscous steamer, an ordinary strainer that fits over a deep, heavy-bottomed saucepan works perfectly well.

1 Heat the oil and fry the spices for 3-4 minutes over moderate heat to bring out their flavor. Add the onion and cook for another 2-3 minutes until it just begins to soften. Mix in the garlic, vegetables and raisins.

2 Put the couscous in a fine-mesh strainer or steamer lined with muslin. Pour boiling water over it so that the grains are all moistened. This will speed up the cooking time considerably.

3 Set the steamer over the vegetables. Cover and cook over gentle heat for 20 minutes, stirring the vegetables occasionally. The steam from the vegetables will cook the couscous in this time.

4 Season both the couscous and the vegetables with salt, adding pepper only if you think it is needed. Transfer the couscous to a serving dish and arrange the vegetables over it.

Ingredients
2 tablespoons sunflower oil
1 teaspoon cayenne
2 teaspoons yellow mustard seeds
1 teaspoon paprika
1 onion, finely chopped
3 cloves garlic, crushed
2 green peppers, seeded and diced
¾ pound zucchini, sliced
2 medium potatoes, diced
6 ounces okra, diced
¾ pound tomatoes, peeled and chopped
2 ounces raisins
1¼ cups couscous
boiling water
salt and pepper

Serves 4-6

★
Photograph
page 106

Barley and tomatoes in sour cream

This is delicious hot but is equally good served cold, without the cheese topping, as an unusual salad.

1 Heat the oil in a large saucepan over moderate heat and fry the barley for 3-4 minutes. Add enough boiling water to cover it by 2 inches. Cover and simmer for 50-60 minutes or until tender. Drain and set aside.

2 Preheat the oven to 375°F.

3 Coarsely chop half the tomatoes and mix them into the barley with the olives, mushrooms, dill weed, sour cream and half the cheese. Season well and turn out into a lightly greased ovenproof dish.

4 Slice the remaining tomatoes and arrange the slices in a layer on top. Sprinkle with the remaining cheese. Bake for 10-15 minutes or until the cheese has melted and begins to brown.

Ingredients
1 teaspoon oil
1 cup whole barley
boiling water
1¼ pounds tomatoes, peeled
2 ounces black olives, pitted and finely chopped
½ pound mushrooms, diced
2 teaspoons dried dill weed
⅔ cup sour cream
1 cup grated Cheddar
salt and pepper

Serves 4-6

★
Photograph
page 106

Polenta with spicy sauce

A traditional Northern Italian dish, perfect polenta should be light and soft on the inside with a crisp outer shell. A sauce that could be used instead of the spicy one given here is the green split pea sauce on page 152. Polenta goes well with steamed green vegetables (snap beans or broccoli) or with sautéed eggplant, zucchini and peppers.

1 Bring the water to the boil. Sprinkle in the cornmeal gradually, stirring well to prevent any lumps forming. Add the salt and butter and continue cooking over low heat, covered, for 20 minutes. Stir the polenta frequently to prevent it sticking to the saucepan or becoming lumpy. When cooked it should be thick and creamy.

2 Pour into a wide, lightly greased dish to cool and set. A dish about 13 x 9 inches is ideal. The polenta should be about ½-inch thick.

3 For the sauce, gently fry the onion and garlic in the oil for 3-4 minutes, or until it begins to soften. Add the chili and red peppers and cook for another 3-4 minutes. Stir in the tomatoes and tomato paste, cover and simmer for 15-20 minutes, or until you have a rich, thick sauce. Season well.

4 When the polenta is quite cold, cut it into small squares. Dip each one first into beaten egg and then into cornmeal. Deep-fry, a few at a time, until brown. Serve hot, covered with the sauce.

Ingredients
4¾ cups water
2 cups yellow cornmeal
1 teaspoon salt
4 tablespoons butter
Red pepper sauce
1 large onion, finely chopped
2 cloves garlic, crushed
2 tablespoons olive oil
¼-½ teaspoon chili powder *or* 1 dried chili, finely chopped
2 red peppers, seeded and diced
1 pound tomatoes, peeled and chopped
1 tablespoon tomato paste
salt and pepper
Coating
1 egg, beaten
extra cornmeal

oil for deep frying

Serves 4

★

Savory millet

If you have never cooked millet before, this simple method makes an excellent introduction. It is particularly popular with children.

1 Heat the oil in a large, heavy-bottomed saucepan and lightly fry the onion, pepper and garlic for 3-4 minutes. Add the millet and cook for a further 2-3 minutes until it just begins to brown.

2 Heat the milk and water together until hot but not boiling. Add to the millet and bring to the boil. Stir once, cover and simmer for 20 minutes, or until the millet is cooked.

3 Quickly stir in the grated cheese and chopped parsley, reserving a little of each for the garnish. Season well and serve immediately, sprinkled with the remaining cheese and parsley.

Ingredients
2 tablespoons sunflower oil
1 onion, finely chopped
1 red pepper, seeded and diced
2 cloves garlic, crushed
1¼ cups millet grains
3 cups milk and water mixed—roughly half and half
1 cup grated Cheddar
4 tablespoons finely chopped parsley
salt and pepper

Serves 4-6

★

Photograph
page 109

Clockwise from top: **Fricassée Argenteuil** (*see p. 104*); **Barley and tomatoes in sour cream** (*see p. 105*); **Polenta with spicy sauce; Couscous** (*see p. 105*)

107

★

Photograph *pages* *188-189*

Ingredients
2 medium eggplants, thickly sliced
olive oil for frying
2 tablespoons tahini
2 tablespoons water
juice of ½ lemon
1 clove garlic, crushed
1 teaspoon shoyu
Millet pilaf
1 small onion, finely chopped
1 tablespoon olive oil
1 large clove garlic, crushed
1 teaspoon ground coriander
1 cup millet grains
4 ounces dried apricots, washed
4 cloves
1 cup white wine or cider
2 cups boiling water
salt and pepper

Serves 4

Byzantine millet pilaf

The combination of apricots and grains, topped with eggplant baked in a sesame sauce, is influenced by Middle Eastern cookery.

1 Preheat the oven to 350°F.

2 Lightly sauté the eggplant slices in the olive oil until just browned and softened. Arrange them in layers in a shallow ovenproof dish.

3 Mix the tahini with the water in a bowl. Add the lemon juice, garlic and shoyu and blend thoroughly. Pour this over the eggplant slices and bake, uncovered, for 20 minutes. Keep warm.

4 Meanwhile, gently fry the onion in 1 tablespoon olive oil for 3-4 minutes, until soft. Add the garlic, coriander and millet and fry for another 2-3 minutes.

5 Cut the apricots into thin slivers. Add them to the skillet together with the cloves, white wine or cider and boiling water. Bring back to the boil and simmer for 20 minutes, or until the millet is cooked. Season well and serve hot with the eggplant.

★

Ingredients
1 teaspoon oil
⅓ cup millet grains
2 cups boiling water
½ cake silken tofu—approx.
    5 ounces
2 tablespoons shoyu
2 ounces almonds, finely chopped
½ cup wheat germ
salt and pepper
1 tablespoon finely chopped parsley
    (optional)
Coating
1 cup millet flakes

oil for shallow frying

Makes 8 patties

Millet and tofu patties

Almonds and wheat germ give texture and flavor to these delicate croquettes. They are best if prepared the previous day and refrigerated overnight, as this makes them easier to handle. You could use regular tofu if you would like a firmer texture.

1 Heat the oil in a large, heavy-bottomed saucepan and gently fry the millet until it turns light brown. Add the boiling water, cover and simmer for 20 minutes, or until the millet is soft. Leave until quite cool. Drain if necessary.

2 Blend the millet, tofu and shoyu to a thick paste in a blender. Turn out into a bowl and beat in the almonds and wheat germ. Season well and add the parsley. Chill thoroughly, preferably overnight in the refrigerator.

3 Divide into 8 pieces and shape these into flat cakes. The texture is quite soft so they need careful handling.

4 Dip each one into millet flakes and shallow-fry for 2-3 minutes on either side until golden brown. Serve immediately, accompanied by a sauce or dip, such as the horseradish and mustard sauce on page 152 or the lime relish on page 155.

From top: **Kasha ring** (*see p. 110*); **Millet and tofu patties; Savory millet** (*see p. 107*); In saucepans: **tomato sauce** (*see p. 72*); **mustard sauce for kasha ring**

★

Photograph
page 109

Ingredients
1 tablespoon sunflower oil
½ pound leeks, diced
½ pound celeriac, diced
½ pound Jerusalem artichokes,
   well scrubbed and diced
½ pound mushrooms, diced
1 clove garlic, crushed
1 teaspoon oil
¾ cup buckwheat groats
2½ cups boiling water
1 teaspoon caraway seeds
1 teaspoon paprika
3 tablespoons red wine
salt and pepper
Sauce
1 cake silken tofu—approx.
   11 ounces
1 clove garlic, crushed
2 teaspoons English *or* Dijon-type
   mustard
½ teaspoon turmeric
1 tablespoon capers

Serves 4-6

Kasha ring

Kasha in Russian means any cooked cereal, but buckwheat is the most usual. Here, it is mixed with vegetables and served with a spicy mustard sauce.

1 Heat the sunflower oil in a heavy-bottomed saucepan and cook the vegetables and garlic over gentle heat, covered, for 10-15 minutes.

2 Meanwhile, in another saucepan, heat 1 teaspoon oil and fry the buckwheat over medium heat for about 3-4 minutes or until it begins to brown. Add the boiling water. Bring back to the boil, cover and simmer for 20 minutes or until the buckwheat is just tender. Drain.

3 Preheat the oven to 350°F.

4 Mix together the cooked buckwheat and vegetables. Stir in the caraway, paprika and red wine. Season well and press the mixture into a lightly greased ring mold of about 2-quart capacity. Cover loosely with foil and bake for 40 minutes.

5 Meanwhile, prepare the sauce by blending the tofu, garlic, mustard and turmeric until completely smooth. Add the capers and blend for another 15 seconds.

6 Heat the sauce very gently, preferably in a double boiler. It must not boil or it will curdle, and it should be warm rather than hot. Turn out the kasha ring on a warmed serving dish and serve with the sauce.

PASTA, PIZZA & PANCAKES

These are all basic ways of cooking flour dough or batter, except for potato pancakes, which use finely grated potato. Wheat flour is the most common, although buckwheat has a long tradition in recipes for pancakes from Brittany to Russia, as well as in a certain type of pasta in northern Italy. Cornmeal is of course the staple flour used for Mexican tortillas.

Some kind of sauce or filling is almost always used. It may be as simple as the oil and garlic sauce for spaghetti, or even just melted butter, or it may be as robust as the refried bean filling for the tortillas. A sauce that will top a pizza will also accompany pasta; fillings for cannelloni or lasagne go well in pancakes, too, and vice versa. You will find recipes here for more unusual sauces, as well as for the indispensable and ever versatile tomato sauce.

PASTA

Store-bought pasta, fresh or dried, is a great standby. It can be made from refined or whole-wheat flour, with or without eggs, plain or colored green with spinach. But if you prefer it homemade, there are machines to help you turn it out in various shapes and sizes. Even without a machine, it is not difficult to make ravioli, lasagne, cannelloni and tagliatelle at home.

Homemade ravioli are a particularly appealing way to start a meal. They can be made quite small, only 1-inch square, as shown in the photographs, or larger. They are also shown made in semicircles, but they can be triangular or twisted into more complicated shapes. Once made and filled, they should be left to dry out for about 30 minutes.

Continued

Pasta continued

Whole-wheat pasta has a denser texture than refined pasta. I use a recipe enriched with eggs in preference to a plain water/flour mixture, as I feel this gives the best flavor.

The sauces in this chapter can in theory be used for any kind of pasta you like. However, as a general guide, thick sauces of the tomato variety go best with spaghetti or tubular pasta such as macaroni, while the smoother, more buttery sauces go better with flat ribbon noodles like tagliatelle.

Ingredients
2⅓ cups whole-wheat flour
large pinch salt
4 eggs
1 tablespoon olive oil
a little beaten egg

**Makes 1 lb 2 oz
(Serves 4 as a main course
or 6 as an appetizer)**

Whole-wheat pasta

Stir the flour and salt together in a large bowl and make a well in the center. Break in the eggs and add the olive oil. Make the dough as shown below. All pasta should be rolled out thinly, but especially whole-wheat pasta as it is so substantial. To make green pasta, substitute about 4 ounces chopped cooked spinach for one of the eggs.

MAKING PASTA DOUGH

1 *Mix the eggs and oil together with a fork, gradually drawing in all the flour from the edges.*

2 *Knead the dough well for a good 5 minutes until it loses all its stickiness and becomes shiny.*

3 *Cover the dough and leave it to rest for half an hour, then roll it out as thinly as you possibly can.*

Cooking pasta
Pasta must always be freshly cooked. Bring a large kettle of water to the boil and put in plenty of salt. If the kettle is big enough, there is no need to add a little oil as some cooks do to prevent the pasta from sticking together. It should be cooked *al dente*—until just tender but offering a very slight resistance to the bite. The only way to be sure of this is to test a piece by biting. Whole-wheat tagliatelle will take from 8-10 minutes to cook, the same as whole-wheat spaghetti. They are much more filling than pasta made with refined flour. As soon as the pasta is cooked, drain and serve immediately.

Cooking directions and times for stuffed pasta (lasagne, ravioli, cannelloni) are given in the appropriate recipes. These can all be cooked in advance, frozen and reheated. To reheat, heat the oven to 350°F. Cover the dish tightly with foil or a lid and bake for 1 hour.

MAKING SQUARE RAVIOLI

1 *Dot teaspoonsful of filling on half the dough at regular intervals. It may help to mark out a grid first in squares of 1-2 inches.*

2 *Brush the edges and in between the rows of filling with a little beaten egg, and carefully cover with the other half of the dough.*

3 *Press firmly along the edges and between the rows to seal, and use a pastry wheel to cut out the individual ravioli.*

Fennel and tomato filling

1 Blanch the fennel in boiling water for 5 minutes and drain.

2 Heat the olive oil and stew the fennel with the garlic for 10 minutes, until quite soft.

3 Add the tomatoes and basil and stew for a further 10 minutes, until the mixture is soft enough to mash. Season well and let it cool before using.

4 To cook the ravioli, bring a large pan of salted water to the boil. Drop in the ravioli and cook, uncovered, for 12-15 minutes. Drain and serve immediately, sprinkled generously with grated Parmesan.

Ingredients
½ pound fennel, finely chopped
2 tablespoons olive oil
1 clove garlic, crushed
½ pound tomatoes, peeled and chopped
2 teaspoon chopped basil
salt and pepper
For serving
grated Parmesan

Serves 4-6

★
Photograph
page 114

Oil, garlic and chili sauce

This is one of the quickest of all pasta sauces. It is made while the pasta is cooking.

1 In a large, heavy-bottomed saucepan, heat the oil and sauté the garlic and chili over moderate heat for 2-3 minutes. The garlic should turn golden but must on no account burn.

2 As soon as the pasta is cooked, drain it, turn it out into the saucepan and mix quickly to coat it with the oil. Mix in the parsley and season with salt (and pepper if you think it needs it). Serve immediately.

Ingredients
2 tablespoons olive oil
2-3 cloves garlic, crushed
1 dried chili, very finely diced
2-3 tablespoons finely chopped parsley
salt and pepper

Serves 4-6

Photograph
*pages
190-191*

Pesto

1 Grind the pine nuts in a blender. Add the basil and garlic and blend again briefly. Add the grated cheese gradually, blending thoroughly.

2 Pour in the olive oil a little at a time, still blending. Season well. Serve with freshly cooked pasta.

Ingredients
3 ounces pine nuts
6-9 tablespoons chopped fresh basil
6 cloves garlic, crushed
1 cup grated Parmesan
⅔ cup olive oil
salt and pepper

Serves 4-6

Walnut and mushroom sauce

1 Heat 1 tablespoon of the oil and gently fry the onion, garlic and spices for 3-4 minutes, until the onion begins to soften.

2 Add the mushrooms, cover and cook over gentle heat for 10 minutes, stirring occasionally. Add the tomatoes and tomato paste, season and cook for another 10 minutes.

3 In a separate pan, heat the remaining oil and fry the chopped walnuts gently for 4-5 minutes, until lightly browned. Stir half the walnuts into the sauce.

4 To serve, mix into freshly cooked pasta, sprinkle with the remaining walnuts and the parsley and serve immediately.

Ingredients
4 teaspoons olive oil
1 large onion, diced
1 clove garlic, crushed
1 teaspoon cinnamon
1 teaspoon allspice
1 teaspoon finely grated gingerroot
½ pound mushrooms, diced
1 pound tomatoes, peeled and chopped
1 tablespoon tomato paste
salt and pepper
4 ounces shelled walnuts, roughly chopped
1 tablespoon finely chopped parsley

Serves 4-6

★

Butter and cream sauce with peas

1 Bring a saucepan of water to the boil. Put in the peas, cover and cook steadily until the peas are tender. Drain.

2 Cream the butter by beating it vigorously in a large mixing bowl until light and fluffy. Gradually beat in the cream, then the grated cheese. Mix the peas into the sauce. Set over very low heat to keep warm.

3 Mix into freshly cooked pasta, season and serve at once.

Ingredients
6 ounces fresh or frozen peas
½ cup butter
4 tablespoons light cream
½ cup grated Parmesan
salt and pepper
For serving
extra grated Parmesan

Serves 4-6

Photograph
page 116

Celery and almond sauce

1 Heat the olive oil and fry the onions and celery with the garlic over gentle heat for 2-3 minutes. Cover and continue cooking for 10-15 minutes, until the vegetables are really tender. Add the stock, cover and cook for another 5-10 minutes, until the sauce is creamy. Season to taste.

2 In a separate pan, heat 1 teaspoon oil and fry the almonds for 4-5 minutes, until lightly browned. Serve the sauce over freshly cooked pasta, sprinkled with the almonds.

Ingredients
4 tablespoons olive oil
8 ounces onions, diced
5 celery ribs, finely chopped
2 cloves garlic, crushed
⅔ cup light vegetable stock (see p. 151)
salt and pepper
1 teaspoon oil
4 ounces slivered almonds (see p. 209)

Serves 4-6

★

Photograph
page 116

Clockwise from top: **Ravioli with fennel and tomato filling** (*see p. 113*); **Pasta with walnut and mushroom sauce; Spaghetti with pesto**

MAKING TAGLIATELLE

1 *Gently fold the sheet of dough over on itself like a jelly roll.*

2 *Cut this carefully into thin strips of about ½ inch. Try not to press too hard.*

3 *Unfold each strip and spread it out to dry for half an hour before it is cooked.*

MAKING LASAGNE AND CANNELLONI

1 *Cut the dough into oblongs about 5 x 4 inches.*

2 *For cannelloni, put 1-2 tablespoons of the filling on each oblong and brush the edge with beaten egg.*

3 *Roll up the oblongs from the long side and press to seal.*

Lasagne with leeks and lentils

If you make your own lasagne, it is easy to make them into strips that will comfortably fit your baking dish. Do not make them too big or they will be clumsy to boil and drain. If you are using store-bought dried lasagne, 8 ounces will be enough.

1 Put the lentils in a saucepan with plenty of water to cover. Bring to the boil and simmer, covered, for 25 minutes. Drain, reserving the stock.

2 Heat the oil and gently fry the leeks, carrot, mushrooms and garlic for 5-6 minutes, or until fairly soft.

3 Add the cooked lentils, tomatoes, herbs and shoyu, cover and cook for 15-20 minutes, adding a little lentil stock if the mixture is too dry. Season to taste.

4 Preheat the oven to 350°F.

Continued

Ingredients
½ cup brown lentils, washed
1 tablespoon olive oil
1 pound leeks, finely diced
1 medium carrot, diced
½ pound mushrooms, diced
2 cloves garlic, crushed
1 pound tomatoes, peeled and
    chopped
1 teaspoon dried oregano
1 teaspoon dried marjoram
1 tablespoon shoyu
salt and pepper
12 ounces to 1 pound fresh lasagne
1¼ cups béchamel sauce
    (see p. 152)
½ cup grated Parmesan

Serves 4

★

Clockwise from top: **Tagliatelle with butter and cream sauce with peas** (*see p. 115*); **Tagliatelle with celery and almond sauce** (*see p. 115); **Lasagne with leeks and lentils.**

117

Lasagne with leeks and lentils continued

5 Meanwhile, cook the lasagne by boiling them in a large kettle of salted water for 8-10 minutes or until just tender. As soon as they are cooked, drain them, run cold water over them and spread them out on a damp cloth. This will help prevent them from sticking.

6 Put a layer of lasagne in a lightly greased baking dish. Cover with a layer of lentil mixture and one of béchamel sauce. Continue in this order until you have used all your ingredients, ending with a layer of sauce. Sprinkle with the grated Parmesan and bake for 30 minutes.

★

Ingredients
¾ pound spinach
1 large onion, diced
1 clove garlic, crushed
1 tablespoon oil
1 green pepper, seeded and diced
4 ounces ground almonds
1¼ cups water
1 teaspoon dried thyme
grated nutmeg
salt and pepper
1-1¼ pound cannelloni
tomato sauce (see p. 72)
½ cup grated Parmesan
For serving
extra grated Parmesan

Serves 4-6

Spinach and almond cannelloni

1 Blanch the spinach in boiling water for 1 minute. Drain thoroughly and chop finely.

2 Gently fry the onion and garlic in the oil for 3-4 minutes until soft. Add the green pepper and cook for 3-4 minutes more.

3 Preheat the oven to 400°F.

4 Stir in the chopped spinach and cook over moderate heat for another 2 minutes. Add the almonds, water and thyme and bring to the boil, stirring. Season with the nutmeg, salt and pepper.

5 Fill the cannelloni with this stuffing as on page 117. Arrange them in a lightly greased dish and cover with tomato sauce. Sprinkle with the grated Parmesan and bake for 20-25 minutes. Serve with extra Parmesan.

Ingredients
1-1¼ pound elbow
  macaroni
¼ pound snap beans, sliced
1¼ cups yogurt
½ pound ricotta or cottage
  cheese
1 bunch scallions, chopped
1 red pepper, seeded and diced
½ teaspoon caraway seeds
2 teaspoons shoyu
salt and pepper
½ cup grated Parmesan cheese

For serving
extra grated Parmesan

Serves 4-6

Pasta with snap beans

1 Preheat the oven to 350°F and bring a large pan of water to the boil.

2 Salt the water and cook the pasta at a rolling boil until just resistant to the bite—about 8-10 minutes. Drain.

3 Blanch the snap beans for 1-2 minutes in boiling salted water and drain.

4 Mix together the yogurt and ricotta or cottage cheese. Add the pasta, the snap beans, scallions and red pepper. Mix well, add the caraway and shoyu and season to taste.

5 Turn out into a lightly oiled ovenproof dish and sprinkle with the Parmesan. Bake for 25-30 minutes. Serve hot.

Clockwise from top: **Spinach and almond cannelloni; Pasta with snap beans; Pasta with chick peas** (*see p. 120*); **Pizza** (*see p. 120*)

Photograph
page 119

Soaking
overnight

Ingredients
1 cup chick peas, soaked
   overnight
1 pound elbow macaroni
2 cloves garlic, crushed
1 tablespoon olive oil
1 tablespoon finely chopped basil
For serving
3 tablespoons freshly grated
   Parmesan

Serves 4-6

Pasta with chick peas

The combination of chick peas with pasta has been known since the time of Horace. Sometimes called "thunder and lightning," this is very simple to make, and the peas and pasta complement each other nutritionally.

1 Drain the chick peas. Put them in a large kettle with plenty of fresh water, bring to the boil and boil rapidly for 10 minutes. Reduce the heat, skim off any scum and simmer, covered, until soft—about 50-60 minutes, depending on the age of the peas.

2 Meanwhile, cook the pasta in a large kettle of boiling salted water until just resistant to the bite—about 8-10 minutes. Drain.

3 In a large, heavy-bottomed saucepan, sauté the garlic gently in the oil for 3-4 minutes without letting it brown.

4 Drain the chick peas and add them, with the pasta, to the saucepan with the garlic. Mix in the basil and stir and turn over low heat for a minute or two to ensure that all the flavors are absorbed and the mixture heated through. Season to taste and serve hot, sprinkled with Parmesan.

PIZZA

Pizzas need little introduction. They can be a very substantial part of a meal or delicious party nibbles. Vary the classic tomato topping by using different vegetables and herbs, and decorate with anything from cheese and artichoke hearts to olives, chopped herbs, capers and green peppercorns.

★

Photograph
page 119

Ingredients
Pizza base
½ ounce compressed yeast
4 tablespoons lukewarm milk
1½ cups whole-wheat flour
pinch of salt
1 large egg, lightly beaten
2-3 tablespoons olive oil

Makes one 10-inch pizza

Tomato and onion topping
1 large onion, diced
2 cloves garlic, crushed
2 tablespoons olive oil
Continued

Pizza with tomato and onion

I use a rich dough, slightly more cake-like than the standard bread dough, which I think makes an excellent pizza base. If you prefer, use a plain whole-wheat dough (see page 174).

1 Preheat the oven to 300°F.

2 Mix the yeast with the milk until creamy.

3 Warm the flour and salt in a large bowl for 5 minutes in the oven. This is not absolutely essential but enables the yeast to work more quickly.

4 Mix the flour, yeast mixture, egg and olive oil together and work into a ball, kneading well. This takes about 5 minutes. The dough should be fairly soft. It it is too sticky, add a little extra flour.

5 Put the dough into a clean bowl to rise. Cover with a damp cloth and leave for 1-1½ hours, until roughly doubled in size and resilient to the touch. Continue as below.

4 celery ribs, diced
1¼ pounds tomatoes, peeled and chopped
2 tablespoons tomato paste
2 teaspoons dried oregano
2 teaspoons chopped fresh basil
salt and pepper
3 ounces mozzarella, sliced
black olives

ROLLING OUT PIZZA DOUGH

1 Punch the dough down with your fist to knock the gas out of it. Knead again for a few minutes until quite smooth.

2 Roll the dough out into a 10-inch circle, or shape into a rectangle 8 x 10 inches.

3 Set the dough on a lightly oiled baking tray. Prick it all over and cover with the topping.

6 While the dough is rising, make the topping. Gently fry the onion and garlic in the oil for 3-4 minutes, until soft.

7 Put in the celery and cook for 5 minutes. Add the tomatoes, tomato paste and herbs, cover and cook for 20-25 minutes. Season to taste.

8 Spread this over the pizza base as shown above. Leave for 10-15 minutes to rest. Meanwhile, preheat the oven to 400°F.

9 Arrange the mozzarella slices and black olives over the pizza and bake for 25-30 minutes.

Mushroom topping for pizza

1 Gently fry the onions and garlic for 3-4 minutes in the oil, until soft.

2 Put in the mushrooms, tomato paste and marjoram and cook, covered, for 20-25 minutes. You should have a thick sauce. If it is too liquid, take the lid off and boil rapidly for a few minutes until it has reduced to the proper consistency. Season to taste.

Ingredients
¾ pound onions, sliced
1 clove garlic, crushed
2 tablespoons olive oil
1 pound button mushrooms, sliced
2-3 tablespoons tomato paste
1 teaspoon dried marjoram
salt and pepper

Photograph
*pages
168-169*

PANCAKES

There is nothing difficult about cooking pancakes. The main essential is a good skillet. Strictly speaking, if there is oil in the batter, the pan does not need greasing, but I find it helps to use just a little oil.

Cooked pancakes, apart from blinis, keep very well. Wrapped carefully in wax paper or plastic wrap, they will keep up to 3 days in the refrigerator or 2 months in the freezer. Single pancakes will thaw within an hour; a stack of pancakes should be left at room temperature for several hours. Filled pancakes can also be frozen. In this case, let the filling cool before use, as otherwise the pancake may become too soggy.

To reheat, put in a lightly oiled ovenproof dish, brush with melted butter or oil, cover with foil or a lid and heat at 350°F for 10-15 minutes if unfilled, 20 minutes if filled.

Buckwheat flour can be used instead of up to half the whole-wheat flour. It produces tasty pancakes with a dark, speckled appearance, which are especially good with strong flavors and sour cream. They are substantial, so make them as thin and lacy as you can.

★

Photograph
page 125

Ingredients
1 cup whole-wheat flour
pinch of salt
1 egg
1¼ cups milk
1 teaspoon oil

oil *or* butter for frying

Makes 8-10 pancakes

Whole-wheat pancakes

This recipe can be used for sweet or savory pancakes. Serve sweet pancakes with maple syrup, or just with a generous squeeze of lemon juice and brown sugar to taste.

1 Mix the flour and salt in a bowl. Beat together the egg, milk and oil. Pour this into the flour, stirring constantly and mixing in the flour until you have a smooth batter. (If you use a blender, first blend the milk, egg, salt and oil for 15-30 seconds, then add the flour and blend for a further 30 seconds to a smooth batter.)

2 Let the batter stand for half an hour or so before making the pancakes. Blend or beat again just beforehand, as some of the flour will almost certainly have settled at the bottom.

3 Heat a little oil or butter—about 1 teaspoon—in a skillet until it smokes. Pour in 2 tablespoons of batter, quickly tipping the skillet so the batter spreads out evenly into a circle.

4 Cook for 2-3 minutes. Flip over and cook the other side for a further 2-3 minutes.

If you are going to eat the pancakes immediately, stack them on top of one another on a lightly oiled plate and keep warm in a moderately hot oven or under a warm broiler. If you are going to keep them to use later, turn each one out on a cool surface as it is cooked. This ensures a good texture. If they are stacked before cooling, their own steam will make them soggy.

Pancake Fillings
All the fillings given here are savory. They can all be made well in advance, and pancakes filled with them freeze well. Other ideas for fillings are some of the pasta sauces already given or small quantities of bean or pea casseroles.

To fill pancakes, put a tablespoon or two of filling on each one, roll up and arrange in a lightly greased ovenproof dish. Brush with a little melted butter or extra oil, cover with foil or a lid and heat for 15-20 minutes in a moderate oven.

Red cabbage and raisin filling

Crisp eating apples are best for this. This filling is also good with the potato pancakes on page 127.

1 Fry the onion gently in the oil until very soft—about 10-15 minutes.

2 Add the cabbage, apple, raisins and spices and cook, covered, for another 5 minutes over moderate heat.

3 Add the red wine and braise over low heat for 15 minutes. Stir occasionally, adding a little water if necessary. Season well.

Ingredients
1 medium onion, finely chopped
1 tablespoon sunflower oil
¾ pound red cabbage, finely shredded
1 medium apple, grated
2 ounces raisins
1 teaspoon paprika
1 teaspoon cinnamon
3 tablespoons red wine
salt and pepper

Enough for 8-10 pancakes

★
Photograph
page 125

Beet and chive filling

1 Scrub and trim the beets. Bring a kettle of water to the boil and cook the beets, covered, until tender. This takes 20-30 minutes, depending on the size of the beets. Drain, peel and dice finely.

2 Gently fry the onion for 3-4 minutes in the oil until soft. Sprinkle with the flour and cook, stirring, for 2-3 minutes.

3 Off the heat, mix in the cooked beets and the herbs. Cool slightly, then stir in the yogurt or sour cream and season.

Ingredients
1 pound fresh beets
1 medium onion, finely chopped
1 tablespoon olive oil
2 teaspoons whole-wheat flour
1 tablespoon snipped chives
3 tablespoons finely chopped parsley
¾ cup yogurt *or* sour cream
salt and pepper

Enough for 8-10 pancakes

Photograph
page 125

★

Ingredients
1 pound broccoli flowerets
1 small onion, finely chopped
1 tablespoon sunflower oil
1 clove garlic, crushed
1 teaspoon ground cumin
1 ounce pine nuts
⅔ cup béchamel sauce
   (see p. 152)
salt and pepper

Enough for 8-10 pancakes

Broccoli and pine nut filling

This also makes a good accompaniment to the mushroom and aduki croquettes on page 96.

1 Lightly steam the broccoli for 5-6 minutes.

2 Gently fry the onion in the oil for 2-3 minutes. Add the garlic, cumin and pine nuts, and continue cooking over moderate heat for 4-5 minutes so that the aroma of the spices is brought out and the pine nuts are lightly toasted.

3 Add the steamed broccoli and cook for another minute or two. Remove the pan from the heat and blend in the béchamel sauce with a wooden spoon. Season to taste.

★

Photograph
*pages
186-187*

Ingredients
8 pancakes (see p. 122)
 Fennel filling
1 pound fennel, finely sliced
4 tablespoons butter
½ cup freshly grated
   Parmesan
salt and pepper
Spinach filling
1 pound fresh spinach, washed
½ teaspoon grated nutmeg
black pepper
Tomato filling
1 onion, chopped
1 clove garlic, crushed
2 tablespoons olive oil
1 pound tomatoes, peeled
 and chopped
3 celery ribs, diced
½ teaspoon aniseeds
1 tablespoon tomato paste
salt and pepper
For serving
extra grated Parmesan

Serves 4

Galette

This makes a spectacular dish for a dinner party.

1 Blanch the fennel for 10 minutes in boiling water. Drain well.

2 Melt the butter in a small saucepan and stew the fennel, covered, for 10 minutes over low heat. Purée it with the grated Parmesan and add salt and pepper to taste.

3 Preheat the oven to 350°F.

4 Cook the spinach in its own juices for 7-8 minutes in a covered saucepan. Chop it very finely and season with nutmeg and black pepper.

5 Gently fry the onion and garlic for 3-4 minutes in the olive oil. Stir in the tomatoes, celery, aniseeds and tomato paste and cook, uncovered, over moderate heat, for 10-15 minutes or until you have a thick sauce. Season well.

6 Assemble the galette in a lightly greased 9-inch spring-form cake pan. Put in one pancake, then sandwich in the different fillings (reserving some of the tomato sauce) between the pancakes. End with a pancake.

7 Bake for 10-15 minutes. Turn out and serve with the remaining tomato sauce and extra grated Parmesan.

Clockwise from top: **Whole-wheat pancakes** (*see p. 122*) with fillings: **beet and chive** (*see p. 123*); **broccoli and pine nut; red cabbage and raisin** (*see p. 123*); **Potato pancakes** (*see p. 127*); **Blinis with sour cream** (*see p. 127*); **Tortillas** (*see p. 126*)

★

Photograph
page 125

Soaking
overnight

Ingredients
Bean Filling
1½ cups red kidney *or* pinto
   beans, soaked overnight
3 tablespoons oil
1 large onion, chopped
3 cloves garlic, crushed
2 teaspoons ground cumin
¼ teaspoon ground coriander
1½ teaspoons salt
1 green pepper, seeded and finely
   diced
pepper
Tortillas
1⅓ cups water
3 tablespoons butter
⅔ cup cornmeal
1¼ cups whole-wheat flour
1 teaspoon salt

Makes 12 tortillas

Tortillas

These are classic Mexican pancakes made here from cornmeal mixed with whole-wheat flour. Refried beans are beans that are first boiled, then fried with spices and vegetables to make a hearty and satisfying filling.

1 Drain the beans. Bring them to the boil in plenty of fresh water and boil rapidly for 10 minutes. Cover and simmer for 40-50 minutes, until soft. Drain and mash.

2 Heat the oil in a skillet and gently fry the onion, garlic and spices with about half the salt for 10 minutes over gentle heat.

3 Put in the green pepper, cover and cook for another 5-8 minutes. Mix with the mashed beans and season well with the rest of the salt and the pepper. Keep warm.

4 Make the tortillas as shown below. Divide the filling among them and serve hot.

MAKING TORTILLAS

1 *Bring the water to the boil and add half the butter. Stir in the cornmeal over low heat. Cover, cook for 5 minutes and stir in the remaining butter until smooth.*

2 *Leave this to cool. Mix the whole-wheat flour and salt together in a bowl. Stir in the cooled cornmeal.*

3 *Knead this to a soft dough. You may need to add a little more water or flour if it is too dry or too sticky.*

4 *Divide into 12 pieces and shape each piece into a ball. Roll each one out into a 6- to 7-inch circle.*

5 *Cook in an ungreased skillet for 2-3 minutes on each side over moderate heat until flecked with dark spots.*

6 *Spoon 2-3 tablespoons of filling into each tortilla.*

Potato pancakes

These are excellent with a sharp or sweet sauce or vegetable. Try the beet and chive filling on page 123 or the red cabbage and raisin filling on the same page.

1 Peel the potatoes and grate them finely. Squeeze out all excess moisture.

2 In a separate bowl, beat the eggs and blend in the miso. Mix in the potatoes and remaining ingredients and season according to taste.

3 Heat the butter and oil in a large skillet. Put in heaping tablespoons of the mixture—you should be able to do 2 or 3 at a time. Fry for about 3-4 minutes on each side, pressing the pancakes down flat as they fry with a wooden spoon. Drain on paper towels and serve hot.

Ingredients
3 large potatoes
2 eggs
1 teaspoon miso
1 small onion, finely chopped
3-4 tablespoons cornmeal
2 teaspoons paprika
salt and pepper
For frying
2 tablespoons butter
2 tablespoons oil

Makes 8-10 pancakes

Photograph
page 125

Blinis

Russian yeast pancakes, traditionally served with sour cream, these are also good with yogurt or the wine and black olive pâté on page 42.

1 Crumble the yeast and sugar together, mix with the warm water and leave for 5 minutes until creamy and frothy. Beat in the egg yolk.

2 Sift the flours together with the salt. Beat the yeast mixture into the flour until quite smooth and the consistency of thick cream.

3 Leave in a warm place until at least doubled in bulk. This will take about 1 hour. Beat the mixture down, using a whisk or wooden spoon.

4 Whip the egg white to a soft peak. Fold 1 tablespoon into the batter and then fold in the rest of the egg white. Leave to rest for 20 minutes.

5 Heat a little butter in a large skillet. Fry tablespoons of the batter over medium heat for 2-3 minutes on each side. You should be able to do 2 or 3 at a time: this batter will not spread out. Keep the first batch warm while you do the next. Serve hot.

Ingredients
¼ ounce compressed yeast
pinch of sugar
½ cup warm water
1 egg, separated
⅓ cup all-purpose unbleached flour
⅓ cup buckwheat flour
pinch of salt
butter for frying

Makes 6-8 blinis

Photograph
page 125

EGGS & CHEESE

At one time eggs and cheese were regarded as a mainstay of the vegetarian diet, and it is still often the case that if you order a vegetarian meal when eating out you end up with either an omelette or a cheese salad. It is true that they seem an obvious replacement for meat, being such a good source of protein, but now we are more aware of the health aspect of diet, and realize that it is not good giving up the hidden fats in meat just to replace them with high-fat dairy products and eggs, which, while important, should play a secondary part.

People who change to a meatless diet sometimes experience a craving for fats. The answer to this can be a little grated cheese. It goes a long way when sprinkled over a bean or grain dish and makes the food more satisfying without upsetting the balance of the diet. There are now an increasing number of cheeses on the market made with vegetable rennet, which is good news for those strict vegetarians whose choice in the past has been limited.

Ingredients
1 clove garlic
2 cups dry white wine
1 tablespoon lemon juice
1 pound grated Emmental *or*
  Gruyère
1-2 tablespoons whole-wheat flour
  (optional)
grated nutmeg
salt and pepper
2 tablespoons Kirsch
For serving
1 large whole-wheat loaf, cut into
  cubes

Serves 4

Fondue

A classic dish, ideal for easy entertaining. It is both rich and sustaining, so accompanying dishes should be light, such as green salads, with fruit or a sorbet to follow. To eat it, each guest spears a piece of bread with a fork and dips in.

1 Rub the inside of a heatproof casserole or fondue pot with the garlic. Pour in the wine and lemon juice and bring slowly to boiling point.

2 Add the grated cheese and the flour, if used—this depends on whether you prefer a thicker consistency. Beat well until the cheese melts and the mixture is completely smooth.
Continued

Top: **Fondue**; bottom: **Blue cheese and onion quiche** (*see p. 130*)

Fondue continued

3 Season with grated nutmeg, salt and pepper. Stir in the Kirsch and serve hot. If the fondue becomes too thick, add a little more hot wine.

Variations
Raw vegetables can be used instead of bread. The basic sauce can be flavored with mustard, paprika or caraway seeds.

★

Photograph
page 129

Ingredients
piecrust made with 1¼ cups
   whole-wheat flour
   (see p. 92)
2 pounds onions, diced
3 tablespoons olive oil
⅔ cup sour cream
2-3 tablespoons white wine
3 eggs, beaten
½ cup grated blue cheese
1 teaspoon caraway seeds
pinch of cayenne

Serves 4-6

Blue cheese and onion quiche

Egg and cheese combinations lend themselves perfectly to quiche or small tart fillings. Stilton is particularly successful here, but Gorgonzola and Danish Blue also work well.

1 Preheat the oven to 400°F.

2 Roll out the pastry to fill a 9-inch pie plate. Prick the base well and bake for 5 minutes to set it.

3 Gently fry the onions for 5-10 minutes in the oil until quite translucent. Let them cool completely.

4 Mix together all the other ingredients. Stir in the onions, pile the filling into the pastry case and bake for 35 minutes. Serve warm or cold.

Variations
Vegetables can be added to the cheese and egg mixture. Broccoli, leeks, spinach, zucchini, asparagus and tomatoes are all ideal. Lightly steam or sauté 1 pound vegetables. Mix them with 1¼ cups milk and the eggs and cheese as above. Season well, pile into the flan case and cover with another ½ cup grated cheese.
Cheddar, Gouda, Emmental and Gruyère are all suitable, on their own or in combination. Cottage cheese, ricotta, sour cream or yogurt can be substituted for some of the milk. Herbs and spices can be added to taste.

Photograph
*pages
180-181*

Ingredients
1 pound greens—spinach, Swiss
   chard, spinach beet or bok choy
4 tablespoons finely chopped parsley
6-8 scallions, finely chopped
8 eggs
2 tablespoons yogurt
2 tablespoons water
salt and pepper
Continued

Frittata verde

A substantial version of an omelette, served flat and not rolled up. It makes a good snack, or it can be eaten with a baked potato and salad for a simple supper.

1 Lightly boil or steam the greens (for cooking times see p. 217). Chop finely and add to the parsley and onions.

2 Beat together the eggs, yogurt and water. Stir the mixture into the vegetables.

3 Heat just enough oil to cover the bottom of a large omelette pan. Pour in the mixture, beating lightly with a fork until it begins to cook.

4 Cook gently for 5-10 minutes. The exact time depends on the size of your pan. The omelette should be well browned on the bottom and thoroughly heated through. This takes longer in a smaller pan, where the mixture is thicker.

5 Sprinkle with the grated Parmesan, if desired, and brown the top for 2 minutes under a hot broiler. Transfer to a serving dish with a spatula. Serve warm or cold.

a little oil (or oil and butter) for frying
2 tablespoons grated Parmesan (optional)

Serves 4

Baked eggs with lentils

A dish inspired by Spain that is ideal for supper or brunch.

1 Bring the lentils to the boil in a large kettle of water and simmer, covered, for 35-40 minutes until soft. Drain.

2 Heat the oil in a large, heavy-bottomed saucepan and fry the onion, garlic and peppers gently until soft—5 minutes.

3 Mix in the cooked lentils and the tomatoes, parsley, bay leaf and water. Season well. Cook over moderate heat, stirring, for 10-15 minutes, or until most of the liquid has evaporated and the mixture is fairly thick.

4 Preheat the oven to 400°F.

5 Spoon the mixture into a lightly greased ovenproof dish, removing the bay leaf. Make four slight hollows with the back of a spoon. Break in the eggs. Sprinkle with the sherry, cover and bake for 20 minutes, or until the egg whites are firm. Serve at once, garnished with the parsley.

Ingredients
½ cup green or brown lentils
2 tablespoons oil, preferably olive
1 medium onion, finely chopped
2 cloves garlic, crushed
1 green pepper, seeded and diced
1 red pepper, seeded and diced
1 pound tomatoes, peeled and chopped
2 tablespoons finely chopped parsley
1 bay leaf
4 tablespoons water
salt and pepper
4 eggs
2 tablespoons pale dry sherry
Garnish
sprigs of fresh parsley

Serves 4

Photograph
page 133

Eggplant and cheese bake

1 Dust the eggplant slices with flour and fry them, a few at a time, in hot oil until just brown and soft. This will take about 2 minutes on each side. When adding more oil, make sure it is well heated before putting in the eggplant. Drain them on paper towels.

2 In the same pan, gently fry the onions for 3-4 minutes until translucent. Put in the tomatoes and cook for a further 10 minutes until the mixture has reduced to a thick pulp. Cool.
Continued

Ingredients
1 pound eggplant, sliced
flour for dusting
oil for frying
¾ pound onions, diced
¾ pound tomatoes, peeled and chopped
2 eggs
4 ounces ricotta
2 tablespoons yogurt
1 teaspoon dried oregano
salt and pepper
¼ cup grated Parmesan cheese

Serves 4

★
Photograph
page 133

*Eggplant and cheese
bake continued*

3 Preheat the oven to 350°F.

4 Beat the eggs with the ricotta and yogurt. Add the tomato and onion mixture and season with oregano, salt and pepper.

5 Lightly grease a 13 x 9-inch baking dish. Put in a layer of eggplant slices, cover with some sauce and sprinkle with a little grated cheese. Continue in this order, ending with a generous sprinkling of cheese. Bake for 25-30 minutes.

Ingredients
1¼ cups milk
1 onion, diced
1 bay leaf
¾ pound zucchini, sliced
3 tablespoons butter
2 tablespoons whole-wheat flour
3-4 eggs, separated
½-⅔ cup grated Cheddar
salt and pepper

Serves 4

Zucchini soufflé

1 Heat the milk with the onion and bay leaf to just below boiling point. Remove from the heat and leave for 20 minutes.

2 Lightly steam the zucchini for 4-5 minutes.

3 Preheat the oven to 400°F.

4 Heat the butter, stir in the flour and cook, stirring, over low heat for 2 minutes. Strain the milk into the pan and bring to boiling point, stirring. Simmer for 2-3 minutes.

5 Off the heat, beat in the egg yolks, one at a time. Mix the zucchini into the sauce. Add the cheese and season lightly.

6 Beat the egg whites until stiff but not dry. Stir 1 tablespoon into the sauce, then gently fold in the remaining egg whites.

7 Spoon into a lightly greased 1½-quart soufflé dish and bake for 25 minutes. The center should be firm. If it is still too soft, give it another 5 minutes. Serve immediately.

Variation
Avocado soufflé
Instead of the zucchini, use 1-2 avocados, diced, sprinkled with lime juice and mixed with 6 green olives, pitted and chopped, and 1 pound tomatoes, peeled and chopped.

Photograph
*pages
190-191*

Ingredients
10 ounces broccoli flowerets
4 tablespoons butter
2½ tablespoons whole-wheat flour
⅔ cup milk
4 eggs, separated
salt and pepper
Filling
tomato sauce (see p. 72)
Continued

Broccoli roulade

1 Steam the broccoli lightly for 5-6 minutes. Chop it finely.

2 Melt the butter, stir in the flour and cook over low heat for 2 minutes. Add the milk and bring to boiling point, stirring well to avoid lumps. Simmer for 2-3 minutes.

3 Preheat the oven to 375°F and line a 15½ x 10½ x 1-inch jelly roll pan with wax paper.
Continued

From top: **Zucchini soufflé**; **Baked eggs with lentils** *(see p. 131)*; **Eggplant and cheese bake** *(see p. 131)*

Broccoli roulade continued

Garnish
3-3½ tablespoons freshly grated
    Parmesan
tomato slices (optional)

Serves 4-6

4 Remove from heat and beat the egg yolks into the sauce, one at a time. Season well and mix in the broccoli.

5 Beat the egg whites until stiff but not dry and gently fold them into the broccoli mixture.

6 Spread this over the prepared jelly roll pan and bake for 17-20 minutes.

7 Turn out onto a clean dish towel covered with a fresh sheet of wax paper. Peel off the old sheet. Spread the filling over the roulade and roll it up, using the dish towel. Don't worry if it cracks slightly. Sprinkle with the grated cheese and put back in the oven for 5 minutes before serving.

Variation
Substitute ½ cup green or brown lentils for the broccoli. Simmer them in plenty of water for 35-40 minutes and drain. For a filling, use the salsify sauce on page 153.

Photograph
*pages
136-137*

Ingredients
¾ cup grated Cheddar
¼ cup grated Stilton
5 cups fresh breadcrumbs
1 tablespoon finely chopped parsley
1 teaspoon finely chopped rosemary
    or thyme
2 eggs
1-2 teaspoons Dijon-type mustard
salt and pepper
oil for deep-frying

Makes 12-16 croquettes

Cheese and herb croquettes

These are deep-fried for a crispy outer coating.

1 Mix the grated cheeses with 4 cups breadcrumbs and the herbs. Add 1 egg and 1 egg yolk and the mustard. Mix well and season to taste.

2 Divide into 12 or 16 pieces and shape into small cylinders. Dip each one into the egg white and then roll it in the remaining breadcrumbs. Deep-fry for 5-7 minutes in hot oil. Drain on paper towel before serving.

Photograph
*pages
44-45*

Ingredients
⅔ cup water
4 tablespoons butter
⅓ cup wheatmeal *or*
    whole-meal flour
½ cup grated Cheddar
2 eggs
pinch of mustard powder
pepper

**Makes 12 medium or 18
    miniature puffs**

Cheese puffs

1 Preheat the oven 425°F and bring the water and butter to the boil in a heavy-bottomed saucepan.

2 Sift the flour into a bowl. Add the bran remaining in the sifter into the bowl. Remove from the heat, add all the flour to the boiling water and butter and beat very well for about 5 minutes, or until the mixture is glossy. Mix in 1 egg at a time, beating thoroughly after each addition, and stir in the cheese, mustard and pepper.

3 Pipe the mixture out into small balls on a lightly greased cookie sheet and bake for 15-20 minutes. Allow to cool before filling. Do not fill the puffs more than an hour or two before eating or they will be soggy.

Cheese puff fillings
Avocado

1 Peel the avocado and remove the pit.

2 Mash it with the lemon juice and mayonnaise.

3 Dice the hard-boiled egg and mix it in. Season to taste.

Ingredients
1 avocado
1 tablespoon lemon juice
2 tablespoons mayonnaise
   (see p. 149)
1 hard-boiled egg
salt and pepper

Photograph
*pages
44-45*

Artichoke hearts

1 Mash the artichoke hearts with the yogurt and dill weed.

2 Season to taste.

Ingredients
6 artichoke hearts
⅔ cup yogurt
1 teaspoon dried dill weed
salt and pepper

Cheese shortbread

1 Preheat the oven to 400°F.

2 Mix the flour with the semolina. Rub the butter in until the mixture is the consistency of fine breadcrumbs. Add the cheese and seasonings.

3 Press into an 8-inch square cake pan and mark into the desired shapes. Bake for 15-20 minutes and allow to cool.

Ingredients
⅔ cup whole-wheat flour
½ cup semolina
½ cup butter
1 cup grated Cheddar
pinch of cayenne
pinch of mustard powder
salt

**Makes nine 3-inch square
biscuits**

★
Photograph
*pages
44-45*

Cheese water biscuits

1 Preheat the oven to 425°F.

2 Mix together the flour, baking powder and salt. Rub in the fat until the mixture is the consistency of fine breadcrumbs.

3 Add just enough milk to make a soft dough. Roll out to a thickness of not more than ¼ inch.

4 Brush with a little extra milk and sprinkle with the grated cheese. Cut into whatever shapes you please. Bake on a cookie sheet for 20 minutes and allow to cool before eating.

Ingredients
1½ cups whole-wheat flour
1½ teaspoons baking powder
½ teaspoon salt
2 ounces vegetable shortening
¼ cup milk
½ cup finely grated Cheddar

Makes about 18-20 small biscuits

★
Photograph
*pages
186-187*

Cheese dip

For a party piece, use a whole Edam cheese. Slice the top third off. Scoop out the centre, leaving a 1-inch shell. Make a dip with the scooped-out cheese, then spoon it back.

Grate the hard cheese very finely. Beat in the cream cheese and cream and finally the other ingredients—some or all of them according to taste. You may not need to add salt, as the cheese will be quite salty already. Serve at room temperature.

Ingredients
6 ounces hard cheese—Edam,
   Cheddar, Swiss or a mixture
2 ounces cream cheese
2 tablespoons light cream
1 tablespoon whole-grain mustard
2 ounces chopped gherkins,
   scallions or olives
cayenne

Photograph
*pages
44-45*

Picnics

Any food that tastes good cold and can be eaten with the fingers or from a container is ideal for picnics, snacks or box lunches: quiches and tarts (the whole-food flamiche shown here is particularly nourishing); rissoles and croquettes based on nuts, eggs or cheese; and all kinds of salads, from a simple green salad to the protein-rich salad shown here, which combines red kidney beans, chick peas, lima beans and snap beans.

Pita bread is perfect for sandwiches (if you prefer homemade bread, try the soda bread on page 178 or the rosemary and walnut scones on page 184). Besides the fillings given here, which combine salad vegetables and cheese, you could use tomato with mozzarella, coleslaws or other salads, particularly the more substantial ones, or the tortilla filling on page 126. Cherry tomatoes make a good accompaniment.

To finish with, fresh fruit is ideal, from apples to cherries, strawberries or little kumquats, which can be eaten whole.

1 Pita stuffed with cottage cheese and bean sprouts in mayonnaise with chopped herbs 2 Red cabbage, carrot and alfalfa salad (*p. 147*) 3 Cheese and herb croquettes (*p. 134*) 4 Salad of raw spinach and young dandelion leaves in vinaigrette dressing with chopped hard-boiled egg 5 Whole-wheat rolls (*p. 175*) 6 Pita stuffed with cubed feta cheese, cucumber, celery and olives 7 Flamiche (*p. 85*) 8 Cashew patties (*p. 40*) 9 Many-bean salad (*p. 142*)

SALADS & DRESSINGS

Salads of fresh, raw vegetables are a rich source of vitamins and minerals and as such play an important part in any healthy diet. Ideally, they should form part of at least one meal a day and can even be the basis of the meal itself.

A growing number of supermarkets and greengrocers are supplying a wider and wider range of vegetables and salad greens, and it's worth searching these out, or growing your own fresh produce if you can. For extra nutrients, add fresh or dried fruit, nuts or sprouts. For a substantial main dish, try a salad with cooked dried beans or peas, pasta or grains. The range of dressings can be varied beyond mayonnaise and vinaigrette. Whatever kind you use, have it ready and toss the salad in it immediately to preserve nutrients. Green salads should be prepared and dressed at the last possible moment.

Soaking
overnight

Ingredients
½ cup wheat berries, soaked
   overnight and drained
½ cup whole barley
2 bananas, sliced
4 dried figs, finely sliced
2 ounces pecans, coarsely chopped
1 fresh green chili, diced
peanut butter dressing (see p. 150)

Serves 4

Mixed grain on lettuce

Other grains—rice, buckwheat, rye—can be used in this salad, in any proportion you like. You could fry the barley first (see page 206) for a few minutes if you prefer.

1 Bring a large kettle of water to the boil. Put in the wheat berries and the barley. Bring back to the boil and simmer, covered, for 50-60 minutes, or until tender. Drain.

2 When cold, mix the grains with the fruit, nuts and chili.

3 Stir the dressing into the salad, and serve, preferably on a bed of crisp lettuce.

Clockwise from top left: **Couscous salad** *(see p. 140)*; **Mixed grain salad with peanut butter dressing; Marinated buckwheat salad** *(see p. 140)*; **Barley salad** *(see p. 140)*; **with basic vinaigrette dressing** *(see p. 149)*

Photograph
page 139

Ingredients
¾ cup buckwheat groats
1 teaspoon oil
2½ cups water
1 orange, peeled and thinly sliced
2 ounces daikon, grated
¼ ounce arame *or* hijiki, soaked
    in warm water for 10 minutes
2 ounces pumpkin seeds
4 ounces firm tofu, finely
    chopped
Marinade
4 tablespoons sunflower oil
1 tablespoon sherry
1 tablespoon shoyu
2 cloves garlic, crushed
juice of ½ lemon
2 teaspoons finely grated gingerroot
4 tablespoons orange juice

Serves 4

Marinated buckwheat

1 Fry the buckwheat in the oil for 2-3 minutes.

2 Bring the water to the boil. Pour it over the buckwheat, stir once, cover the pan and simmer for 20 minutes. All the water should be absorbed. If not, drain the buckwheat.

3 Mix together all the marinade ingredients and pour them over the warm buckwheat. Let cool.

4 When the buckwheat is cool, add the other ingredients. Chill the salad in the refrigerator for about half an hour before serving.

Photograph
page 139

Ingredients
½ cup whole barley
2 ounces hazelnuts
1 small cauliflower, divided into
    small flowerets
½ cucumber, diced
1 tablespoon blue poppy seeds
6 tablespoons vinaigrette dressing
    (see p. 149)
salt and pepper

Serves 4

Barley

The hazelnuts can be used fresh, but they taste even better if you toast them gently first. The barley could be fried, too, as in the first salad recipe.

1 Boil the barley in plenty of water for 50-60 minutes. Drain.

2 Toast the hazelnuts for 2-3 minutes under the broiler or in a moderate oven and chop them coarsely.

3 Mix the barley and hazelnuts with the cauliflower, cucumber and poppy seeds. Stir in the dressing and season to taste.

Photograph
page 139

Soaking
overnight

Ingredients
½ cup chick peas, soaked overnight
1¼ cups couscous
1 teaspoon miso
2½ cups boiling water
2 tablespoons olive *or* walnut oil
1 tablespoon sesame oil
1 tablespoon lemon juice
2 cloves garlic, crushed
4 tablespoons chopped coriander
    leaves
12-15 scallions, chopped
salt and pepper

Serves 4

Couscous

Couscous and chick peas combine to make a substantial main salad. Without the chick peas this makes a lighter side salad which goes well with any bean or vegetable dish.

1 Drain and rinse the chick peas. Put them in a large saucepan with plenty of fresh water, bring to the boil and boil hard for 10 minutes. Reduce the heat, skim off any foam and simmer, covered, until soft—about 50-60 minutes. Drain and set aside.
Continued

2 Put the couscous in a large, heavy-bottomed saucepan. Mix together the miso and the boiling water and pour this over the couscous. Stir well, bring back to the boil and simmer, covered, for 5 minutes, stirring occasionally. Remove from the heat and let cool. All the water should have been absorbed. If not, drain off the excess.

3 When the couscous is cool, fluff it up with a fork. Mix in the chick peas, oils, lemon juice, garlic, chopped coriander and scallions. Reserve a little chopped coriander for a garnish if you like. Season with salt and plenty of pepper.

Spiced rice

1 Gently fry the onion in the oil for 3-4 minutes, until soft.

2 Put in the spices and rice and fry for another 2-3 minutes.

3 Add the boiling water, bring back to the boil and simmer until all the water is absorbed and the rice is tender— about 25-30 minutes.

4 Meanwhile, steam the green beans for 3-4 minutes, until barely tender.

5 Mix all the dressing ingredients together and pour over the warm rice. Season well and let cool.

6 When the rice is cool, mix with the remaining ingredients.

Ingredients
1 onion, finely chopped
1 tablespoon sunflower oil
1 teaspoon turmeric
¼ teaspoon cayenne
⅔ cup long-grain brown rice
1¾ cups boiling water
¼ pound green beans, chopped
¼ pound pineapple, diced
3 tablespoons grated creamed
  coconut
10-12 radishes, quartered
Dressing
2 tablespoons sunflower oil
1 tablespoon white wine vinegar
3 tablespoons pineapple juice
½ teaspoon grated gingerroot
salt and pepper

Serves 4

Photograph
page 143

Lentil and mint in yogurt

This salad quite definitely improves with keeping and is even better eaten the day after it is made.

1 Cook the lentils in plenty of boiling water until tender. This takes 35-40 minutes. Drain and let cool.

2 Heat a very small amount of oil—just a few drops—and fry the fenugreek and cardamom seeds for 3-4 minutes, or until they turn dark. Crush them well.

3 Mix together the crushed spices, yogurt, curd cheese and garlic. Stir this into the cooled lentils. Add the chopped scallions and herbs and season well.

Photograph
page 143

Ingredients
⅔ cups green lentils
a little oil
1 teaspoon fenugreek seeds
6 cardamom seeds
⅔ cup yogurt
4 ounces curd cheese
1 clove garlic, crushed
12 scallions, chopped
1 tablespoon finely chopped mint
1 tablespoon finely chopped parsley
salt and pepper

Serves 4

Paprika pasta

Ingredients
¼ pound pasta—shells *or* elbow
    macaroni
2 ounces black olives, pitted and
    sliced
4 tomatoes, peeled and chopped
1 small fennel bulb, diced
Dressing
⅔ cup yogurt
2 tomatoes, peeled and coarsely
    chopped
juice of ½ lemon
1 teaspoon paprika
dash of shoyu
2 teaspoons chopped basil

Serves 4

Lettuce or chicory goes well with this salad, but radicchio looks particularly good and echoes the Italian touches of pasta and basil.

1 Bring a large saucepan of water to the boil, salt it and cook the pasta until just tender to the bite—this may take from 7 to 15 minutes depending on the kind of pasta. Drain and cool.

2 Blend all the ingredients for the dressing together until smooth and stir into the cooled pasta.

3 Mix with the olives, tomatoes and fennel.

Photograph
*pages
136-137*

Soaking
overnight

Many-bean

Ingredients
⅓ cup red kidney beans, soaked
    overnight
⅓ cup chick peas, soaked
    overnight
⅓ cup lima *or* cannellini beans,
    soaked overnight
¼ pound snap beans, cut into
    ½-inch lengths
Marinade
¼ cup white wine vinegar
⅓ cup mixed olive and
    sunflower oil
1 tablespoon lemon juice
1 teaspoon grated lemon rind
2 cloves garlic, crushed
1 tablespoon white wine
1 dried red chili, very finely chopped
1 bunch scallions, chopped

Serves 4

The kidney beans should be soaked and cooked separately unless you want the whole salad to be pink.

1 Drain the beans and peas. Cover with fresh water, bring to the boil and boil rapidly for 10 minutes. Reduce the heat and simmer until tender. The kidney beans will take 35-40 minutes, the chick peas and lima beans up to an hour, depending on how fresh they are. Drain.

2 Steam the snap beans for 3-4 minutes. They should be still quite crunchy, only just beginning to be tender.

3 Combine together all the marinade ingredients.

4 Mix all the beans and peas together and pour the marinade over them. Leave for several hours in a cool place before serving. Drain off any excess dressing.

Photograph
*pages
54-55*

Spinach, apple and potato

Ingredients
1 pound spinach, washed
½ pound potatoes
½ pound crisp eating apples,
    diced
2 ounces blue cheese
⅔ cup yogurt
salt and pepper

Serves 4

Cauliflower, lightly cooked and divided into flowerets, can be substituted for the potato. It can be left raw and the spinach, too, in which case vinaigrette would be better than the yogurt.

1 Cook the spinach in a covered pan without adding any extra water for about 6 minutes, until just tender. Chop coarsely.

2 Boil the potatoes until just tender. Drain, peel and cut into cubes. Leave to cool and mix with the spinach and apple.

3 Mash or blend the blue cheese with the yogurt. Gently mix this dressing into the salad and season to taste.

From top: **Paprika pasta salad; Spiced rice salad** *(see p. 141);* **Lentil and mint salad in yogurt** *(see p. 141)*

Green salads

Ingredients
Lettuce
Endive, Batavian and curly
Belgian endive
Radicchio
Young spinach leaves
Watercress
Sorrel
Nasturtium leaves
Lovage
Celery leaves
Young dandelion leaves
Aragula

Aim for a variety of contrasting tastes and textures. In addition to the various kinds of lettuce, add chicory for a slightly bitter crispness and its relative, radicchio, for color. Endive, curly or Batavian, is very popular in France, as are young dandelion leaves. So is sorrel, which, with its strong, acid taste, needs to be used in moderation, like celery leaves. Lovage tastes of celery too, but is milder. Young spinach leaves are firm and crunchy. Both watercress and nasturtium leaves have a peppery tang. If you can find aragula, you will realize why the Italians love it.

I like to keep a wooden bowl for salads and rub garlic into the wood as a first step. The bowl never needs washing, only wiping with paper towels. The flavors of the dressing thus seep gradually into the wood.

To add extra interest to a green salad, use sprouted seeds, thinly sliced onions or shallots, nuts or thin slices of fruit— the pale white-green of a crisp apple, the softer green of avocado or melon, or darker green kiwi fruit.

Avocado and kiwi

*Photograph
pages
186-187*

Ingredients
2 large avocados, diced
4 kiwi fruit, peeled and sliced
1 tablespoon finely chopped parsley
1 tablespoon snipped chives
6 tablespoons vinaigrette
    dressing (see p. 149)
½ small cucumber, cut into julienne
    strips (see p. 222)
2 celery ribs, cut into julienne
    strips (see p. 222)
1 head of lettuce
1 bunch watercress, cleaned—
    approx. 2 ounces

Serves 4

1 Toss the avocados and kiwi fruit with the herbs and half the vinaigrette dressing.

2 Toss the julienne of cucumber and celery in the remaining vinaigrette dressing.

3 To serve, arrange the lettuce leaves and watercress in a dish. Pile on the avocado and kiwi fruit and arrange the cucumber and celery on top.

Endive, orange and watercress

*Photograph
pages 54-55*

Ingredients
3 heads Belgian endive
2 bunches watercress, cleaned—
    approx. 4 ounces
2 oranges, peeled and sliced
2 ounces cream cheese
⅓ cup yogurt
2 tablespoons snipped chives
salt and pepper

Serves 4

1 Separate the endive into blades. Arrange it on a serving dish or in a bowl with the watercress and orange slices. Chill for half an hour.

2 Beat together the cheese and yogurt. Stir in the chives and season to taste. Just before serving, pour the dressing over the salad.

Celeriac and zucchini

1 Cut the celeriac into julienne strips, see page 222 (they need not be as small as a normal julienne), and toss in the lemon juice to prevent discoloration.

2 Cut the other vegetables into strips of the same size. Mix all the ingredients with the dressing.

Ingredients
1 small celeriac
juice of ½ lemon
½ pound zucchini
1 small rutabaga
1 small daikon
tahini and orange dressing (see p. 150)

Serves 4

Photograph
page 146

Olive and orange

1 Blend the dressing with the honey and cayenne.

2 Mix the oranges, olives and scallions with the dressing and chill for an hour or two.

3 Just before serving, arrange the watercress or young spinach leaves in a bowl and pile the salad on top.

Ingredients
6 tablespoons basic vinaigrette dressing (see p. 149)
1 teaspoon honey
pinch of cayenne
4 large oranges, peeled and divided into segments
1-2 ounces green olives, pitted and finely sliced
1 bunch scallions, chopped
For serving
watercress *or* young spinach leaves

Serves 4

Photograph
page 146

Cucumber and strawberry

1 Mix together the yogurt, garlic and herbs.

2 Arrange the cucumber and strawberries in a bowl and gently mix in the dressing. Chill for 1 hour before serving.

Ingredients
1¼ cups yogurt
1-2 cloves garlic, crushed
2 tablespoons finely chopped mint
1 tablespoon finely chopped parsley
1 large cucumber *or* 2 small ones, diced or sliced
1 pint strawberries, coarsely chopped

Serves 4

Photograph
page 146

Beet, celery and apple

1 Mix the beet, celery and apple well. The beet can be finely chopped instead of grated if you prefer.

2 Moisten with the olive oil and lemon juice and season.

Ingredients
8 ounces raw beets, peeled and grated
4 celery ribs, chopped
½ pound crisp dessert apples, peeled and chopped
2 tablespoons olive oil
juice of ½ lemon
salt and pepper

Serves 4

Photograph
page 146

COLESLAWS

Shredded cabbage—red, green or white—makes an excellent base for substantial salads. A food processor is ideal for preparing them. If you shred the cabbage by hand, cut the pieces as finely as possible. Allow ½ pound cabbage for 4 people and use the same weight of other ingredients: fresh or dried fruits, nuts and seeds, grated root vegetables, crisp celery or fennel, sprouts and herbs. Serve with a vinaigrette or mayonnaise dressing (see pages 148-149).

Coleslaw with apricots

1 Toast the cashew nuts for 2-3 minutes under a hot broiler until lightly browned.

2 Cut the apricots into very fine slivers. Mix with all the other ingredients. The poppy seeds can be sprinkled over the top if you prefer, and any of the alternative dressings could be substituted.

Ingredients
2-3 ounces cashew nuts
2-3 ounces dried apricots
½ pound red *or* white cabbage, shredded
4 celery ribs, chopped
2 teaspoons blue poppy seeds (optional)
6 tablespoons mayonnaise (see p. 149)

Serves 4

Coleslaw with fennel

Mix all the ingredients together. The dill weed could be used to garnish.

Ingredients
½ pound white cabbage, shredded
4 ounces fennel, chopped
3 ounces mung bean sprouts
1 ounce pumpkin seeds
1 tablespoon dried dill weed
6 tablespoons mayonnaise (see p. 149)

Serves 4

Red cabbage, alfalfa and carrot

1 Mix together the oil, lemon juice and apple juice concentrate and season to taste. Mix half with the red cabbage and half with the grated carrot, keeping them separate.

2 Arrange the salad in rings with the red cabbage on the outside, then the grated carrot, and the alfalfa sprouts in the center.

Ingredients
3 tablespoons sunflower oil
3 tablespoons lemon juice
1 tablespoon apple juice concentrate
salt and pepper
¾ pound red cabbage, finely shredded
½ pound carrots, finely grated
2 ounces alfalfa sprouts

Serves 4

Photograph
pages 136-137

From top: **Beet, celery and apple** *(see p. 145);* **Celeriac and zucchini in tahini and orange dressing** *(see p. 145);* **Cucumber and strawberry** *(see p. 145);* **Olive and orange** *(see p. 145);* **Coleslaw with apricots; Coleslaw with fennel**

Photograph
*pages
186-187*

Mushroom salad in tofu

Ingredients
¾ pound button mushrooms, sliced
1 tablespoon oil
1 clove garlic, crushed
2 ounces shelled walnuts
½ cake silken tofu—approx.
    5 ounces
1 tablespoon lemon juice
salt and pepper
3-4 scallions, sliced lengthwise

Serves 4

1 Toss the mushrooms in the oil with the garlic.

2 Toast the walnuts for 2-3 minutes under a hot broiler. Chop them coarsely.

3 Mix together the tofu and lemon juice. Season well and stir into the mushroom slices.

4 Either mix in the scallions and toasted walnuts or arrange them on top as a garnish.

Photograph
*pages
188-189*

Bean sprouts Oriental

Ingredients
4 tablespoons sunflower oil
1 tablespoon red wine vinegar
2 teaspoons shoyu
salt and pepper
4 ounces mung bean sprouts
¼ pound button mushrooms, diced
1 red or yellow pepper, diced
4 celery ribs, diced

Serves 4

1 Combine the oil, vinegar and shoyu and season to taste.

2 Mix together the other ingredients. Toss with the dressing and chill before serving.

DRESSINGS

In addition to the usual vinaigrette and mayonnaise dressings, yogurt or tofu, flavored with cheese, tahini, shoyu or miso, can be used. It is worth making your own mayonnaise, not only for the taste but because you can be sure of avoiding the additives contained in commercial brands.

The term "vinaigrette" covers a multitude of combinations. As a guide, start with 3 parts of oil to 1 part of vinegar or lemon juice. Walnut oil and sesame oil give characteristic nutty tastes; sunflower and safflower oil are good for lighter dressings. Herbs and spices can be added, for example, tarragon, parsley, chives, horseradish, cayenne, chili and garlic. Bear in mind the type of salad you are dressing: bland food, such as beans, needs a good sharp vinaigrette dressing, while crisper salad greens benefit from a richer mixture. My own preference is for a sharp yet light dressing, as in the basic vinaigrette recipe opposite.

Basic vinaigrette

Mix all the ingredients together and shake well. I use a jar with a screw top.

Variations

Add a peeled and mashed avocado and blend until smooth. The result is more like a mayonnaise than a vinaigrette dressing. Good with a simple green or tomato salad or with a coleslaw.

Add 1-2 tablespoons soy flour and 1 teaspoon honey and blend until smooth. This looks like egg mayonnaise and is a useful recipe for those who prefer not to eat dairy products. Other non-dairy mayonnaise substitutes are the avocado vinaigrette dressing above and the almond dip on page 43.

Ingredients
4-6 tablespoons oil (olive *or* sunflower *or* a mixture to taste)
1 tablespoon wine or cider vinegar
1 tablespoon lemon juice
1 large clove garlic, crushed
large pinch of mustard powder
salt and pepper

Makes ⅓ to ½ cup

Mayonnaise

1 Beat the egg yolks. These should be at room temperature, as otherwise the mayonnaise may curdle.

2 Add up to half the oil drop by drop, beating the mixture constantly. I find it easiest to add the oil with a fork.

3 When half the oil has been added, beat in 1 tablespoon vinegar. Then beat in the remaining oil, about a tablespoon at a time, until the mixture is very thick.

4 Thin down with some or all of the remaining vinegar and season to taste.

Mustard, garlic, tarragon and other flavorings can be added to taste. For a lower-fat dressing, mix equal quantities of mayonnaise and yogurt.

Ingredients
2 egg yolks
1¼ cups oil (sunflower, olive *or* a mixture, according to preference)
2 tablespoons white wine vinegar
salt and pepper

Makes about 1½ cups

Cottage cheese

Blend all the ingredients together until smooth and season to taste.

Ingredients
½ pound cottage cheese
2 tablespoons mayonnaise
juice of ½ lemon
1 tablespoon honey (optional)
2 tablespoons chopped herbs— chives, parsley or watercress
salt and pepper

Makes about 1¼ cups

Photograph
page 139

Ingredients
8 tablespoons peanut butter
⅔ cup water
2 teaspoons miso
pinch of cayenne
up to 1 teaspoon honey *or*
    lemon juice (optional)

Makes about 1¼ cups

Peanut butter

Blend the peanut butter, water, miso and cayenne together until smooth. Blend in the honey or lemon juice to taste for a sweeter or a sharper dressing. This goes well with cold grains or pasta.

Ingredients
2 tablespoons tahini
2 tablespoons water
1 tablespoon sunflower oil
juice of ½ orange
1 teaspoon finely grated gingerroot

Makes about ½ cup

Tahini and orange

1 Mix the tahini and water together. You need to do this or the tahini may curdle.

2 Add all the other ingredients and mix thoroughly. Good with grains, raw vegetables and green salads.

Variation
Omit the oil and ginger and add ⅔ cup yogurt. This makes about ¾ cup. Lemon juice could be used instead of orange.

STOCKS, SAUCES & RELISHES

Vegetable stock can be every bit as rich in flavor and as wholesome as a meat-based one. Recipes are given for a light and a dark version, either of which can replace milk or water to add flavor to sauces and soups.

Of the sauces here, the most adaptable is béchamel, made with whole-wheat flour, which provides the basis for a range of variations. The rich brown sauce is a good example of how to create a tasty gravy substitute without using meat products. Nut-based sauces play a large part in vegetarian cuisine and supply extra protein.

Sauces need not be thickened with flour. Vegetable purées make delicious bases, as in the celery and dill or tomato sauce. A version of tomato sauce using orange is given here, but for a basic one use the recipe given on page 72.

Stock

Other root vegetables can be added to this—turnip, celeriac and parsnip are all good. Green vegetables, such as cabbage or broccoli, have a strong flavor and should be added sparingly, if at all, but the water they have cooked in could be used. The strained vegetables can be puréed and added to a thick soup.

Light stock

1 Heat the oil and cook all the vegetables and herbs very gently for 5 minutes. Take care not to let the vegetables color.

2 Add the water, bring to the boil and simmer, covered, for 1½-2 hours. Strain and cool. This will keep for 3-4 days in the refrigerator, or it can be frozen.

Continued

★

Ingredients
1 tablespoon olive oil
4 potatoes, coarsely chopped
2 carrots, coarsely chopped
1 large onion, coarsely chopped
1 celery rib, coarsely chopped
1 bay leaf
sprig of thyme
6 cups water
For dark stock
miso *or* shoyu to taste

Makes about 6 cups

Stock continued

Dark stock
Instead of gently cooking the vegetables, fry them until well browned, especially the onions. Add the miso or shoyu, bring to the boil and simmer as before. Instead of water, use liquid from cooking aduki beans, black-eyed peas or red kidney beans, or from soaking dried mushrooms.

★
(*including variations*)

Ingredients
1¼ cups milk
½ onion
6 peppercorns
1 bay leaf
3 tablespoons butter
2 tablespoons whole-wheat flour
salt and pepper

Makes 1¼ cups

White (béchamel) sauce

Strictly speaking "white sauce" is a misnomer, as whole-wheat flour makes a speckled beige sauce. You can also use cornmeal: this gives a lighter, golden version, more like a custard; which is suitable as a basis for a sweet sauce. I find a ratio of more fat than flour gives a smoother mixture, it is easier to stir in the milk, and the finished result is lighter. For a less rich sauce, use skim milk, soy milk, or half milk and half stock. For a cream sauce, add 2-3 tablespoons cream.

1 Bring the milk gently to the boil with the onion, peppercorns and bay leaf. Remove from heat and let stand, covered, for 10 minutes. Strain.

2 Melt the butter and when it foams sprinkle with the flour. Cook this mixture over gentle heat for 2-3 minutes, stirring. Add the milk, about a quarter at a time, stirring well to prevent lumps and making sure all the uncooked roux (the flour and butter mixture) is incorporated.

3 Bring to boiling point and simmer, stirring occasionally, for 3-5 minutes. Season to taste.

Variations
Green split pea sauce with cayenne
Cook ¼ cup green split peas until quite soft—about 45 minutes. Drain and purée. Stir into the white sauce and season to taste with cayenne. This is a good way of adding extra protein to a plain grain or vegetable dish.

Horseradish and Mustard
As the white sauce is coming to the boil, stir in 1 tablespoon grated horseradish and ¼ teaspoon mustard powder. Serve with croquettes, pancakes or simple steamed vegetables.

Cheese or Herb
While the sauce is hot, add ⅔-1½ cups grated Cheddar or 1-2 tablespoons chopped herbs, such as dill, tarragon or parsley. Cook, stirring, for another minute or two, until the cheese has melted or the herbs have flavored the sauce.

Salsify sauce

Use as a filling for the lentil roulade on page 134 or as sauce for the baked cabbage on page 66.

1 Boil the salsify for 20-25 minutes. Peel and dice.

2 Gently fry the onions and garlic in the butter for about 3-4 minutes, until soft, add the salsify and cook for another 2-3 minutes, until lightly browned.

3 Stir in the flour, yogurt and lemon juice. Mash until you have a fairly smooth but not perfectly blended consistency.

Ingredients
2 pounds salsify, scrubbed
2 medium onions, diced
2 cloves garlic, crushed
3 tablespoons butter
2 teaspoons whole-wheat flour
6 tablespoons yogurt
lemon juice to taste

Makes about 1¼ cups

★

Rich brown sauce

A good brown sauce using no liquid other than water is quick and simple to make. The fried vegetables are essential to the flavor and the miso and shoyu add color as well as seasoning. Whole-wheat flour adds its own delicious taste, but must be thoroughly cooked if the result is not to be gluey.

1 Melt the butter in a saucepan and gently cook the vegetables, covered, for 10 minutes.

2 Sprinkle with the flour and cook, stirring, for 3-4 minutes. Put in the water and bay leaf. Bring to the boil, still stirring, and simmer for 4-5 minutes.

3 Dissolve the miso in a tablespoon of the sauce and mix this back into the pan. Add the shoyu and simmer for a further few minutes. Taste for seasoning and add more miso or shoyu if desired. Remove the bay leaf before serving.

Ingredients
3 tablespoons butter
1 ounce mushrooms, minced
2 celery ribs, minced
1 small carrot, minced
1 small onion, minced
¼ cup whole-wheat flour
2½ cups water
1 bay leaf
2 teaspoons miso
1 teaspoon shoyu

Makes about 3 cups

★

Photograph
page 154

Cashew sauce

This goes well with the mushroom brioche on page 88.

1 Toast the cashew nuts under the broiler for 3-4 minutes until golden brown.

2 Grind to a fine powder in a blender. Pour in 2½ cups water and blend until the mixture resembles a very thin milk.

3 Heat the oil in a small saucepan, add the flour and cook over low heat for 3 minutes. Gradually pour in the cashew milk and bring to the boil, stirring constantly.

4 Add shoyu and seasoning. Cook gently for a further 10 minutes. Stir occasionally and add more water if necessary.

Ingredients
4 ounces cashew nuts
2½-3⅔ cups water
2 tablespoons oil
2 tablespoons flour
2 teaspoons shoyu
salt and pepper

Makes 2½-3⅔ cups

★

Photograph
pages 86-87

★

Chestnut and wine sauce

This is an ideal accompaniment for pastry dishes.

Ingredients
2 ounces dried chestnuts, soaked
  for 1 hour
2 tablespoons butter
2 ounces mushrooms, finely
  chopped
⅓ cup red wine
1 tablespoon brandy
1 bay leaf
sprig of thyme
salt and pepper

Makes about 1¼ cups

1 Boil the chestnuts in their soaking water until soft. This takes about 40 minutes. Purée the chestnuts with 4 tablespoons of their cooking liquid.

2 Heat the butter and gently sauté the mushrooms in it for 5 minutes. Add the chestnut purée, red wine, brandy, bay leaf and thyme and simmer for 5 minutes. Season to taste and serve hot, discarding the bay leaf and thyme.

★

Photograph
*pages
54-55*

Tomato and orange sauce

A fresh-tasting variation on basic tomato sauce, that will keep for 3-4 days in the refrigerator.

Ingredients
1 large onion, finely chopped
1 clove garlic, crushed
2 tablespoons olive oil
1 pound tomatoes, peeled and
  chopped
2 teaspoons dried oregano
juice and grated rind of 1 orange
salt and pepper

Makes 1¼ cups

1 Lightly fry the onion and garlic in the oil for 3-4 minutes. Add the tomatoes and oregano and cook, covered, for 20 minutes, stirring occasionally.

2 Stir in the orange rind and juice and cook, covered, for a further 5 minutes. Season to taste and serve hot.

Clockwise from top right: **Date and orange relish; Avocado and fennel sauce; Chestnut and wine sauce; Celery and dill sauce; Rich brown sauce** *(p. 153)*

Celery and dill sauce

★

Buttermilk goes well with the distinctive flavor of dill, but you can omit it if you would prefer a thicker, not too sharp sauce.

1 Heat the butter and in a saucepan and gently cook the celery, covered, for 10 minutes.

2 Add the dill weed and stock and simmer for 5 minutes. Allow to cool a little.

3 Put through a blender. Add the buttermilk and season to taste. Reheat gently before serving.

Ingredients
2 tablespoons butter
4 celery ribs, finely chopped
4-6 teaspoons fresh dill weed
⅔ cup light vegetable stock
 (see p. 151)
⅔ cup buttermilk
salt and pepper

Makes about 1¼ cups

Avocado and fennel sauce

★

If no extra liquid is added, this makes a good dip. Yogurt or tofu can be blended in for a creamier consistency.

1 Heat the oil and sauté the fennel briskly for 3-4 minutes. Add boiling water to cover and simmer for 10 minutes. Drain, reserving the liquid.

2 Blend the fennel and avocado with a little of the cooking liquid until smooth. Add more liquid until you have the required consistency. Season. Reheat gently before serving.

Ingredients
1 teaspoon oil
½ pound fennel, very finely
 chopped
1 ripe avocado, chopped
salt and pepper

Makes about 1 cup

Lime relish

★

Photograph
*pages
180-181*

Wash the lime well but do not peel it. This relish will keep for a day or two but is best eaten as soon as possible. It goes well with couscous, curry, samosas and croquettes like the mushroom and aduki croquettes on page 96.

Mix the vegetables, lime and ginger together and toss them in the vinegar. Season to taste.

Ingredients
¼ pound carrot, grated
½ cucumber, peeled and grated
6 scallions, finely chopped
½ lime, very finely chopped
1 teaspoon grated gingerroot
1 tablespoon white wine vinegar
salt and pepper

Makes about ¾ cup

Date and orange relish

★

A simple recipe that can be eaten immediately. It is excellent as a chutney in cheese sandwiches or as an accompaniment to the croquettes on page 96.

Put all the ingredients into a heavy-bottomed saucepan. Cover and cook gently for 30-45 minutes, stirring occasionally to break the mixture down, and adding a little extra liquid if necessary. Allow to cool before serving.

Ingredients
2 oranges, peeled and chopped
½ pound dried dates, chopped
3 tablespoons vinegar
2 tablespoons dark raw sugar
juice and rind of ½ lemon
1 teaspoon mustard seeds
1 tablespoon powdered cinnamon
pinch of cayenne
2 tablespoons water *or* orange
 juice

Makes about 2 cups

PUDDINGS

From a whole-food point of view, if not strictly a vegetarian one, desserts make a very positive contribution to a meal. If the main course has been light and lacking in protein, serve cheesecake made with tofu, a soufflé, mousse or roulade using eggs, or a milk pudding. If you prefer to avoid cream, try a cashew "cream" (made with cottage cheese), yogurt, or custard made with cornmeal as an accompaniment, and use yogurt also to make delicious ice cream.

Fresh fruit salad is one of the best possible endings to a meal. Base it on a color theme—green and white looks cool and refreshing, red soft fruit with peaches or nectarines is lovely for a party—or on a simple contrast of fruits, such as pomegranate and banana. Dried fruits really come into their own in desserts, whether individually, as mixed fruit compotes or puréed, and give a nutritious as well as delectable final touch to a meal.

★ *(sauce)*

Ingredients
4 medium pears, ripe but still firm
¼ cup honey
1¼ cups orange juice
2½ cups water
1 vanilla bean
Sauce
¼ cup butter
¼ cup carob powder
1 egg
½ teaspoon vanilla extract
2 tablespoons maple syrup

Serves 4

Pears with carob sauce

Carob powder makes an excellent substitute for chocolate in this version of poires Belle Hélène.

1 Peel the pears, leaving the stalks. Dissolve the honey in the orange juice and water over low heat, add the vanilla bean and poach the pears, covered, for 15-20 minutes, or until tender. Allow to cool completely in the syrup. Remove the vanilla bean.

2 For the sauce, melt the butter, stir in the carob powder and beat in the egg, vanilla extract and maple syrup. Stir over gentle heat for 10 minutes, until the sauce thickens slightly and is completely smooth. You may need to add a little of the pear syrup to thin to a coating consistency. Coat each pear liberally with the warm sauce.

Millet pudding with apricots

Those who like rice pudding, but do not care for it made with brown rice, will find this a delicious alternative. The soy milk gives it a rich, creamy quality. It is good on its own or with puréed or stewed fruit.

1 Preheat the oven to 325°F.

2 Gently fry the millet in the oil for 4-5 minutes until golden brown. Pour over the soy milk, bring to the boil and simmer for 5 minutes.

3 Transfer to an ovenproof dish, sprinkle with the cinnamon (and any or all of the optional extras listed with the ingredients) and bake for 45-60 minutes.

4 Stew the apricots in their soaking water for 10 minutes, or until warm. Serve in a separate bowl.

Ingredients
½ cup millet grains
1 teaspoon oil
2½ cups soy milk
1 teaspoon powdered cinnamon
Optional extras
2 teaspoons honey
2 ounces roasted hazelnuts
2 ounces raisins
2 ounces crystallized ginger, chopped

8 ounces Hunza apricots, soaked in hot water for 1 hour—ordinary dried apricots can be used if Hunza apricots are not available

Behind: **Millet pudding with apricots**; foreground: **Pears with carob sauce**

★ *(sauce)*

Photograph
*pages
188-189*

Ingredients
1 large firm pear
1 tablespoon granulated brown sugar
¾ cup red wine
1¼ pounds rhubarb, chopped
    into 1-inch lengths
1 pink grapefruit, peeled and
    chopped
1-2 tablespoons honey
Cashew cream
4 ounces cashew nuts
4 ounces cottage cheese
1-2 tablespoons honey
⅔ cup water

Serves 4

Rhubarb with cashew cream

*Made with low-fat cottage cheese, the nut "cream" makes a
perfect accompaniment to cooked fruit.*

1 Peel the pear and cut it into chunks. Dissolve the sugar
in the wine in a small pan and stew the pear, covered,
over very low heat for 15 minutes. Strain, reserving the juice.

2 In a separate pan, stew the rhubarb and grapefruit with the
honey over low heat for 10 minutes, or until the rhubarb
is tender but not disintegrating. Strain, reserving the juice.

3 Put the pear juice and rhubarb juice in a pan together and
boil rapidly until reduced by at least half and beginning
to thicken. Combine the pear, rhubarb and grapefruit in
a serving bowl and pour the juice over. Leave to cool.

4 To make the cashew cream, blend all the ingredients
together until very smooth. Serve with the rhubarb.

★

Photograph
*pages
86-87*

Ingredients
8 ounces golden seedless raisins
3 tablespoons fruit juice, warmed
½ cup rolled oats
⅓ cup self-rising whole-wheat
    flour
6 tablespoons vegetable shortening,
    grated
¼ teaspoon ground nutmeg
½ teaspoon grated gingerroot
½ teaspoon ground allspice
1 ounce crystallized ginger, finely
    chopped
juice and rind of ½ orange
juice and rind of ½ lemon
3 eggs
3 tablespoons sherry *or* brandy

Serves 4-6

Rich fruit pudding

Rich but sugar free, this makes an ideal Christmas pudding.

1 Soak the raisins for 15-30 minutes in the fruit juice.

2 Mix together the oats and flour. Rub in the fat, add
the spices and ginger and mix well. Add the raisins
and the orange and lemon rind and juice.

3 In a separate bowl, beat the eggs thoroughly. Add them to
the mixture with the sherry or brandy and stir very well
for at least 5 minutes.

4 Butter a 1-quart bowl and pour in the pudding mixture.
Cover with wax paper and a double layer of foil and steam
for 1½-2 hours.

Photograph
*pages
168-169*

Ingredients
1¼ cups fruit juice
1 teaspoon agar powder
¼ pound fresh fruit, chopped

Makes 4 small jellies

Fruit jelly

*I use orange juice or red grape juice for this. Most soft fruit
are suitable. Apples and bananas must be tossed in lemon juice
to prevent discoloration.*

1 Bring the fruit juice to the boil with the agar. Beat
thoroughly and boil until the agar has dissolved. Let to
cool slightly.

2 Stir in the prepared fruit, pour into molds and leave
to set. Dip the molds into cold water first if you are going
to turn out the jellies.

Fruit compote

*This is good both at breakfast and at the end of a meal. It needs
to be started the day before but is very easy to make.*

1 Soak the dried fruit overnight with the spices in the water
and fruit juice concentrate.

2 Next day, bring to the boil and simmer for 25 minutes.
Remove the spices, add the seeds of the pomegranate
and cook for a further 5 minutes, adding more water if
necessary. Serve the compote warm or cold, sprinkled with
the chopped pistachios.

Variation

For a more substantial version, which is also good hot, spoon
the compote into an ovenproof dish. Cover with 2 cups
muesli (see p. 206), stirring some of it into the fruit, and
bake at 350°F for 30-35 minutes.

Ingredients
½ pound dried apricots
2 ounces prunes
2 ounces dried pears
2 ounces dried figs
2 ounces golden seedless raisins
6 cloves *or* allspice berries
1 cinnamon stick
2½ cups water
1 tablespoon fruit juice concentrate
1 fresh pomegranate
Garnish
2 ounces shelled pistachios,
 chopped

Serves 4

★

Photograph
*pages
180-181*

Soaking
overnight

Shortcake

*Frozen raspberries are suitable for this. You can use sugar-free
jam and omit the whipped cream if you like.*

1 Preheat the oven to 375°F and line an 8-inch round cake
pan with wax paper.

2 Beat the eggs and sugar thoroughly until they turn pale
yellow and become thick and frothy. Do not overbeat.

3 Fold in the flour carefully and thoroughly. Spoon the
mixture into the prepared cake pan and bake for 25 minutes.
Turn out and cool.

4 When cold, split the cake in half and spread with the jam.
Sandwich together again and cut into small pieces.

5 Put these in a serving dish, cover with the raspberries
and sprinkle with the sherry or liqueur. Spread the custard on
top and leave to set. Serve chilled, decorated with whipped
cream and toasted almonds if desired.

Ingredients
2 eggs
⅓ cup light raw sugar
⅓ cup wheatmeal flour *or* 2½
 tablespoons each whole-wheat
 flour and all-purpose white flour
 mixed
2-3 tablespoons jam
½ pound raspberries
sherry *or* liqueur to taste
1¼ cups egg custard *or* cornmeal
 custard (see p. 160)
Garnish (optional)
whipped cream
toasted slivered almonds

Serves 4

★

Photograph
*pages
168-169*

Custard

A traditional custard must be heated very gently and not allowed to come near boiling point; a double boiler is ideal for cooking it. Cornmeal custard is a simple alternative that omits the eggs and sugar.

★

Ingredients
2 eggs
¼ cup light raw sugar
1¼ cups milk

Makes 1¼ cups

★

Photograph
*pages
168-169*

Ingredients
1½ tablespoons cornmeal
1 tablespoon maple syrup
1¼ cups milk
1 vanilla bean

Makes 1¼ cups

Traditional custard
Beat the eggs and sugar together. Add the milk and heat gently until thick enough to coat the back of a spoon.

Cornmeal custard
1 Mix the cornmeal and maple syrup with a little of the milk to make a smooth paste.

2 Heat the remaining milk with the vanilla bean until nearly boiling. Pour this over the cornmeal paste and mix until smooth.

3 Return to the pan and reheat gently until thick, stirring constantly. Remove the vanilla bean before serving.

For a thinner custard, use only ¾ tablespoon cornmeal.

Photograph
*pages
54-55*

Ingredients
½ pound cranberries
1 cup orange juice
2 cloves
¼ teaspoon ground cinnamon
6 tablespoons granulated brown
   sugar
2 tablespoons water
2 teaspoons agar powder
6 eggs, separated
½ teaspoon vanilla extract
⅔ cup heavy cream
1 tablespoon brandy *or* rum

Serves 4

Spiced cranberry soufflé

You can use fresh or frozen cranberries for this, or any soft fruit—strawberries or raspberries that do not look quite good enough to serve as they are would be ideal.

1 Put the cranberries in a small pan with the orange juice and spices. Cover and simmer until they have turned to a thick sauce. Remove from the heat and allow to cool.

2 Boil 4 tablespoons of the sugar with the water and agar for 4-5 minutes, or until you have a thick caramel sauce.

3 Beat the egg whites until stiff. Still beating pour in the caramel. Add the vanilla, beat again and chill for 1 hour in the refrigerator.

4 Fold the cranberry sauce into the egg whites. Pile into a 1½ quart soufflé dish and chill.

5 Beat the egg yolks with the rest of the sugar until pale yellow and frothy. Add the cream and the brandy or rum and beat again thoroughly. Serve this sauce with the soufflé.

Prune and brandy mousse

1 Stew the prunes in just enough water to cover until soft. This takes about 35-40 minutes.

2 Drain the prunes and purée them with the brandy, egg yolks and yogurt until smooth.

3 Beat the egg whites until stiff and fold in. Spoon into individual glasses and chill before serving.

Ingredients
½ pound prunes, soaked for 3-4 ⅔ hours or overnight and pitted
1 tablespoon brandy
2 eggs, separated
⅔ cup yogurt

Serves 4

Photograph
page 162

Lemon and whisky roulade

1 Preheat the oven to 375°F and line a 15½ x 10½-inch jelly roll pan with oiled wax paper. (See also Broccoli roulade, page 132.)

2 Beat together the eggs, honey and lemon rind in a bowl over a pan of hot water until thick and mousse-like. Still beating, add the lemon juice very gradually. This will take 10-15 minutes.

3 Remove from the heat and fold in the flour carefully and thoroughly. Pour into the prepared pan and level out. Bake for 15-20 minutes, until just firm.

4 Tip the roulade out on a clean sheet of wax paper, roll it up with the paper and allow to cool.

5 Whip the cream and fold in the whisky and sugar.

6 Unroll the cold roulade, spread the cream over it and roll up again. Decorate with extra cream and/or lemon slices or lemon zest.

Ingredients
4 eggs
1¼ tablespoons honey
grated rind and juice of 1 small
   lemon
⅔ cup wheatmeal flour *or* ⅓ cup
   each whole-meal flour and
   all-purpose white flour mixed
1 cup whipping cream
1¼ tablespoons whisky
2½ teaspoons light raw sugar
Garnish
extra whipping cream
lemon slices
lemon zest

Serves 4-6

★
Photograph
page 162

Tofu cheesecake

This is a light flan with the look of traditional cheesecake. The filling is delicate so handle it carefully.

1 Preheat the oven to 350°F.

2 Melt the butter, honey and sugar together in a pan, bring to the boil and stir in the oats.

3 Press the mixture into a 9-inch flan ring, preferably one with a removable base, and bake for 15-20 minutes.

4 Blend all the ingredients for the filling until smooth. Pour over the base and chill for 24 hours before serving.

Ingredients
Base
½ cup butter
1 tablespoon honey
1-2 tablespoons granulated brown
   sugar
2 cups rolled oats
Filling
1 cake silken tofu—about 11
   ounces
4 ounces cottage cheese
2 bananas, peeled
2 teaspoons honey
juice and rind of ½ lemon

Serves 4

Photograph
page 162

Green and white fruit salad

A refreshing sweet for a summer day. The pear should be of a firm type, such as Comice. Other possibilities are green or white figs, sliced in half lengthwise, plums or bananas.

1 Scoop out the melon pulp into balls. Peel the lychees and remove the pits, then halve the fruit. Mix all the fruit together about 2 hours before eating.

2 Blend all the ingredients for the dressing together. Mix with the fruit and chill.

Ingredients
½ honeydew melon
½ pound lychees
½ pound seedless green grapes
2 kiwi fruit, sliced
1 small firm pear, diced
Dressing
2 tablespoons lemon juice
1 tablespoon honey
1 tablespoon Pernod
150 ml (¼ pint) white grape juice

Serves 4

Peach and claret water ice

A good alternative when peaches are out of season is persimmon. This ice can be served on its own or with extra fresh fruit— one peach or persimmon per person—peeled and cut into thin slivers.

1 Simmer the peaches in the water with the sugar and the lemon rind and juice for 15 minutes.

2 Strain, pressing some of the peach pulp through the strainer if you like. Add the claret and freeze until mushy— about 1 hour.

3 Beat the egg white and fold it in. Freeze again.

Ingredients
6-8 medium peaches, peeled and
  very finely chopped
2½ cups water
⅔ cup brown granulated sugar
rind and juice of 1 lemon
½ cup claret
½ egg white

Serves 4

★
Photograph
pages
86-87

Black-currant yogurt ice cream

Red currants, blackberries, bilberries or gooseberries could also be used, as could pitted black cherries.

1 Mix together the yogurt, vanilla extract and honey and freeze until mushy—about 1 hour.

2 Put the black-currants in a saucepan with the orange juice and sugar. Cover and simmer over low heat for 5 minutes (gooseberries would take about 10 minutes).

3 Remove from the heat and let the fruit steep for 30 minutes. Strain and allow to cool completely.

4 Stir the fruit into the yogurt. Freeze for an hour. Beat the egg whites until stiff, fold them in and freeze for 1-2 hours, or until firm.

Ingredients
2½ cups yogurt
1 teaspoon vanilla extract
2 tablespoons honey
4-6 ounces black-currants,
  trimmed
2 tablespoons orange juice
3 tablespoons light raw sugar
2 egg whites

Serves 6

★
Photograph
pages
186-187

Clockwise from top left: **Prune and brandy mousse** *(see p. 161)*; **Green and white fruit salad; Lemon and whisky roulade** *(see p. 161)*; **Tofu cheesecake** *(see p. 161)*

CAKES, BISCUITS & PASTRY

Whole-food cakes may not be as light as traditional sponge cakes, but they have a compensating richness of texture and flavor. The cakes in this chapter use whole-wheat or soy flour and oat flakes; only one—parkin—uses any sugar. The others are sweetened with dried fruit, carob powder, fruit juice, grated carrot, honey or molasses, all of which make excellent sweeteners without the health problems associated with sugars. Three of them—the carob, banana and rich fruit cakes—are made without eggs, showing how easy it is to use substitutes and cut down the cholesterol intake. The banana bread also uses oil as a fat rather than butter, helpful for those on a diet low in saturated fats.

Of the biscuits, none uses sugar. The pastries are enriched with sugar and egg yolk but there is no sugar in the toppings or fillings. All these recipes are suitable for freezing, and keep well for several days in airtight containers.

★

Ingredients
8 ounces dried figs
1¾ cups apple juice
8 tablespoons butter
2 eggs
2 cups self-rising whole-wheat
  flour
2½ teaspoons ground allspice
¾ teaspoon fennel seeds
10 ounces carrots, grated

Carrot and fig cake

1 Stew the figs for 30 minutes in the apple juice, drain and purée.

2 Preheat the oven to 325°F and line an 8-inch round cake pan with wax paper.

3 Beat the butter until creamy.

4 Beat the eggs, mix with the flour and spices and beat into the butter.

5 Stir in the carrot and the fig purée. Spoon into the prepared pan and bake for 1 hour. Allow to cool for 10 minutes and turn out.

Clockwise from top right: **Parkin** *(see p. 166)*; **Carrot and fig cake**; **William's carob cake** *(see p. 166)*

★
Photograph
page 165

Ingredients
5 ounces carob powder
3 ounces desiccated coconut
¾ cup soy flour
½ cup rolled oats
⅓ cup whole-wheat flour
8 ounces raisins
1 tablespoon powdered cinnamon
½ cup butter, cut into small pieces
3 tablespoons oil
1¼ cups apple *or* grape juice
Filling
2 tablespoons carob powder
2 tablespoons tahini
1 tablespoon honey

William's carob cake

1 Preheat the oven to 325°F and line an 8-inch square cake pan with wax paper.

2 Mix together the dry ingredients and mix in the butter and oil until smooth.

3 Stir in the fruit juice and spoon the mixture into the prepared cake pan. Cover with foil. Bake for 50-60 minutes, or until a knife inserted into the center comes out clean. This cake does not rise. Cool for 10 minutes and turn out.

4 Mix the carob powder and tahini with a little water to a paste. Add the honey and more water until the filling has a spreading consistency. You could enrich it with a little cream if you like.

5 Split the cake and spread the filling thinly over the center and on the top. Sandwich together again.

Variation (filling)
Mix together 2 tablespoons tahini, 2 tablespoons apple juice concentrate and 1-2 teaspoons carob powder. Let stand for 30-60 minutes. This has a glossy look and makes a very good icing. It can also be used in sandwiches.

★
Photograph
page 165

Ingredients
⅔ cup whole-wheat flour
2¾ cups rolled oats
1 cup coarse oatmeal
pinch of salt
½ teaspoon bicarbonate of soda
¼ teaspoon baking powder
3 teaspoons ground ginger
1½ cups butter
⅔ cup molasses
2½ tablespoons dark raw sugar
1 tablespoon honey
⅓ cup milk
2 eggs, beaten
⅓ cup apple juice

Makes 9 squares

Parkin

A traditional oatmeal and ginger cake from the North of England, where it is often eaten with cheese and apples.

1 Preheat the oven to 325°F and line an 8-inch square cake pan with wax paper.

2 Mix the first 7 ingredients together in a bowl.

3 Put the butter, molasses, sugar and honey in a saucepan and bring to boiling point, stirring occasionally. Pour this over the dry ingredients and mix thoroughly.

4 Put the milk, eggs and apple juice in the same saucepan. Heat until very warm, stirring until well-blended. Do not worry if the mixture curdles.

5 Add this to the contents of the bowl, mix well and spoon into the prepared cake pan. Sprinkle a little extra milk on the surface if you prefer it glazed. Bake for 30-35 minutes or until a knife inserted into the center comes out clean. Cut into 9 squares and serve from the tin.

Banana bread

You could substitute other fruit for half the banana: pear, apple, apricot or pineapple are particularly good. They must be very finely chopped to give the best flavor.

1 Preheat the oven to 375°F.

2 Mix all the ingredients together. The consistency should be soft and moist. Spoon into a greased ½ quart loaf pan and bake for 50-60 minutes, or until a knife inserted into the center comes out clean. Cool for 10 minutes before turning out.

Ingredients
1 pound ripe bananas, mashed
2 ounces chopped nuts
½ cup sunflower oil
4 ounces raisins
⅔ cup rolled oats
1 cup whole-wheat flour
½ teaspoon almond essence
pinch of salt

★
Photograph
*pages
168-169*

Rich fruit cake

Made without sugar or eggs, this is nevertheless an ideal cake for special occasions—birthdays, Christmas or weddings.

1 Preheat the oven to 325°F and line a 9-inch square cake pan with wax paper.

2 Cream the honey and oil together.

3 Mix the soy flour with the water and gradually add to the oil and honey mixture, beating well. Beat in the rum and the grated rind and juice of the orange and lemon. Add the almonds, figs and dates.

4 Mix the flour with the salt and spice and mix together the currants and raisins.

5 Stir half the flour and half the currant mixture into the soy cream, then stir in the remainder. Spoon into the prepared pan and bake for 3¼-3½ hours, or until a knife inserted into the center comes out clean. Cool for 10 minutes and turn out.

Ingredients
½ cup clear honey
¾ cup oil
¾ cup soy flour
1¼ cups water
1 tablespoon rum
grated rind and juice of 1 orange
grated rind and juice of 1 lemon
2 ounces slivered almonds
4 ounces dried figs, chopped
4 ounces dried dates, chopped
1½ cups whole-wheat flour
pinch of salt
2 teaspoons mixed spice
8 ounces currants
8 ounces golden seedless raisins
8 ounces dark seedless raisins

★
Photograph
pages 86-87

Sunflower crunch

1 Preheat the oven to 400°F and lightly grease a 15½ x 10½-inch jelly roll pan.

2 Mix together all the dry ingredients.

3 Melt the butter and honey and boil together for 3-4 minutes. Pour this over the dry ingredients and mix well. Press firmly into the prepared jelly roll pan and bake for 15-20 minutes. Allow to cool before cutting.

Ingredients
7½ cups rolled oats
5 tablespoons granola (see p. 182)
3¾ tablespoons sunflower seeds
3¾ tablespoons sesame seeds
3¾ tablespoons chopped nuts
5 tablespoons whole-wheat flour
1¼ teaspoon baking powder
⅔ cup butter
3½ tablespoons honey

Makes 12-15 squares or fingers

★
Photograph
*pages
168-169*

Children's parties

Food for children's parties can be healthy yet still appeal to a sweet tooth—there is no need for it to be rich in sugar.

Even the traditional jellies and shortcake can have a whole-food slant. Make the jellies with fresh fruit and set them with agar; use a wheatmeal cake as the basis for the shortcake —it doesn't have to be decorated with whipped cream. For the birthday cake, try a banana bread decorated with yogurt-coated raisins, or the carob cake on page 166.

Spread sandwiches with peanut butter and mashed banana, or with dates, puréed and mixed with cream cheese and sesame seeds.

Fill buns or rolls with herb-flavored croquettes. Miniature pizzas are always popular; so are carob bourbon biscuits, cut into shapes, and sunflower seed biscuits made with crunchy oatmeal. Savory popcorn is easy to make: heat a little oil in a heavy saucepan, add a handful of corn at a time, put the lid on and keep the pan covered until all the corn has popped. Toss it in a little shoyu.

1 Apple juice 2 Wheatmeal shortcake with cornmeal custard (*pp. 159 and 160*) 3 Mushroom and aduki croquettes (*p. 96*) 4 Banana bread (*p. 167*) with carob icing (*p. 166*) 5 Carob bourbon biscuits (*p. 170*)
6 & 11 Sandwiches made with whole-wheat bread (*p. 174 and above*) 7 Lemonade 8 Popcorn (*see above*)
9 Yogurt milk shake 10 Sunflower crunch (*p. 167*)
12 Pizzas (*p. 120*) 13 Fruit jellies (*p. 158*)

Carob truffles

★
Photograph pages 188-189

Ingredients
6 ounces cake *or* biscuit crumbs
1-2 ounces raisins, chopped
1½ ounces hazelnuts, finely chopped
2 ounces ground almonds
4 tablespoons black-currant jam, preferably sugar-free
1 tablespoon brandy
Coating
10 ounces carob chocolate

Makes 25-30 truffles

If you melt only a little carob chocolate—2 or 3 squares at a time—it's easier to give each truffle a thin coating. Use two forks to turn the truffles over.

1 Mix all the ingredients except the carob chocolate thoroughly. Divide into walnut-sized balls.

2 Melt the carob chocolate over low heat. Dip each truffle in and turn it until coated. Leave to set.

Carob bourbon biscuits

★
Photograph pages 168-169

Ingredients
10 tablespoons butter
2 tablespoons honey
2 egg yolks
1¼ cups whole-wheat flour
2 tablespoons cornmeal
1 tablespoon carob powder
½ teaspoon vanilla extract
Filling
1 tablespoon butter
1 tablespoon tahini
1 tablespoon peanut butter
1 tablespoon thick honey

Makes about 20 pairs of biscuits

This can be cut into the traditional bourbon "fingers" about 3 x 1-inch or, for a party, they look pretty if differently shaped pastry cutters are used.

1 Preheat the oven to 350°F and lightly grease a cookie sheet.

2 Beat together the butter, honey and egg yolks until creamy.

3 Mix in the flour, cornmeal, carob powder and vanilla extract.

4 Roll out to a thickness of ¼ inch on a floured board, prick with a fork and cut into the desired shapes. Bake for 10-15 minutes. Turn out on a rack and allow to cool.

5 For the filling, beat all the ingredients together and sandwich a little between each pair of biscuits.

Brownies

★

Ingredients
½ pound dried dates, chopped
½ cup butter
2 ripe bananas, mashed
2 eggs
½ cup whole-wheat flour
2 ounces carob powder
4 ounces chopped walnuts
1 teaspoon vanilla extract

Makes 16 squares

1 Preheat the oven to 350°F and lightly grease an 8-inch square baking pan.

2 Cook the dates in just enough water to cover for 20 minutes, or until soft and reduced to a stiff purée. Cool. Then beat them with the butter until light and fluffy.

3 Beat in the bananas and then the eggs, one at a time.

4 Stir in the flour, carob powder, walnuts and vanilla extract and mix gently but thoroughly.

5 Turn out into the prepared baking pan and bake for 40 minutes. Allow to cool in the pan before cutting.

Clockwise from top left: **Brownies; Orange daties** *(see p. 172);* **Apricot slice** *(see p. 172)*

★
Photograph
page 171

Ingredients
1 pound dried dates, chopped
1 unpeeled orange, washed and
    finely chopped
½-⅔ cup water
2¼ cups whole-wheat flour
3½ cups rolled oats
1½ cups butter *or* solid
    vegetable fat
2 tablespoons honey

Makes about 18 slices

Orange daties

*Date purée gives these slices a moist quality and rich flavor,
highlighted by a fresh orange tang. They will keep 4-5 days
in an airtight container, and also freeze well.*

1 Preheat the oven to 400°F and lightly grease a
15½ x 10½-inch jelly roll pan.
2 Put the dates and orange in a saucepan with the water.
Cook gently, covered, for 20 minutes or until soft. Cool
slightly and liquidize until smooth.

3 Mix together the flour, oats, butter and honey. Spread
half of this over the prepared jelly roll pan and press down
evenly.

4 Cover with the date mixture and then with the remaining
dough. It is easier to do this if you roll it out first on
wax paper. Bake for 25-30 minutes and allow to cool before
cutting into slices.

★
Photograph
page 171

Ingredients
½ pound dried apricots
piecrust (p. 92) made with
    1¼ cups flour
Topping
4 ounces slivered almonds
4 ounces ground almonds
1 teaspoon vanilla extract
2 eggs
2 tablespoons apple juice
    concentrate

Makes 12 slices

Apricot slice

*Instead of ordinary piecrust, you could use the rich pastry
given in the next recipe (for mince pies).*

1 Stew the apricots in just enough water to cover for 35-40
minutes, until soft.

2 Preheat the oven to 400°F and lightly grease a 13 x 9-inch
cookie sheet.

3 Roll the pastry out to about 9-inches square and place it
on the cookie sheet. Prick it all over and bake for 4 minutes
to set it.

4 Reduce the oven to 375°F.

5 Purée the apricots and spread them over the pastry base.

6 Mix the topping ingredients together, spread them over the
apricots and bake for 20 minutes. Cool and cut into slices.

Mince pies

The quantity of mincemeat given is much more than is needed for the mince pies, as it is not worth making in small amounts. It keeps in the freezer for 2-3 months, bottled for 2-3 weeks. If you are bottling it, leave overnight in a cool place first.

1 Stew the apples with the spice and fruit juice for about 10 minutes, until soft, adding a little water only if necessary.

2 Remove from the heat and mix in the other ingredients.

3 For the pastry, mix the flour and salt together, make a well in the center and add the remaining ingredients.

4 Gradually incorporate the flour into the ingredients, rubbing lightly with the fingertips, until you have a soft dough. Wrap in wax paper and chill for 1 hour.

5 Preheat the oven to 400°F.

6 Roll the pastry out to a thickness of ¼ inch and cut out 18 3-inch rounds for bases and the same number of 2½-inch rounds for lids. Line 2½-inch muffin-pan cups with the bases and half fill with mincemeat. Cover with the lids and bake for 15-20 minutes. Turn out on a rack to cool.

Ingredients
Mincemeat
1½ pounds cooking apples, peeled and chopped
1 tablespoon mixed spice
1 tablespoon fruit juice
¾ cup honey
8 ounces raisins
8 ounces currants
4 ounces mixed peel, finely chopped
4 ounces slivered almonds
1-2 tablespoons brandy
2 tablespoons molasses

Makes 2½ pounds mincemeat

Pastry
3 cups whole-wheat flour
pinch of salt
6 ounces brown sugar
1 cup butter, chopped
4 egg yolks
2-3 drops vanilla extract

Makes 18-20 mince pies

★

Photograph
pages
86-87

Oatcakes

These can be made any size you like. Small rounds 2 inches in diameter are good for cocktail parties; 3 inches is a useful size for cheese biscuits. You could also make them square or oblong.

1 Preheat the oven to 400°F and lightly grease a cookie sheet.

2 Mix together the dry ingredients. Rub the fats into the mixture and add enough milk to bind into a stiff dough.

3 Roll out to a thickness of just under ½ inch. Cut into the required shapes and bake for 12-15 minutes, or until crisp. Cool on a rack.

Ingredients
1 cup fine oatmeal
1½ cups whole-wheat flour
1 teaspoon salt
½ cup vegetable shortening, grated
½ cup butter, cut into small pieces
a little milk to mix—approx. 3-4 teaspoons

Makes about 25 small biscuits

★

Photograph
pages
186-187

BREAD

Making your own bread is by no means a time-consuming chore: the longest part is the rising, but don't forget that while this is happening it is the yeast that is doing the work and not you.

All you need is flour, water (or milk) and yeast, with salt to taste. Soft whole-wheat flour makes a dense loaf that keeps well; strong flour gives a lighter texture. The inclusion of a little rye or barley flour adds a distinctive flavor. Cornmeal can be used on its own or mixed with wheat flour.

Compressed (cake) yeast is specified here; if you are using dried yeast, you need only half the amount. Other rising agents—baking soda or baking powder—are used for quick breads, mixed and baked in under an hour. Molasses or honey is added for flavor and texture, but is not needed to activate the yeast. (See also page 204.)

★

Photograph
page 177

Ingredients
4½ cups whole-wheat flour
1 teaspoon salt
1 ounce compressed yeast
1 teaspoon molasses
¼ cup soy flour
2 cups warm water
1 tablespoon sunflower oil

Makes approx. 2¼ pounds

Whole-wheat bread

This is a simple, basic recipe—delicious as it is, or you can vary it by adding grains, herbs or cheese. The soy flour adds taste as well as protein.

1 Combine the flour and salt in a warm dry bowl.

2 Mix together the yeast, molasses and soy flour until creamy. Add ⅔ cup of the warm water and beat vigorously until the yeast has dissolved. Leave in a warm place for 5 minutes or so until the surface is frothy.

3 Pour the yeast mixture over the flour. Add the remaining water and oil and stir with a spoon until the dough starts to form. Continue as shown opposite.

MAKING BREAD

1 *Knead until the individual ingredients combine. The point to watch for is the change in texture. The dough should take on a uniform smoothness and feel velvety.*

2 *Leave in a bowl, covered with a damp cloth, in a warm place free from drafts. After about an hour the dough should roughly double in size. It will be spongy but firm in texture and will come away cleanly from the sides of the bowl.*

3 *Tip the dough out of the bowl and punch your fist into the center to knock out all the gas. This is called punching down. Knead again for a few minutes.*

4 *For loaves, cut the dough into 1 pound lumps. Shape into loaves and set in greased pans to rise a second time.*

5 *To make a braid, divide each lump into three, roll into long cylinders and twist together. For a round loaf, shape the dough into a ball.*

6 *To make rolls, cut the dough into 3-ounce pieces. Shape into rounds or crescents, or slash the sides with scissors to make "daisy wheels."*

4 When shaped, leave bread to rise in a warm, draft-free place. Loaves take 20-30 minutes, rolls 10-15, to double in size. Preheat oven to 425°F.

5 Bake loaves for 35-40 minutes if in a loaf pan, 30-35 minutes if on a cookie sheet; bake rolls for 15-20 minutes. The bread is done if it sounds hollow when tapped with knuckle. Turn out on a wire rack to cool.

Variations
Sprouted and cooked grains
These add flavor and texture to a basic dough. Sprouted wheat or rye gives a light, slightly sweet loaf, while cooked grains make the bread moist and chewy. After the first rising, and before shaping the dough knead in 2-3 ounces of cooked or sprouted grains for each pound of dough. Let rise and bake as above.

Savory breads
Cheese and thyme
A savory bread can be made in the same way by kneading in ¼ cup of grated Cheddar with 2 teaspoons dried thyme before the second rising. Glaze the loaf if you like by brushing it with a little beaten egg or milk just before you put it in the oven. Sesame seeds make a good decoration.

Cheese and garlic
As above, but use garlic powder instead of thyme. Poppy seeds are an attractive decoration for this.

Cheese and onion
As above, but adding 1 very finely chopped onion instead of the herbs. Sprinkle the top with extra grated cheese.

★

Photograph
*pages
188-189*

Ingredients
2 ounces compressed yeast
1 tablespoon molasses
3 cups warm water
3⅔ cups whole-wheat flour
4½ cups rye flour
1½ teaspoons salt
4 tablespoons oil
1 tablespoon carob powder
1 tablespoon caraway seeds

Makes four 1-pound loaves

Rye bread

This uses the batter method, a good way of dealing with a dough containing low-gluten flour. The yeast, water and whole-wheat flour form a batter and the yeast ferments for an hour with the flour, reacting with the gluten in it, before being kneaded with the low-gluten flour (rye in this recipe). The resulting dough is lighter, softer and easier to handle.

1 Mix the yeast and molasses with the warm water in a large bowl. Stir in the whole-wheat flour and beat thoroughly to form a smooth batter. Leave for 1 hour to ferment.

2 Beat in the remaining ingredients to form a soft dough. Knead for a few minutes until the dough feels smooth. Add a little extra flour if necessary, but the dough should not be too dry.

3 Divide into four pieces and shape each piece into a long loaf. The bread will be less sticky if you release some of the moisture in the dough by pricking it all over with a fork. Let rise for 45-60 minutes. Rye bread is usually baked on a cookie sheet rather than in a loaf pan.

4 Preheat the oven to 425°F.

5 Bake the bread for 30-35 minutes, or until it sounds hollow when tapped. Turn out on a rack and allow the bread to cool completely.

Clockwise from bottom left: **Whole-wheat bread** (*see pp. 174-176*)—rolls shaped in daisy wheels or crescents, sliced plain loaf, whole loaf with cooked rice, round loaf with sprouted wheat, braid, and cheese and garlic rolls; **Oaten rolls** (*see p. 178*)

Photograph
page 177

Ingredients
1 ounce compressed yeast
1 tablespoon honey
2 cups warm milk
1 cup coarse oatmeal
3 cups whole-wheat flour
1 teaspoon salt

Makes twelve 3-ounce rolls

Oaten rolls

The oats are softened by a preliminary soaking. They give the rolls a rich, sweet flavor and a pleasantly moist texture.

1 Mix together the yeast and honey. Beat in the warm milk, stir in the oatmeal and leave to stand for 45-60 minutes, by which time the oats will have swelled and softened slightly and the surface of the mixture will be frothy.

2 Stir in the flour and salt to form a soft dough. Knead thoroughly. If the mixture is a little sticky, add more flour, but not too much—the texture should be soft but not dry. Leave in a clean bowl to rest for 30 minutes.

3 Knead again lightly for 2 minutes. Divide into 12 pieces and shape into rounds. Make an indentation in the center of each one with the handle of a wooden spoon.

4 Put to rise on a greased cookie sheet for 30 minutes. They will rise slightly, but not as much as a whole-wheat loaf. Preheat the oven to 425°F.

5 Bake the rolls for 15-20 minutes, or until they sound hollow when tapped, and turn them out on a rack to cool.

Photograph
page 183

Ingredients
3 cups whole-wheat flour
4 cups fine whole-wheat (pastry or chapatti) flour
2 teaspoons baking soda
1 teaspoon salt
2-2½ cups butter, cut into pieces
2 cups buttermilk

Makes one large 2½-pound round *or* **two small ones**

Soda bread

Buttermilk gives a distinctive taste and texture. The bread freezes well but tastes best of all still warm from the oven.

1 Preheat the oven to 425°F.

2 Mix together the flours, the baking soda and the salt. Rub in the butter.

3 Make a well in the middle and gradually add the buttermilk until you have a soft but not sloppy dough. You may need a little extra buttermilk—it will depend on the flour.

4 Knead the dough quickly and lightly, just enough to shape it into a rough ball. Place on a floured cookie sheet and flatten it out to a circle about 1½ inches thick.

5 With a floured knife, cut two slashes in the form of a cross almost, but not quite, through it, to divide it into quarters.

6 Bake for 25 minutes, then reduce the oven to 375°F and bake for 25 minutes, or until the crust is browned. The exact time depends on how wet the dough is.

Heaven's rolls

Linseeds are popular in Austria and are used, like the wheat germ, to add flavor as well as nutrients.

1 Mix the yeast and honey until creamy. Beat in ⅔ cup water and leave to ferment for 5 minutes in a warm place.

2 Mix together the dry ingredients.

3 Stir the yeast mixture into the dry ingredients with the remaining water, add the oil and knead well for 5-7 minutes, adding a little more flour if the mixture is sticky. Leave in a clean bowl, covered, to rise for 30 minutes.

4 Punch the dough down with your fist, knead briefly and divide into 12 pieces. Shape each piece into a roll, put on a greased cookie sheet and let rise for 10-15 minutes. Preheat the oven to 425°F.

5 Bake for 15-20 minutes or until the rolls sound hollow when tapped. Turn out on a wire rack to cool.

Ingredients
1 ounce compressed yeast
2 tablespoons honey
1¼ cups warm water
3⅔ cups whole-wheat flour
2 ounces sunflower seeds
2 ounces linseeds
2 ounces wheat flakes
½ cup wheat germ
1 teaspoon salt
1 tablespoon oil

Makes twelve 3-ounce rolls

★
Photograph
pages
180-181

Cornbread

Yellow cornmeal gives a golden color as well as an appetizing nutty flavor and crisp texture. You can use a mixture of cornmeal and wheat flour for different tastes and consistencies.

1 Preheat the oven to 400°F.

2 Mix the cornmeal thoroughly with the baking soda and the salt.

3 Beat the egg thoroughly, add the yogurt, honey and oil and beat again until well mixed.

4 Mix all the ingredients together to make a soft batter. If it seems too runny, add a little more flour. Spoon into a lightly greased sandwich tins or muffin-pan cups and bake for 20-25 minutes, or until risen, golden brown and firm to the touch. Turn out on a rack to cool.

Variations
Milk and baking powder can be used instead of yogurt and baking soda. More eggs will give a lighter, richer, more cake-like mixture. For a sweeter bread, use extra honey and add dried fruit. For a savory bread, add grated cheese, chopped peppers or onion with paprika or chili powder.

Ingredients
3 cups cornmeal
3 teaspoons baking soda
1½ teaspoons salt
1 egg
1¼ cups yogurt
4 teaspoons honey
4 tablespoons oil

Makes two 6-inch rounds *or* **9 buns**

★
Photograph
pages
54-55

Brunch

A meal to enjoy on a lazy Sunday morning, most of which, including the khichhari, croquette mixture and pancake batter, can be prepared in advance. To start with serve homemade muesli and granola (the latter also used in special muffins); fruit compote and fruit juice; rye bread with honey, apple butter or peanut butter, or rolls made with sunflower seeds, linseeds, wheat flakes and wheat germ. These could be followed by boiled eggs or by an omelette with an Italian name but which might also derive from Persian cookery, generously filled with a mixture of fresh herbs and greens: sorrel, spinach, lovage, mint, parsley or chives.

For those who arrive nearer lunchtime, khichhari, ancestor of the traditional British breakfast dish kedgeree, or strongly spiced bean and mushroom croquettes make more filling dishes. Pancakes are delicious with either yogurt or maple syrup. Cream cheese, Gjetost and Jarlsberg make a varied selection of cheeses.

As an alternative to coffee there is a wide range of herb teas; rose hip with hibiscus or mint with lime are particularly refreshing.

1 & 7 Granola (*p. 182*) **2** Rye bread (*p. 176*)
3 Pancakes (*p. 122*) **4** Lime relish (*p. 155*)
5 Mushroom and aduki croquettes (*p. 96*)
6 Muesli (*p. 206*) with yogurt
8 & 14 Fruit compote (*p. 159*) **9** Frittata verde (*p. 130*)
10 Heaven's rolls (*p. 179*) **11** Granola muffins (*p. 182*)
12 Yogurt (*p. 220*) **13** Khichhari (*p. 104*)

Photograph
*pages
180-181*

Ingredients
Granola
½-⅔ part oil
½-⅔ part honey
3 parts rolled oat flakes
1 part wheat germ
1 part bran
1 part soy flour
1 part whole-wheat flour
1 part sesame seeds
1 part sunflower seeds
1 part chopped nuts
powdered cinnamon to taste
Muffins
1½ cups whole-wheat flour
4 ounces granola
½ cup wheat germ
½ cup bran
3 teaspoons baking powder
1 teaspoon salt
3 small eggs
1¼ cups milk
4 tablespoons maple syrup

Makes 9-12 muffins

Granola muffins

You can use a simpler granola mix if you like, but the one given here is particularly good and can also be used as a cereal, a quick crumble topping, or mixed with yogurt for a nutritious snack. It keeps several weeks in an airtight container.

Granola

1 Preheat the oven to 300°F.

2 Beat together the oil and honey and mix thoroughly with the dry ingredients.

3 Spread on a lightly greased cookie sheet or baking dish and bake for ½-1 hour, turning the top layer under from time to time so that the entire mixture browns evenly.

Muffins

1 Preheat the oven to 400°F.

2 Mix together all the dry ingredients.

3 In a separate bowl, beat the eggs thoroughly and add the milk and maple syrup. Beat the mixture again and mix with the dry ingredients.

4 Spoon the mixture into greased deep muffin-pan cups and bake for 18-20 minutes. Serve warm. Delicious for brunch.

Ingredients
2 large eggs
¾ pound carrots, cooked and
    mashed
2 unpeeled eating apples, grated
8 tablespoons sunflower oil
1⅓ cups whole-wheat pastry flour
4 teaspoons baking powder
pinch of salt
½-⅔ cup light raw sugar
1 teaspoon powdered cinnamon
2 teaspoons gomashio (optional)

Makes 9 muffins

Carrot and apple muffins

The sweetness of carrots combines well with apples to make these muffins—an excellent way of using up leftover carrots. Eat them with soups or salads.

1 Preheat the oven to 400°F.

2 Beat the egg thoroughly and mix with the carrots, apple and oil.

3 Mix together the flour, baking powder, salt, sugar and cinnamon, with the gomashio if used. Stir into the egg mixture until smooth and thick, like batter. If it is too sloppy, add a little extra flour.

4 Fill 9 greased muffin-pan cups and bake for 15-20 minutes until firm. Serve warm.

Clockwise from top: **Carrot and apple muffins; Soda bread** *(see p. 178)*; **Malted fruit loaf** *(see p. 184)*; **Rosemary and walnut scones** *(see p. 184)*

Photograph
page 183

Ingredients
2¼ cups whole-wheat flour
4 teaspoons baking powder
½ teaspoon salt
2 ounces walnuts, finely chopped
1½ tablespoons finely chopped
   rosemary
¼ cup sunflower oil
1 large egg, beaten
¾ cup milk

Makes 10-12 scones

Rosemary and walnut scones

*A subtle variation on traditional English scones, good with soup
or as a lunchtime snack.*

1 Preheat the oven to 425°F.

2 Mix together the flour, baking powder and salt and add
the chopped walnuts and rosemary.

3 Combine the oil, egg and milk. Add to the dry ingredients
and mix to a soft dough.

4 Pat out to a thickness of ¾ inch and cut into 2-inch
rounds. Bake for 10 minutes and serve warm.

Photograph
page 183

Ingredients
3 cups whole-wheat flour
1 teaspoon salt
1 ounce mixed spice
2 ounces dark raw sugar
1 ounce compressed yeast
1 tablespoon malt extract
¼ cup soy flour
1¼ cups warm water
1 tablespoon sunflower oil
4 ounces raisins
1 egg, lightly beaten with a little
   salt
Glaze
1 tablespoon malt extract
1 tablespoon apple juice
   concentrate

Makes two 1-pound loaves

Malted fruit loaf

*I buy good-quality mixed spice—ground cloves, nutmeg and
cinnamon—and add extra ground cinnamon, but you
could use any combination you like. Ginger, coriander and a
little pepper can all be added.*

1 Mix together the flour, salt, spices and sugar.

2 Mix the yeast with the malt extract, soy flour and warm
water and leave to ferment in a warm place for 5 minutes
or until the surface of the liquid is bubbly.

3 Add the yeast mixture and the oil to the dry ingredients.
Mix well with a wooden spoon and then knead well for 5-7
minutes. Lightly knead in the raisins, put into a clean
bowl and let rise for 30 minutes, covered with a damp cloth.

4 Punch the dough down with your fist, knead again lightly
and divide it between two greased loaf pans. Let rise for 30
minutes.

5 Heat the oven to 400°F. Brush the tops of the loaves with
the beaten egg and bake them for 30-35 minutes.

6 While still hot from the oven, brush with the malt extract
mixed with the apple juice. You may not need quite all of it.

MENU AND MEAL PLANNER

Whether you're a full-time vegetarian or would merely like a vegetarian meal as an occasional change from a meat-based one, it can be difficult to structure a meal, to decide what to serve with what. This part of the book is designed to help you prepare varied and interesting meals, well balanced in taste, texture and nutrients. There are menus to help you entertain; menus for a weekend, combining simply prepared meals with more elaborate ones; and menus for a whole week for a family, with the emphasis on simpler cooking while providing balanced, nutritious meals. There is a section on buying, storing, preparing and cooking ingredients, including ideas for garnishes and tips on how to choose the most suitable kitchen equipment. Finally there is a section on daily nutritional requirements and how best to supply them.

★ *indicates that the dish is suitable for freezing*

Summer dinner party

Contrasting fillings make a multicolored centerpiece for a light summer evening meal. The vegetable-based menu is given substance by the whole-wheat pancakes and more protein is provided by the vegetarian cheeses and the tofu in the salad dressing.

Button mushrooms are garnished with walnuts and scallions in a tofu and lemon dressing (*see p. 148*).

A layered galette of whole-wheat pancakes with three different vegetable fillings—spinach, fennel, and tomato and onion (*see p. 124*). The pancakes can be made in advance and frozen; the fillings will keep for 1-2 days in the refrigerator. Serve sprinkled with grated Parmesan.

Black-currant yogurt ice cream looks rich and creamy, but is low in fat and sugar. Its clean sharp taste is enhanced with orange (*see p. 163*).

Avocado and kiwi salad with a julienne of celery and cucumber, tossed in a herb vinaigrette dressing (*see p. 144*).

Globe artichoke served with an individual bowl of lemon and garlic sauce is a quick and easy first course, which can be prepared well in advance (*see p. 37*).

A selection of cheeses—from the top: Coulommiers, blue cheese, goat's cheese—all made without animal rennet and served with oatcakes (*see p. 173*) and cheese water biscuits (*see p. 135*).

Winter dinner party

Rich, thick soup, subtly spiced pilaf with millet and eggplant, individual spinach darioles, salad and a compote of winter fruit make a substantial meal, most of which can be prepared in advance.

Spinach leaves are stuffed with tomatoes and flavored with basil (or oregano, if desired and with scallions) (*see p. 67*).

Byzantine millet pilaf with coriander, apricots and eggplant in sesame sauce can be prepared in advance and frozen (*see p. 108*).

Rye bread uses both whole-wheat and rye flour. Molasses, carob powder and caraway add color and spice (*see p. 176*).

Mushroom soup with red wine, flavored with parsley, bay leaf, marjoram and tarragon, can be made in advance and frozen (*see p. 57*).

Mung bean sprouts are combined with
sweet peppers, button mushrooms and
celery in a shoyu-flavored dressing
to provide a colorful salad
(*see p. 148*).

Rhubarb, pink grapefruit
and pears in wine can be served
hot or cold. The "cream" to
go with them is based on cashew
nuts and cottage cheese (*see p. 158*).

Carob truffles are a delicious
mixture including chopped
fruit and nuts with a coating
of melted carob chocolate
(*see p. 170*).

189

Impromptu dinner party

If special guests turn up unexpectedly and you have only
a couple of hours to prepare a meal, this menu can be created quickly and
easily from what you might have at hand.

Tomato sauce is easy
to make in quantity and
keeps well, whether
frozen or in the
refrigerator
(*see p. 72*).

Spaghetti aglio, olio e peperoncino
is the Italian name for this
quickly-made dish
of pasta with
garlic and
chili, much
liked in its
native land.
Grated
cheese is
optional (*see p. 113*).

Potatoes, lightly steamed and
sprinkled with toasted almonds,
are a good accompaniment to the
roulade, but steamed
carrots or celery
would be good too
(*see p. 217*).

Make an **impromptu salad**
with whatever you have at
hand: use leftover grains or
beans, and nuts or raisins,
as well as fresh salad
vegetables as here,
dressed with
vinaigrette
dressing
(*see p. 149*).

A **roulade** always looks
impressive, but in fact is
easy to make once you have
mastered the technique—it
only needs one or two
practice runs (*see p. 132*).

Oranges,
sliced and
marinated in
orange and lemon
juice with honey and Grand Marnier to taste,
and decorated with the orange zest.

191

Menu organizer

A frequent criticism of vegetarian food is that it takes so long to prepare. The secret of success is organization—making sure that the beans are put to soak in advance and that time is allowed for preparation. To help with this, a countdown is given for each menu showing exactly what needs to be done and when (apart from dishes that are self-explanatory, such as quickly assembled salad or fruit combinations). Many dishes freeze well, so, as with non-vegetarian food, it's a good idea to make extra quantities to freeze for a later meal.

The following fifteen menus are suitable for dinner parties for all seasons of the year and all occasions, from Christmas dinner to informal gatherings. The first three are illustrated in detail on the preceding pages. Of the others, the first Christmas menu is shown on pages 86-87 and the Thanksgiving menu on pages 54-55.

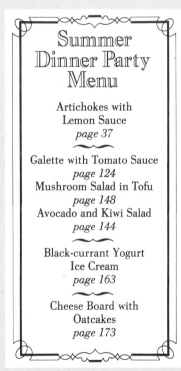

Summer Dinner Party Menu

Artichokes with
Lemon Sauce
page 37

~

Galette with Tomato Sauce
page 124
Mushroom Salad in Tofu
page 148
Avocado and Kiwi Salad
page 144

~

Black-currant Yogurt
Ice Cream
page 163

~

Cheese Board with
Oatcakes
page 173

PREPARATION IN ADVANCE
★ **Galette:** make, assemble and freeze *or* make **pancakes** and **fillings** and store separately in refrigerator 1-2 days in advance.
★ **Black-currant yogurt ice cream:** make and freeze.
★ **Oatcakes:** make and freeze

or store in an airtight container.
Vinaigrette dressing: make and keep in a screwtop bottle in the refrigerator for 1-2 days.

EVENING BEFORE
Lemon sauce: make and refrigerate.
Thaw galette and oatcakes if frozen.

ON THE DAY
Prepare salad ingredients.
Assemble **mushroom salad in tofu,** toss in dressing and keep cool.
Do not assemble the avocado and kiwi salad until the last moment.
One hour before serving boil and prepare **artichokes.**
Assemble the **galette** if not from the freezer.
Thirty minutes before serving preheat the oven to 350°F and put in the galette.
Reheat the lemon sauce for the artichokes.
Reheat the extra tomato sauce for the galette.
Assemble the **avocado and kiwi salad.**
Remove the ice from the freezer when you serve the first course.

Winter Dinner Party Menu

Mushroom Soup with
Herbs
page 57
Rye Bread
page 176

~

Byzantine Millet Pilaf
page 108
Spinach Darioles
page 67
Bean sprouts Oriental
page 148

~

Rhubarb with Cashew
Cream
page 158
Carob Truffles
page 170

PREPARATION IN ADVANCE
★ **Mushroom soup:** make and freeze *or* make 1-2 days in advance and refrigerate.
Bean sprouts: start a week in advance and grow bean sprouts (see page 216). Store in refrigerator.

★ **Rye bread:** make and freeze *or* make 1-2 days in advance and refrigerate

★ **Carob truffles:** freeze *or* make 3-4 days in advance and store in airtight container.

EVENING BEFORE

Thaw soup and bread if frozen. Make the **cashew cream** and refrigerate.

ON THE DAY

Make the **rhubarb dessert** and refrigerate.
Make the **bean sprout salad** and refrigerate.
Make the **pilaf** and put in a baking dish. Prepare the **eggplant** for the topping.
Prepare the **spinach darioles.**
Take the dessert, cashew cream and truffles out of the refrigerator.
Forty minutes before serving preheat the oven to 350°F and put in the **darioles.**
Thirty minutes before serving cover the pilaf tightly with foil and put in the oven. Bake the eggplant.
Gently reheat the soup and the rhubarb dessert.

IMPROMPTU DINNER PARTY

This meal is based on ingredients you are likely to have in your kitchen: pasta, potatoes, a fresh vegetable (although lentils could be used here instead of broccoli), salad and fruit. The only other assumption made is that you have some tomato sauce ready in the refrigerator, but even this too could be made in the time available.

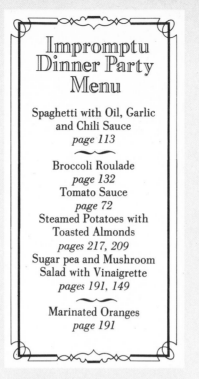

Impromptu Dinner Party Menu

Spaghetti with Oil, Garlic and Chili Sauce
page 113

Broccoli Roulade
page 132
Tomato Sauce
page 72
Steamed Potatoes with Toasted Almonds
pages 217, 209
Sugar pea and Mushroom Salad with Vinaigrette
pages 191, 149

Marinated Oranges
page 191

Two hours before serving prepare the broccoli and sauce for the **roulade base,** the **oranges,** and the vegetables for the **salad.**
Forty-five minutes before serving bring a pan of water to the boil and put the **potatoes** to steam. Preheat the oven to 375°F. Finish making the **roulade base** and put it in to bake.
Put on the water for the spaghetti. Assemble the salad. Heat the **tomato sauce.**
Fifteen minutes before serving fill the **roulade,** roll it up and put it back in the oven.
Put the **almonds** in to toast. Reduce the oven to 325°F. Add the **spaghetti** to the boiling salted water. Make the **oil, garlic and chili sauce.** As soon as the spaghetti is ready, drain, mix with the sauce and serve.

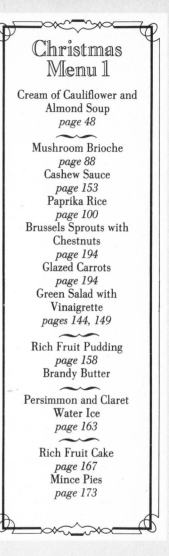

Christmas Menu 1

Cream of Cauliflower and Almond Soup
page 48

Mushroom Brioche
page 88
Cashew Sauce
page 153
Paprika Rice
page 100
Brussels Sprouts with Chestnuts
page 194
Glazed Carrots
page 194
Green Salad with Vinaigrette
pages 144, 149

Rich Fruit Pudding
page 158
Brandy Butter

Persimmon and Claret Water Ice
page 163

Rich Fruit Cake
page 167
Mince Pies
page 173

PREPARATION IN ADVANCE

★ **Mushroom filling for brioche:** make and freeze *or* make and refrigerate the day before.
★ **Cashew sauce:** freeze *or* make the day before and refrigerate.
Vinaigrette: make and store in a screwtop jar in the refrigerator.
★ **Rich fruit pudding:** prepare the pudding, put it into a bowl and cover in readiness to cook. Cook and freeze *or* refrigerate, uncooked, for 1-2 days.

★ **Persimmon and claret ice:** make and freeze.
Rich fruit cake: make well in advance, wrap in foil and store in an airtight container.
★ **Mince pies:** make and freeze *or* store in an airtight container 1-2 days in advance.

EVENING BEFORE
Mushroom brioche: prepare the dough, put in a bowl, cover and leave overnight in a cold place.
Paprika rice: prepare and cook the rice and refrigerate. If frozen, take the pudding and brioche filling out of the freezer to thaw.
Put the **chestnuts** to soak in water overnight.

ON THE DAY
Thaw the cashew sauce and mince pies if frozen. Remove pudding from refrigerator if not frozen.
Make the **soup.**
Wash and prepare the **salad** ingredients, wrap in a dish towel and keep in refrigerator.
Take the rice out of refrigerator.
Prepare **sprouts** and **carrots.**
Two hours before serving have water boiling in the steamer and put the **pudding** in to steam.
One hour before serving preheat the oven to 400°F. Reheat the filling and assemble the **brioche.** Bake and when cooked set aside to cool slightly before serving. Cook the **chestnuts** for 40 minutes and keep warm.
Thirty minutes before serving put the **rice** in a greased ovenproof dish, cover tightly with foil and heat through in the oven (or reheat in a steamer).
Take **persimmon ice** out of the freezer, scoop into individual bowls and put in refrigerator.

Gently reheat the soup and cashew sauce.
Steam the **carrots** for 15-20 minutes, season, toss in butter and keep warm in serving dish.
Steam **sprouts** for 6-10 minutes. Toss with **chestnuts,** a little butter and seasonings and keep them warm.
Toss salad in dressing.
Warm the mince pies a little.

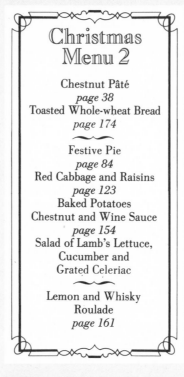

Christmas
Menu 2

Chestnut Pâté
page 38
Toasted Whole-wheat Bread
page 174

Festive Pie
page 84
Red Cabbage and Raisins
page 123
Baked Potatoes
Chestnut and Wine Sauce
page 154
Salad of Lamb's Lettuce,
Cucumber and
Grated Celeriac

Lemon and Whisky
Roulade
page 161

PREPARATION IN ADVANCE
★ **Chestnut pâté:** make and freeze *or* make a day in advance and refrigerate.
★ **Festive pie:** make the pastry and freeze *or* refrigerate (it will keep for 2-3 days).
★ **Red cabbage and raisins:** make and freeze *or* make 1-2 days in advance and refrigerate.
★ **Bread:** bake and freeze *or* refrigerate 1-2 days in advance.
★ **Lemon roulade:** make, decorate

and freeze *or* make the sponge the day before, roll it up and when cool, keep in an airtight container.

EVENING BEFORE
Pâté: thaw if frozen.
Festive pie: make filling and refrigerate.
Red cabbage: thaw if frozen.
Sauce for potatoes: make and refrigerate.

ON THE DAY
Assemble **pie** but do not bake. Defrost the roulade well in advance *or* if it is not frozen, assemble it.
One hour before serving prepare the **salad** and refrigerate.
Gently heat the red cabbage.
Preheat the oven to 425°F and put potatoes and pie in to bake, potatoes at the top, pie at the bottom. Gently reheat the sauce.

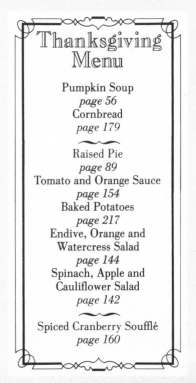

Thanksgiving
Menu

Pumpkin Soup
page 56
Cornbread
page 179

Raised Pie
page 89
Tomato and Orange Sauce
page 154
Baked Potatoes
page 217
Endive, Orange and
Watercress Salad
page 144
Spinach, Apple and
Cauliflower Salad
page 142

Spiced Cranberry Soufflé
page 160

This is practicable only if you have a really large oven (or a double oven) or can share the preparation with a friend, as the pumpkin takes up rather a lot of space.

PREPARATION IN ADVANCE
★ **Filling for raised pie:** make and freeze *or* refrigerate for up to 3 days.
★ **Tomato and orange sauce:** make and freeze *or* refrigerate for 3-4 days.
★ **Cornbread:** make and freeze *or* make a day in advance and either keep chilled *or* wrap well and keep in an airtight container.

EVENING BEFORE
Pumpkin soup: scoop out the insides and make the soup. Refrigerate. Wrap the shell carefully in plastic wrap and keep cool.
Thaw pie filling, sauce and bread, if frozen.

ON THE DAY
Make **cranberry soufflé** and chill. Prepare ingredients for **salads.** Assemble and chill.
Make pastry for the **pie** and assemble.
An hour and a half before serving preheat the oven to 400°F and put in the pie.
Put in the **potatoes** to bake at the bottom of the oven.
Forty-five minutes before serving put the pumpkin shell with the soup in the oven.
Make the **sauce** for the soufflé.
With ten minutes to go warm the cornbread.
Gently reheat the tomato and orange sauce.

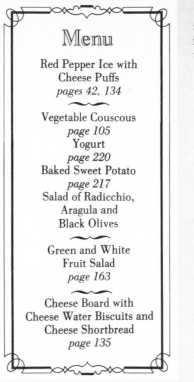

Menu

Red Pepper Ice with
Cheese Puffs
pages 42, 134

Vegetable Couscous
page 105
Yogurt
page 220
Baked Sweet Potato
page 217
Salad of Radicchio,
Aragula and
Black Olives

Green and White
Fruit Salad
page 163

Cheese Board with
Cheese Water Biscuits and
Cheese Shortbread
page 135

PREPARATION IN ADVANCE
★ **Red pepper ice.**
★ **Water biscuits** and **shortbread:** if not frozen, both will keep for 4-5 days in an airtight container.
Vinaigrette dressing: if you have none ready, make extra and keep it chilled.

ON THE DAY
Thaw biscuits and shortbread if necessary.
Prepare all vegetables for the **couscous** and the **salad,** and the fruit for the **fruit salad.**
Make the **cheese puffs.**
They do not need a filling.
About one and a half hours before serving preheat the oven to 400°F.
Put the **sweet potato** in to bake.
Make the **couscous.**
Assemble **radicchio and aragula salad** and **fruit salad.**

Twenty minutes before serving scoop out red pepper ice into individual bowls and put in the refrigerator.

Menu

Lentil and Eggplant
Pâté
page 38
Rye Bread
page 176

Broccoli and Pine Nut
Pancakes
pages 122, 124
Cheese Sauce
page 152

Steamed Potatoes with
Fresh Herbs
page 196
Beet, Celery and
Apple Salad
page 145
Mixed Green Salad
page 144
Avocado Dressing
page 149

Fresh Pears and Plums
in Sour Cream with
Cinnamon and Honey

PREPARATION IN ADVANCE
★ **Lentils:** cook and freeze *or* refrigerate for 1-2 days.
★ **Rye bread:** make and freeze *or* make 1-2 days in advance and store or chill.
★ **Pancakes:** make both pancakes and filling. If making the day before, chill pancakes and filling separately; if freezing, assemble and freeze.

EVENING BEFORE
Pâté: thaw lentils if frozen. Make pâté and refrigerate.
Cheese sauce: make and refrigerate.
Avocado dressing: make and chill.

ON THE DAY
Thaw out bread and pancakes if frozen; bring pâté to room temperature.
Prepare all vegetables for **salads** and fruit for **dessert;** chop **herbs** for potatoes.
Forty-five minutes before serving preheat the oven to 400°F. Put in the pancakes, tightly covered.
Put the **potatoes** on to steam.
Assemble the **salads** and **dessert.**
Reheat the cheese sauce.
When the potatoes are ready, put them in a heated serving dish and keep warm.
Just before serving the potatoes, sprinkle with the chopped herbs.

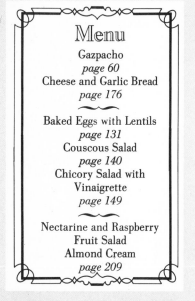

Menu

Gazpacho
page 60
Cheese and Garlic Bread
page 176

Baked Eggs with Lentils
page 131
Couscous Salad
page 140
Chicory Salad with
Vinaigrette
page 149

Nectarine and Raspberry
Fruit Salad
Almond Cream
page 209

PREPARATION IN ADVANCE
★ **Gazpacho:** make and freeze *or* keep chilled for 1-2 days.

Cheese and garlic bread: make 1-2 days in advance and keep chilled.
★ **Chick peas (for couscous salad):** if not frozen, soak overnight and cook.
★ **Almond cream:** make and freeze, *or* keep chilled for 3-4 days.

EVENING BEFORE
Couscous salad: thaw chick peas if frozen, cook couscous and assemble salad. Chill.
Cook **lentils** for main course.
Vinaigrette: make and chill.

ON THE DAY
Thaw gazpacho, bread and almond cream if necessary.
Not more than 2 hours before serving, prepare the **chicory** and mix the **raspberries and nectarines.**
Prepare the **baked eggs and lentils** and bake at 350°F for 20 minutes.
Toss the chicory in the vinaigrette dressing.

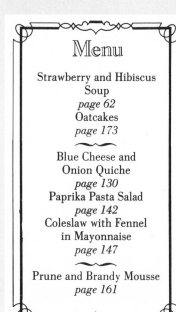

Menu

Strawberry and Hibiscus
Soup
page 62
Oatcakes
page 173

Blue Cheese and
Onion Quiche
page 130
Paprika Pasta Salad
page 142
Coleslaw with Fennel
in Mayonnaise
page 147

Prune and Brandy Mousse
page 161

PREPARATION IN ADVANCE
Soup: make and keep in refrigerator (it will keep for 3-4 days).
★ **Oatcakes:** make and freeze *or* store in an airtight container.
★ **Pastry base for quiche:** prepare as described on page 92 and freeze, *or* prepare the day before and refrigerate.
Mayonnaise: make and keep in the refrigerator (it will keep for 3-4 days).
★ **Prunes:** soak, cook and purée. Freeze *or* keep in the refrigerator (4-5 days).

EVENING BEFORE
Prune mousse: make the mousse and spoon into individual glasses. Keep chilled.

ON THE DAY
Take the oatcakes and pastry base out of the freezer well in advance to thaw.
Toast **almonds** for soup garnish.
Cook the **pasta,** drain and cool.
Toss pasta in dressing and set aside in a cool place.
Prepare the vegetables for the **coleslaw,** toss with the mayonnaise, put in a bowl and refrigerate.
Make the filling and assemble the **quiche.**
Forty-five minutes before serving preheat the oven to 400°F and put in the quiche. Set aside after cooking to cool slightly.
Ten minutes before serving reheat the **soup** just enough to warm it slightly.

Menu

Avgolemono with
Cheese Water Biscuits
pages 57, 135

Cauliflower Moussaka
page 72
Baked Potatoes
page 217
Lentil and Mint Salad
in Yogurt
page 141
Celeriac and Zucchini
Salad in Tahini and
Orange Dressing
page 145

Apricot Slice
page 172

Goat's Cheese with Celery

*One and a quarter hours before
serving* preheat the oven to 375°F
and put in the **potatoes.**
Thirty minutes before serving put
the moussaka in the oven.
Fifteen minutes before serving
finish making the **soup.**

PREPARATION IN ADVANCE
Cheese water biscuits: make and
store in an airtight container
up to a week before.
Lentil salad: cook the lentils and
refrigerate 1-2 days in advance.
★ **Apricot slice:** make and freeze
or store in an airtight container
for 2-3 days.
EVENING BEFORE
Avgolemono: complete steps 1
and 2 of the recipe then strain
and refrigerate.
Lentil salad: prepare, assemble
and refrigerate.
Apricot slice: thaw if frozen.

ON THE DAY
Prepare, assemble and refrigerate
the **celeriac and zucchini salad.**
Prepare and assemble the
moussaka.

Make the **tahini and orange
dressing** and mix with the salad
not too far in advance.

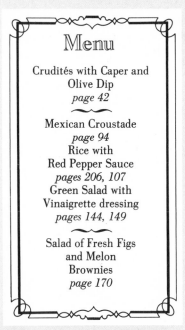

Menu

Crudités with Caper and
Olive Dip
page 42

Mexican Croustade
page 94
Rice with
Red Pepper Sauce
pages 206, 107
Green Salad with
Vinaigrette dressing
pages 144, 149

Salad of Fresh Figs
and Melon
Brownies
page 170

PREPARATION IN ADVANCE
Caper and olive dip: prepare and
refrigerate 1-2 days in advance.
★ **Red kidney beans for
croustade:** prepare and freeze *or*
cook 2-3 days in advance and
refrigerate.
★ **Brownies:** make and freeze *or*
store in an airtight container for
2-3 days.
Vinaigrette: prepare and store in
a screwtop jar in the refrigerator.

EVENING BEFORE
Croustade: make the crust and
keep in an airtight container or
in the refrigerator.
Red pepper sauce: make and
refrigerate.

ON THE DAY
Thaw **beans** and **brownies** if
frozen.
Prepare the **fruit salad.**
Prepare the green salad but do
not dress it until the last minute.
Keep both salads chilled.
Cook and mash the **sweet potatoes**
and assemble the croustade.
Take the caper and olive dip
out of the refrigerator and leave
to warm to room temperature.
Prepare the **crudités** and keep
chilled.
Cook the **rice** and keep hot.
Thirty minutes before serving,
preheat the oven to 375°F. Cover
the croustade lightly with foil
and put in the oven to heat
through.
Gently reheat the red pepper
sauce.

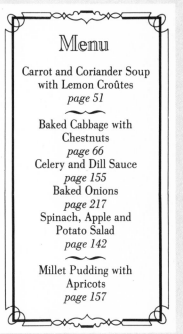

Menu

Carrot and Coriander Soup
with Lemon Croûtes
page 51

Baked Cabbage with
Chestnuts
page 66
Celery and Dill Sauce
page 155
Baked Onions
page 217
Spinach, Apple and
Potato Salad
page 142

Millet Pudding with
Apricots
page 157

PREPARATION IN ADVANCE
Chestnuts: soak and cook.

EVENING BEFORE
Carrot soup: make and refrigerate.

Apricots: soak and cook; refrigerate.

ON THE DAY
Assemble the **cabbage.**
Make the **dill sauce.**
Lightly cook the **potato** and **spinach** and let cool.
Assemble the **salad** and toss in its dressing.
Two hours before serving prepare the **millet pudding.** Preheat the oven to 350°F and bake the pudding.
One hour before serving put in the cabbage and **onions.**
Prepare the **lemon croûtes** for the soup.
Gently reheat the dill sauce and the apricots.
Reheat the soup and garnish just before serving.

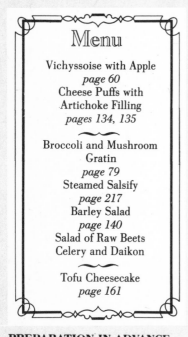

Menu

Vichyssoise with Apple
page 60
Cheese Puffs with
Artichoke Filling
pages 134, 135

Broccoli and Mushroom
Gratin
page 79
Steamed Salsify
page 217
Barley Salad
page 140
Salad of Raw Beets
Celery and Daikon

Tofu Cheesecake
page 161

PREPARATION IN ADVANCE
Barley salad: cook barley and refrigerate 2-3 days in advance.
★ **Vichyssoise:** freeze *or* make and refrigerate 1-2 days ahead.

★ **Tofu cheesecake:** freeze *or* make and refrigerate 1-2 days in advance.

EVENING BEFORE
Cheese puffs: make the filling and refrigerate.
Beet salad: prepare, assemble and refrigerate.

ON THE DAY
Make the **cheese puffs.** Take the filling for the puffs out of the refrigerator.
Prepare, assemble and refrigerate the **barley salad.**
Prepare the **raw salad** but do not assemble until just before serving.
One hour before serving steam the **salsify.**
Prepare and assemble the **gratin.**
Forty-five minutes before serving preheat the oven to 400°F and bake gratin.
Fill the **cheese puffs.**

Menu

Spiced Lentil Soup
with Coconut
page 48
Cornbread
page 179

Stuffed Vine Leaves
page 67
Tomato Sauce
page 72
Steamed Zucchini with
Toasted Sunflower
Seed Garnish
pages 217, 209
Olive and Orange Salad
in Vinaigrette dressing
page 145

Shortcake with Custard
pages 159, 160

PREPARATION IN ADVANCE
★ **Soup:** make the soup up to the point of adding the coconut milk. Freeze for up to 2 weeks *or* keep in the refrigerator for up to 2 days.
★ **Cornbread:** make and freeze *or* make a day ahead and either keep chilled *or* wrap well and keep in an airtight container.
★ **Tomato sauce:** make and freeze *or* keep in the refrigerator for 3-4 days.
★ **Vinaigrette dressing:** make and store in a screwtop bottle in the refrigerator.
★ **Shortcake:** make and freeze *or* make the sponge the day before and keep in an airtight container.
★ **Custard:** make and freeze *or* keep chilled for 2 days.

EVENING BEFORE
Stuffed vine leaves: cook the filling and refrigerate.
Shortcake and **custard:** thaw and refrigerate if frozen *or* make and refrigerate.

ON THE DAY
Thaw the **soup** if frozen and finish making it.
Stuff the **vine leaves** and put in baking dish.
Thaw the tomato sauce and cornbread if frozen.
Toast the **sunflower seeds** (see page 209).
One hour before serving prepare and dress the **salad** and prepare the **zucchini.**
Forty-five minutes before serving preheat the oven to 350°F and bake the **vine leaves.**
Fifteen minutes before serving, heat the soup and the tomato sauce and warm the cornbread. Lightly steam the **zucchini,** sprinkle with the sunflower seeds and keep warm.

WEEKEND ENTERTAINING

Whether you're having people to stay or just catering for yourself and the family, there's no need to spend the whole time in the kitchen in order to provide interesting and nutritionally balanced meals. If you haven't a freezer it would help if you had a little time during the previous week to make some of the basics such as bread, cakes and biscuits and some of the more substantial dishes such as soups or casseroles. Friday dinner is simple but tasty and filling; Saturday lunch is fairly light; Saturday dinner offers a choice of main dishes; and Sunday lunch would appeal to many a meat-eater.

Friday

Dinner
Gumbo
page 57

Lentil and Spinach Quiche
page 92
Mixed Grain Salad on
Lettuce
page 138
Green Salad with
Avocado Dressing
pages 144, 149

Fruit Crumble
page 219

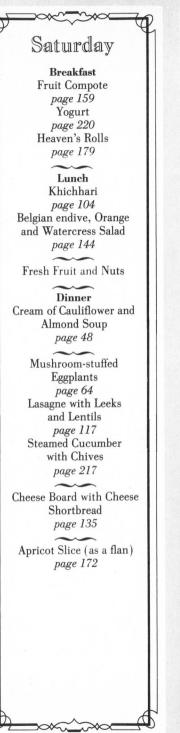

Saturday

Breakfast
Fruit Compote
page 159
Yogurt
page 220
Heaven's Rolls
page 179

Lunch
Khichhari
page 104
Belgian endive, Orange
and Watercress Salad
page 144

Fresh Fruit and Nuts

Dinner
Cream of Cauliflower and
Almond Soup
page 48

Mushroom-stuffed
Eggplants
page 64
Lasagne with Leeks
and Lentils
page 117
Steamed Cucumber
with Chives
page 217

Cheese Board with Cheese
Shortbread
page 135

Apricot Slice (as a flan)
page 172

Sunday

Breakfast
Fruit Juice
Granola Muffins
page 182
Muesli
page 206

Lunch
Cream of Broccoli Soup
page 49

Hazelnut and
Zucchini Bake
page 73
Red Pepper Sauce
page 107
Lentil and Mint Salad
in Yogurt
page 141
Steamed Carrots with
Sesame Seeds
page 217

Peach and Claret
Water Ice
page 163

PREPARATION IN ADVANCE
★ **Heaven's rolls, granola muffins,** and any **bread** you will need: if not frozen, can be made 3-4 days in advance and stored in tins.
★ **Cheese shortbread** and **apricot slice** can also be made 2-3 days ahead if not frozen.
Crumble topping can be made 3-4 days ahead and kept in a screwtop jar.
★ **Gumbo, khichhari** and **lasagne** can be made a day or two ahead if not frozen.
One or two days in advance, cook and refrigerate: **grains** for salad, **fruit compote** and the **red pepper sauce.**

★ Make and freeze **peach water ice.** You can also freeze **lentil and spinach quiche, broccoli soup, stuffed eggplants, hazelnut and zucchini bake** and **red pepper sauce.**

THURSDAY
EVENING
Quiche: if not frozen, make the pastry base, prick and bake for 5 minutes; refrigerate.

FRIDAY
MORNING
Thaw gumbo and quiche for tonight if frozen, or finish preparing quiche.
Broccoli soup for Sunday: if not from freezer, make and refrigerate but do not garnish.
Grain salad: assemble and chill.
Green salad: prepare ingredients and chill but toss in dressing at the last moment.
Fruit crumble: assemble.

EVENING
One hour before serving dinner preheat the oven to 350°F and put in the crumble.
Forty-five minutes before serving put the quiche in the oven. Let it cool slightly before serving.
Fifteen minutes before serving reheat the gumbo gently.

Thaw the heaven's rolls and khichhari for next day, if frozen.

SATURDAY
MORNING
If frozen, defrost the stuffed eggplants, lasagne, cheese shortbread and apricot slice.
Cauliflower soup: make and chill.
Lentil and mint salad: make and chill.

MIDDAY
Endive, orange and watercress salad: prepare and refrigerate.
For dinner: prepare and stuff the **eggplants** if not frozen.

EVENING
Thirty minutes before dinner preheat the oven to 350°F and put in the eggplants and lasagne to bake and/or heat through.
Steam the **cucumber** and sprinkle with the chives.
Remember to thaw the granola muffins for Sunday breakfast and the broccoli soup, hazelnut and zucchini bake and red pepper sauce for lunch, if frozen.

SUNDAY
If not frozen, prepare the **hazelnut and zucchini bake.**
Forty minutes before lunch preheat the oven to 350°F and put in the dish to bake or heat through.
Prepare and cook the **carrots.**
Reheat the red pepper sauce.
Reheat the soup: steam the **broccoli flowerets** and add to the soup with the cream.
Take the water ice out of the freezer when the soup is served.

MEALS FOR A WEEK

Planning ahead a week at a time is sensible for the busy family cook to minimize the work and time spent in the kitchen. In these sample menus, as far as possible, the preparation for the day's meals is done the night before—it has not been assumed that the cook can spend the entire day in the kitchen. All the weekday lunch menus can be quickly prepared and are adaptable as box lunches to take to work or school.

This sort of family cooking relies to a large extent on dishes that can be frozen or made in advance and that are versatile even if left over —for example, grains make good bases for salads or croquettes; pasta can be added to salads or soups; beans, peas or lentils can be used for all of these or, mashed up, as sandwich spreads or refried beans. Although a freezer is a real asset, the preparation notes here do not assume that you will automatically have one.

If you do have a freezer, it makes sense to cook double batches of those dishes that can be frozen, and do double quantities of grains and beans for use as suggested above. Other ways to take advantage of a freezer include the following:
★ grate Cheddar cheese in quantity and freeze in 1 cup packs for quick toppings, fillings and sauces;
★ make crumble topping in quantity and freeze for use in both savory dishes and puddings;
★ purée fruit in season and freeze for ices, puddings and sauces;
★ keep a stock of bread, rolls, cakes and biscuits; cooked beans and

grains; croquettes and other assembled dishes; stocks, soups and sauces.

The sample menus suggested here are balanced, nutritious and tasty. They include a cross-section of nutrients: *grains* (whether whole, flaked, in bread, puddings or cakes): wheat, rye, rice, buckwheat, millet, oats and corn; *beans:* lima, red kidney and aduki; split peas and chick peas; *nuts and seeds:* walnuts, almonds, cashews, hazelnuts, sunflower and pumpkin seeds. Each day includes a salad and/or steamed or stir-fried vegetables, and fresh or dried fruit.

As an alternative to the cooked meals suggested here, a quickly prepared and nutritious offering could be chunks of tofu, cheese and nuts (the best of convenience foods), perhaps served with a simple salad and fresh fruit. A baked potato is another useful and filling standby.

SUNDAY
EVENING
★ Thaw **croquettes** *or* make and chill overnight.
★ Thaw bread or muffins if frozen. Put **muesli** to soak; also **dried fruit** for compote.
Make **granola** if not on hand.

MONDAY
MORNING
Cook **muffins** if not from freezer. Make **compote.**
★ Take double quantities lima beans and red kidney beans from freezer *or* put to soak (separately).

MIDDAY
Make **soda bread** if no bread already in freezer.

EVENING
Cook **red kidney beans** and **lima beans** separately. Use half the lima beans for the casserole and mix the rest with half the red kidney beans and the marinade for Tuesday's **many-bean salad.** Refrigerate; freeze the rest of the kidney beans until Friday.
Make **broccoli and walnut bake.** Steam double quantity **green beans;** use half tonight, cool and

Breakfast (for all days)

Fruit/Fruit Juice

Fruit Compote
page 159
Muesli/Granola/
Hot Cereal
pages 182, 206

Bread/Muffins
pages 174 to 184

Yogurt

Tea/Coffee/Herb Teas

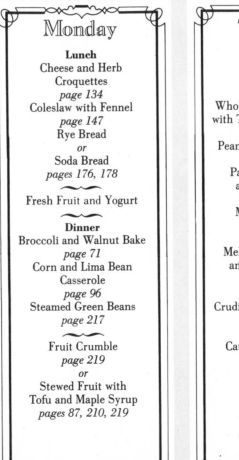

Monday

Lunch
Cheese and Herb Croquettes
page 134
Coleslaw with Fennel
page 147
Rye Bread
or
Soda Bread
pages 176, 178

Fresh Fruit and Yogurt

Dinner
Broccoli and Walnut Bake
page 71
Corn and Lima Bean Casserole
page 96
Steamed Green Beans
page 217

Fruit Crumble
page 219
or
Stewed Fruit with Tofu and Maple Syrup
pages 87, 210, 219

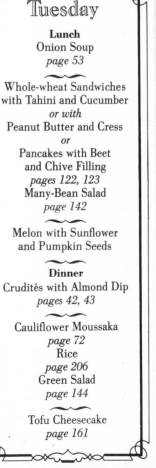

Tuesday

Lunch
Onion Soup
page 53

Whole-wheat Sandwiches with Tahini and Cucumber
or with
Peanut Butter and Cress
or
Pancakes with Beet and Chive Filling
pages 122, 123
Many-Bean Salad
page 142

Melon with Sunflower and Pumpkin Seeds

Dinner
Crudités with Almond Dip
pages 42, 43

Cauliflower Moussaka
page 72
Rice
page 206
Green Salad
page 144

Tofu Cheesecake
page 161

refrigerate other half for Tuesday's bean salad.

Prepare **crumble** or **stewed fruit.**

Make **onion soup** for Tuesday if not from freezer.

TUESDAY
MORNING
★ Thaw **onion soup** if frozen.
★ Thaw **pancakes** if frozen.
★ Thaw double batch of **chick peas** *or* put to soak.
★ Thaw **moussaka** if frozen.
Make **almond dip** and **tofu cheesecake.**

MIDDAY
Reheat **soup** and **pancakes** *or* make **pancakes** fresh.
Assemble **bean salad.**

EVENING
Make **moussaka** if not frozen.
Cook **chick peas** for Wednesday's **salad** and Thursday's **hummus.**

WEDNESDAY
MORNING
★ Thaw **shortbread** for lunch, **soup, bread** and **buckwheat** for supper if frozen.
Bake **bread** and make **shortbread** if not frozen.

MIDDAY
Cook **potatoes** and **spinach** for salad.
Make **jelly** and leave to set.

EVENING
If not frozen, cook **soup** and **buckwheat.**
Prepare **vegetables** to be **stir-fried.**
Assemble **buckwheat salad.**
★ Make **carob cake** for Thursday *or* thaw over night if frozen.

THURSDAY
MIDDAY
Make **hummus** and keep extra for a sandwich spread.

Wednesday

Lunch
Salad of Chick Peas and Tomatoes
Spinach, Apple and Potato Salad
page 142
Cheese Shortbread
page 135

〜

Strained Yogurt with Honey and Nuts

Dinner
Miso Julienne
page 53
Whole-wheat Bread with Cheese and Onion
page 176

〜

Stir-fried Vegetables with Tofu
page 80
Marinated Buckwheat Salad
page 140

〜

Fruit Jelly with Mangoes
page 158

Thursday

Lunch
Hummus with Pita Bread
page 43

〜

Frittata Verde
page 130
Salad of Tomato, Cucumber and Grapefruit

〜

William's Carob Cake
page 166

Dinner
Carrot and Coriander Soup
page 51

Pasta with Yogurt and Snap Beans
page 118
Steamed Zucchini
page 217

〜

Peaches in White Wine

Friday

Lunch
Fresh Pea Soup with Mint
page 59

〜

Rye Sandwich with Mashed Kidney Bean, Garlic and Tahini Filling
or
Pizza with Tomato and Onion
page 120
Endive, Orange and Watercress Salad
page 144

〜

Cheese Board

Dinner
Aduki Beans in Wine
page 97
Steamed Carrots and Celery
page 217
Green Salad
page 144

〜

Millet Pudding with Apricots
page 157

Make the **frittata**—instead of green herbs you could use any vegetables left from the previous day: tomato, spinach or potato, with onion.

★ Thaw **carrot and coriander soup** for supper if frozen. Marinate **peaches** (peeled if fresh—see p. 218—*or* dried) in **white wine** for supper.

EVENING
If not from freezer, cook **carrot and coriander soup**.
Make **pasta with beans**.
Steam **zucchini**.

★ Thaw **kidney beans** for sandwiches for next day.

FRIDAY
MORNING
★ Thaw **filling** for Saturday's tortillas and double quantity **aduki beans** *or* put **beans** to soak, including those for **tortilla filling**.
★ Thaw **fresh pea soup** and **pizza** (*or* **pizza base**) if frozen.

MIDDAY
Make **fresh pea soup** if not from freezer.
Make **pizza** if not frozen. (If you made extra tomato sauce for

the moussaka on Tuesday, use this for the pizza.)

EVENING
Cook the **aduki beans in wine**.
Make **millet pudding with apricots**.
Steam **carrots** and **celery**.
For Saturday: make **brown sauce** and cook **beans** for **tortillas** if not from freezer.

SATURDAY
MORNING
★ Thaw (or make) for lunch: **croquettes; oaten rolls; banana bread**.
★ Thaw **brown sauce** if frozen.
★ Thaw **tofu dip** and **tortillas** (filled or unfilled) for supper.

EVENING
Make **tofu dip** if not from freezer; also **tortillas** and/or **filling** if not frozen.
★ Thaw/make **cashew cream**.
Soak **prunes** for Sunday lunch.
★ Thaw **kasha ring** *or* put buckwheat to soak overnight.
★ Thaw **mustard sauce** if frozen.

SUNDAY
MORNING
★ Thaw **flageolet soup** if frozen *or* put **flageolets** to soak.
Make **gnocchi** and refrigerate.
Make **prune mousse** and chill.

MIDDAY
Make **kasha ring** and **sauce** if not from freezer.
★ Thaw **cornbread** if frozen.

EVENING
Make **flageolet soup** and **cornbread** if not from freezer.
Steam **broccoli**.

Saturday

Lunch
Mushroom and Aduki Croquettes
page 96
Rich Brown Sauce
page 153
Oaten Rolls
page 178
Grilled Tomatoes
page 217

Banana Bread
page 167

Dinner
Avocado with Tofu Dip
page 43

Tortillas
page 126
Salad of Green and Red Peppers

Pineapple and Fresh Dates
Cashew Cream
page 158

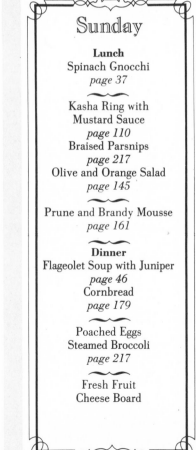

Sunday

Lunch
Spinach Gnocchi
page 37

Kasha Ring with Mustard Sauce
page 110
Braised Parsnips
page 217
Olive and Orange Salad
page 145

Prune and Brandy Mousse
page 161

Dinner
Flageolet Soup with Juniper
page 46
Cornbread
page 179

Poached Eggs
Steamed Broccoli
page 217

Fresh Fruit
Cheese Board

INGREDIENTS

GRAINS

Wheat, rice, barley, oats, millet, rye and corn
are the world's major food grains or cereals,
and all belong to the immense family of grasses.
The other grain of culinary interest, buckwheat, is
the seed not of a grass but of a herbaceous plant.

For thousands of years cereals have been the
staple foods that have kept people alive: wheat,
rye, barley and oats in temperate climates; rice,
corn and millet in the tropics and subtropics.
Most of the world's populations still eat the staple
that grows in their backyard, but in the affluent
countries meat has pushed cereals out of their
primary position, and grains have been refined and
processed to the point where all the fiber and
many of the nutrients have been lost, along with
two other important ingredients: taste and texture.

Unrefined cereals (whole grains) still contain
the germ, an important source of oils, proteins and
minerals, and bran, a source of fiber. They may
be bought whole or cracked, flaked, parboiled,
steamed or toasted, all of which help to shorten
cooking time and make them easier to digest.

Wheat

The most universally grown and the most important
of all food grains, wheat is available in various
forms, from the whole berry to flour, and wheat
flour is used more than any other for making
bread, cakes, pastry and pasta. The whole grain or
berry is by far the most nutritious form. It
retains its outer covering, or bran, which contains
valuable vitamins, minerals and fat as well as
fiber, and the germ, which is only 2 percent of the
grain but contains the bulk of the nutrients.
The rest of the grain, some 70 percent, is known
as the endosperm and consists mainly of starch.

Flour is the form in which wheat is most easily
available. Most of today's flour is produced by
roller-milling, a process that involves high
temperatures and consequent loss of vitamins and
flavor. For this reason, stone-ground flour is
generally considered preferable.

Bread is the end product of most of the world's flour.
Yeast bread is made mainly from wheat, the
only grain high in gluten, a protein that stretches

to form an impermeable skin over the thousands of
bubbles of gas formed when yeast ferments. Bread
made with strong or hard flour has a lighter
consistency than bread made with soft flour. Whole-
wheat flour gives a dense loaf; unbleached white
flour one with a light texture and some percentage
of the nutrients still intact. Wheatmeal flour
contains 81 or 84 percent of the grain and is often
considered a good compromise.

> **YEAST** Compressed, or cake, yeast specified in all the
> recipes in this book, is usually the easiest for the
> beginner to work with. Try to buy it in one piece: it
> should be pale beige, look smooth and have a pleasant,
> fresh smell. Yeast that smells stale or that is crumbly
> and beginning to dry out will not work as well.
> Store it wrapped up, in the refrigerator, for up to
> 10 days (or freeze it—small pieces, separately wrapped,
> are convenient; to revive it, put it in lukewarm
> water for 15 minutes). It will also keep if submerged
> in cold water.
> Dried yeast is usually sold as granules. It gives the
> same results as compressed yeast if used properly.
> Use only a third to a half as much as compressed yeast.
> To reactivate it, sprinkle it into a cup of hot water
> with a little sugar, stir well and leave in a warm
> place for 10-15 minutes. It will keep for up to a
> year if stored in a cool, dry place.

Rice

Rice can be divided into two main categories,
long-grain and short-grain. Properly cooked
long-grain rice has dry, separate grains, usually
associated with curries or pilafs. Short-grain rice
has a softer texture and is stickier when cooked.
Brown (whole-grain) rice has a chewy texture and
nutty flavor that make white rice seem bland,
stripped as it is of the outer layers and germ, and
with them most of the nutrients.

Rice can also be found in the form of flakes and
flour; the flour has a light consistency and small
quantities are good in bread and cakes. The bran
and germ removed when rice is milled are sold
as rice polish, an excellent source of the B vitamins
as well as minerals and protein. Small quantities
can be added to cakes, biscuits or crumble toppings.

Wild rice is not a rice at all, although it is a member of the grass family. It is often served on its own so as not to mask its characteristic delicate, subtle flavor, a little like that of artichokes. It is also good mixed with brown rice.

Corn

This originated in Central America, where it was the staple grain of the Incas, Mayas and Aztecs. Its popularity has spread not only to North America but to Europe, where it is used for such national dishes as polenta in Italy and mamaliga in Rumania. Unlike other whole grains it is not usually dried but is eaten fresh. There are three main varieties: dent corn, which supplies commercial cornmeal; sweet corn, or corn on the cob, the form in which we know it as a fresh vegetable; and popcorn.

Cornmeal is available finely or coarsely ground. Stone-ground or water-ground is best, as the germ is not removed. It is too low in gluten to make yeast bread, but mixes well with wheat to give muffins and breakfast quick breads a distinctive taste and color. Other important products of corn are cooking oil (see page 219) and corn syrup, used for sweetening (see page 212).

Barley

The complete grain is known as whole barley. Pearl barley has been polished and has lost most of the bran, germ and vitamin B. Low in gluten, barley flour will not make yeast bread (unless mixed with wheat flour), but the grayish flat bread made from it is sweet-tasting and delicious. Barley syrup, sometimes known as malt extract, is used as a sweetener.

Oats

Still a popular food in Scotland, northern England and Ireland, oats probably originated in Northern Europe. They are made into oatcakes and parkin, or used for soups, as well as for the traditional hot cereal. They are higher in protein and fats than other grains and rich in B vitamins and iron.

Oats are most often found as flakes or meals, which cook quickly. Flakes can be used for cereals, granola, muesli and crumble toppings, as well as for oatcakes, to which they add a crunchy texture. Oatmeal is used for cereals and oatcakes and as a crunchy coating for croquettes. It is often mixed with wheat flour to improve the taste of bread.

Rye

The groats can be treated like rice or wheat berries, or cracked to produce grits or flakes, which cook more quickly. Rye is a good source of B vitamins, especially B_2 and B_3, and the minerals potassium and magnesium. It also contains rutin, once known as vitamin P, which is good for circulatory complaints.

Millet

Richer than other grains nutritionally, millet is a particularly good source of iron and the B vitamins. Its delicate flavor can seem bland at first, but it combines well with other flavors and makes an excellent alternative to rice in risottos or milk puddings.

Buckwheat

This is not a cereal grain at all but the seed of a herbaceous plant related to dock and rhubarb. It is high in iron and other minerals and in all the B vitamins, as well as containing rutin. Kasha, the porridge-like cooked cereal popular in Russia, is usually made from roasted buckwheat.

BUYING

Most health-food stores sell grains in all their forms from berries to flour, bread and pasta. Choose a store where you can rely on the stock being fresh. Supermarkets often have a some variety, if not such a wide one. You may find unbleached flour and/or white flour treated with caramel or other coloring: it may have the nutrients that were milled out of it added back as synthetic vitamins and minerals. Do, therefore, read the labels and make sure you are getting the whole grain or its product, or that you know exactly what proportion of it you are buying. Also, if you care about organically grown food, check where the flour comes from. Most of the world's bread wheat comes from North America and is not organically grown. Organically grown flour is likely to be soft, giving a dense-textured but well-flavored loaf.

STORING

Whole grains keep indefinitely in cool, dry conditions in an airtight container, but the longer they are stored, the longer they take to cook. Flakes and flours do not keep so long and are best used within 3-6 months, since the oil contained in the germ eventually goes rancid, particularly in oats; wheat germ itself should be used within 2-3 weeks.

COOKING

To cook whole grains, first rinse them to remove surface dust. Choose a saucepan with a close-fitting lid, or use a pressure cooker. Rub a little oil around the pan to prevent the grains from sticking—this will also make the pan easier to clean. One cup is enough for 2-3 people.

Put some water in the saucepan (see the table below for quantities) and bring to the boil. Put in the grains, bring to the boil again, then cover the pan and simmer very gently until the water is absorbed. Do not stir unnecessarily, as this tends to make the grains sticky, and do not add salt until just before the end of the cooking time.

There are simple ways to vary the basic method. Sauté the grain lightly in a little oil or shoyu before adding boiling water (this is good with barley, buckwheat and millet in particular); add spices and vegetables for flavor, particularly saffron, ginger, coriander, garlic or onions. Mix different grains—rice with wheat or barley—for more texture and taste.

The softer grains—millet, rice and buckwheat—make excellent croquettes, Rice, barley and millet are good for sweet puddings, and buckwheat, wheat and oats for substantial breakfast cereals. Cracked grains absorb water more easily and cook quickly. Bulgur wheat, which is steamed, cracked and toasted, needs soaking but no further cooking.

Flakes and meals are used in breakfast cereals (muesli or granola) and as versatile toppings for either sweet or savory dishes. For a crumble topping, try the topping for the winter hotpot on page 76. You can vary the proportions of flakes to flour. Substitute granola (see recipe on page 182) for the flakes if you want a sweet crumble.

Muesli is generally a combination of various flakes, mainly oats, with seeds, nuts and dried fruit. I prefer a version nearer to the original Bircher-Benner muesli, with more emphasis on fresh fruit. For one person, soak 2 tablespoons rolled oats in 2 tablespoons water for 1-2 hours (or overnight). Just before eating, stir in the juice of an orange, a tablespoon of ground almonds and a whole unpeeled apple, grated.

Leftover cooked grains make excellent salads when mixed with beans or vegetables, or they can be added to soups or casseroles. Cooked grain keeps for two days in the refrigerator and can be successfully frozen. To reheat, first thaw, either overnight in the refrigerator or for several hours (the exact time depends on how large a portion you are thawing) at room temperature. Turn out into an oiled dish, cover with foil and heat in a moderate oven (350°F) for 15-20 minutes.

PREPARATION AND COOKING TIMES FOR WHOLE GRAINS

TYPE OF GRAIN	PREPARATION BEFORE COOKING	AMOUNT OF LIQUID PER CUP OF GRAIN	AVERAGE COOKING TIME	PRESSURE COOKING
Wheat	soak overnight (8-12 hours)	4 cups	50-60 minutes	20 minutes
Rice long-grain short-grain	can be toasted or lightly fried	1¾-2 cups 1¾-2 cups	25-30 minutes 20-25 minutes	10 minutes 8-10 minutes
Wild rice		3 cups	50-60 minutes	20 minutes
Corn		plenty of water	5-10 minutes	
Barley	toast	4 cups	50-60 minutes	20 minutes
Oats	can be toasted	3 cups	30-35 minutes	12 minutes
Rye	soak overnight (8-12 hours)	3 cups	50-60 minutes	20 minutes
Millet	can be toasted or lightly fried	2½-3 cups	20 minutes	8 minutes
Buckwheat	toast or lightly fry	2-2½ cups	20 minutes	8 minutes

BEANS, PEAS AND LENTILS

Sometimes collectively known as legumes, these have the advantage that they are cheap to buy, readily available (although some of the less common ones may not be so easy to find) and keep well. Most tend to be bland in taste, but cooked in combination with other ingredients they have a capacity for blending well with them, especially with stronger flavors, and enhancing them: chick peas with tahini (sesame seed paste), lentils with spices, butter or haricot beans with onions, tomatoes, peppers. Cooked dishes generally improve on being left for several hours or overnight for the full development of flavor before reheating. They may not be the answer if you need to prepare a meal or a snack in a hurry, but they are ideal if you prefer to do the preparation beforehand.

One common objection to legumes is that they tend to cause intestinal gas. The best way to counter this is to accustom yourself to eating them gradually, making sure they are thoroughly cooked. Lentils and smaller beans are sometimes found to be more easily digestible.

BUYING AND STRONG

It is becoming easier nowadays to find good quality dried beans and peas. Buy from somewhere with a good turnover: although they do keep well, if they have spent a year sitting on a shelf they will take a very long time to cook. Choose beans or peas that look plump, brightly colored and unwrinkled. They are worth buying in bulk as they will keep in good condition for up to six months.

Keep up to 6 months (1 month if in glass jars).

All legumes keep best in cool, dry, dark conditions in airtight containers. If you have a fairly rapid turnover—say within a month—they can be kept in glass jars, as long as they are not exposed to full sun, which impairs flavor and nutrients.

PREPARATION

You do need to pick them over (lentils especially) for stones and grit and give them a rinse to wash off the surface dust. Lentils and split peas can then be cooked immediately, but beans and whole peas should be soaked before cooking. Use plenty of water, remembering that legumes absorb water and will swell up to between two and three times their original bulk. There is a quick method, which is the equivalent of an overnight soak: bring to the boil in plenty of water, boil for 3-5 minutes and let stand in the water for an hour.

COOKING

After soaking, drain and rinse again. Some vitamins will be lost in the soaking water, but this is not crucial. Put in a saucepan, cover with plenty of fresh water and bring to the boil. Skim off any scum. Do not salt the water: salt toughens the outer skin and cooking will take longer. Vegetables, herbs, spices or flavorings can be added: onions, garlic, carrots, other root vegetables, black peppercorns, ginger or chili peppers. The addition of anise, dill, fennel or caraway seeds—1 teaspoon per cup of legumes—or a strip of the sea vegetable kombu (see page 212) helps digestion. After the preliminary boiling (see note on chart on page 208), turn the heat down, cover the pan, but not too tightly, and simmer. If you add a little oil this will prevent the beans or peas from boiling over and will also give them a smoother texture. The cooking time depends on the kind of legume, how long it has been stored, and whether you want it for a salad or a purée: those for salads should be just tender, while those for a purée need longer cooking. Use the times given in the chart as a guide, and test for tenderness by pressing lightly.

An alternative cooking method is in a pressure cooker (see the chart for times). It cuts the cooking time by about two-thirds, and there is no need to worry about fast boiling, as this happens automatically. Don't cook more than about half a 2 cups at a time, or they may froth up and block the safety valve. Even a little overcooking may result in a purée, so use an ordinary saucepan if you are making, say, a bean salad, where the appearance is important.

SERVING AND KEEPING

All beans, peas and lentils can be used as a basis for casseroles and can be served as a simple side dish, perhaps as a purée: aduki beans, flageolets or mung beans have a subtle taste and are particularly suitable. Haricots, lima or butter beans and the other kidney beans (see illustration on page 12) are often cooked with spices, herbs and vegetables for a contrast in flavor. For croquettes, the most suitable are aduki beans, lentils, mung beans and black-eyed peas. All of them can also be used in soups, and this is the most common use for peas, both split and whole. Almost all beans and lentils are good eaten cold in salad, with the exception of broad beans and soybeans.

Once cooked, beans, peas and lentils keep well: several days in a covered container in the refrigerator, or they can be frozen—they retain their flavor very well. Cool and open-freeze them, then pack in plastic containers and label. For soups,

a handful or two can be removed and put straight into the soup near the end of the cooking time. For salads, allow to thaw for about an hour at room temperature, or overnight in the refrigerator, then mix with the other vegetables or herbs and the dressing. Croquettes, cooked or uncooked, also freeze well; shape into patties, open-freeze on trays and pack in plastic containers or bags with wax paper between them. Thaw overnight in the refrigerator or for two hours at room temperature.

The cooking liquid is well worth keeping. Any toxins will have been destroyed, and it is excellent for soups, stews and sauces, particularly if flavored with vegetables or spices. It will keep for 4-5 days in the refrigerator, and can be frozen.

SOAKING AND COOKING CHART FOR BEANS, PEAS AND LENTILS

TYPE OF BEAN	RECOMMENDED SOAK OVERNIGHT*	AVERAGE COOKING TIME	PRESSURE COOKING
Aduki beans	yes	45 minutes	15 minutes
Black-eyed peas	yes	45-50 minutes	15 minutes
Black beans	yes	50-60 minutes	20 minutes
Broad beans	yes	1½ hours	40 minutes
Butter or lima beans	yes	60-90 minutes	25-30 minutes
Cannellini	yes	45-50 minutes	15 minutes
Flageolets	yes	45-50 minutes	15 minutes
Ful medames	yes	60 minutes	20 minutes
Haricot beans	yes	50-60 minutes	20 minutes
Mung beans	yes	30-45 minutes	15 minutes
Pinto beans	yes	60-90 minutes	25-30 minutes
Red kidney beans	yes	45-50 minutes	15 minutes
Soybeans	yes	2-2½ hours†	45-50 minutes
Chick peas	yes	60-90 minutes	25-30 minutes
Whole green peas	yes	60-90 minutes	25-30 minutes
Split peas	no	40-45 minutes	—
Whole lentils	no	30-45 minutes	12-15 minutes
Split lentils	no	15-30 minutes	—

*"Overnight" here means approximately 8-12 hours. All times given are only a rough guide, as cooking times can vary considerably depending on the age and origin of the crop. The first ten minutes' cooking of all except lentils and split peas should be done at a fast boil, uncovered, to destroy any toxic elements on the outer skin, except †soybeans, which should boil hard for the first hour. Although lentils and split peas need not be soaked overnight, they will cook faster if they are first steeped in boiling water for 15-30 minutes. Drain before cooking them.

NUTS AND SEEDS

Botanically, nuts and seeds are the same: both have kernels containing the whole future plant in embryo and are a concentrated source of food.

A combination of mixed nuts and cereals with green vegetables makes a nutritionally adequate main course, and nuts give taste and texture to salads, cooked vegetables and grains. By themselves, or with sunflower or pumpkin seeds, they make a good snack. Watermelon and pomegranate seeds are also edible.

BUYING

It is better to buy nuts in their shells: this protects the kernels and keeps them fresh. If you do want them shelled, buy loose nuts, preferably whole, as these tend to be of better quality. Avoid nuts that have been coated in fat and salted. Seeds should always be bought whole.

STORING

Store in a cool place. Unshelled nuts will keep up to six months. Keep seeds and shelled nuts in an airtight container; whole, they will stay in good condition for up to three months, unless kept in a warm place, when their high fat content means they are liable to go rancid quickly. Split, chopped or ground nuts will go stale more quickly still and should be eaten within 4-6 weeks.

PREPARATION

Nuts can be blanched to remove the dark skin; roasted or toasted to improve their flavor (although there is a certain amount of nutrient loss); ground, which also makes them easier to digest; or, in the case of coconut, grated. Seeds, especially sunflower and sesame, are also good toasted.

To blanch nuts, except for hazelnuts, put them in a bowl, cover with boiling water and leave for a few minutes, or until they can be popped out of their skins when gently pressed. If you are not using the peeled nuts immediately, drop them in cold water to keep them white. Hazelnuts should be baked in the oven (or toasted under the broiler) for 5 or 6 minutes. If they are then rubbed in a cloth, the fibrous skin will come away.

To roast nuts or seeds in the oven, spread them out in a single layer on a shallow tray or cookie sheet. Sprinkle with a small amount of oil. Put in a moderate oven for about 10 minutes, and shake the tray or sheet two or three times to turn them and ensure even browning. You can also fry them. Use a heavy pan and just enough oil to grease the bottom lightly. Shake or stir the nuts or seeds over gentle heat until evenly browned. If you are prepared to watch them carefully, they will toast under a hot broiler in 2 or 3 minutes but must be turned before they burn.

To skin sweet chestnuts, slash each one with a sharp knife (take care, as the skins can be tough), drop them into boiling water and leave them for about 10 minutes, by which time both the outer and inner skins should come away. Dried chestnuts do not need shelling.

Nuts are easily ground: use a small grater, a nut mill or a blender. A coffee grinder, kept specially for the purpose, is ideal. Nuts tend to grind unevenly and it is easier to do a few at a time. Walnuts and Brazil nuts have a tendency to be greasy, and you may need to scrape around the sides of the mill once or twice.

COOKING

In addition to being eaten raw, nuts and seeds are used in roasts, bakes, croquettes and casseroles, and in cereal mixtures and crumble toppings. Peanut butter is the best known nut butter, but cashews, hazelnuts and almonds also make good spreads and dips. Blend them with a little oil and salt to taste, or mix equal quantities of nuts and water with a little oil and salt and blend. Nut butters will keep in the refrigerator for 4-6 weeks if made with only oil, for 3-4 days if made with water. They can also be frozen.

Nut creams and milks are easy to make and can form the basis for sauces or substitutes for cream to serve with puddings or cakes. Almond milk can be made by blending together 1½ tablespoons blanched ground almonds, ¾ cup water and 1 teaspoon honey. There is a recipe for cashew cream on page 158. Both will keep in the refrigerator for up to 3-4 days.

COCONUT CREAM To make 1¼ cups coconut cream, grate 3-4 ounces of the creamed coconut block, cover with boiling water and leave for half an hour (or put in a blender for half a minute). Stir well and strain before using. For coconut milk, use twice the amount of water. Season with a little salt and use with curries and other rice dishes.

DRIED FRUIT

It takes up to six pounds of tree fruit (or two pounds of grapes) to produce a pound of dried fruit, so the vitamin, mineral and sugar content is highly concentrated. Dried fruit should not be reconstituted in liquids with extra sugar added.

Sulfur is often added to preserve color and maintain water content, thus keeping the fruit plumper. It also prevents fermentation and decay, and helps retain vitamins A and C (although it destroys B vitamins). There is no evidence that this is harmful—sulfur, in small quantities, is an essential mineral. Where possible health-food stores will stock fruits that have not undergone unnecessary chemical treatment.

BUYING AND STORING

Choose plump unblemished fruit. No fruit, sun-dried or otherwise, should be rock-hard. It will keep for up to a year in airtight containers, although it is best when used within six months. A piece of orange or lemon peel in the container helps to keep the fruit moist. Dried fruit can also be frozen, and will keep for up to a year. Reconstituted dried fruit will keep frozen for 2-3 months.

PREPARATION

Much fruit sold these days is already cleaned but it is still wise to rinse again under running water to remove any traces of preservative. Drain well. If it is for a cake mix, where the fruit may sink if damp, clean it by sifting with some flour.

Sifting currants with flour   *Plumping raisins*

To plump raisins and currants, soak them in hot liquid—water, fruit juice or wine—for 5 minutes. Drain, pat dry and use at once. Plumped vine fruits give a juicy texture to cakes and puddings. To reconstitute tree fruits, cover with liquid and leave to soak for 8-12 hours. You may need to add more liquid. A quicker method is to put the fruit in a pan, cover it with liquid and bring it to the boil; simmer, covered, for 10-15 minutes and leave for an hour. It may be eaten at this stage or cooked until soft, whichever you prefer.

COOKING

Stew or cook the fruit for 30-40 minutes or until tender: use the soaking liquid, which now contains valuable nutrients, for cooking. It will keep for 3-4 days in the refrigerator.

Cooked fruit can be eaten hot as fruit compote or puréed for use as a sweet pastry filling or in cakes, or it can be added to breakfast cereals, salads, stuffings and savory dishes such as curries.

Apples are unusual in that they do not lose vitamin C in the drying process. They are mostly used in fruit compotes.

Apricots are sold whole, halved, or in pieces. The pieces are cheaper and are good for purées and jams. Hunza apricots, from the Himalayas, are small, unsulfured and pale beige in color. They are sold whole and unpitted: the pit can be cracked and the delicious kernel, tasting rather like an almond, extracted.

Bananas have an excellent flavor. Good mixed with dates and figs for rich fruit purées to use in sauces or cakes, they can also be baked in rum or deep-fried.

Dates should be plump and moist with thin skins. Cooking dates are compressed into blocks; break them up before use to check for pits, as it is not uncommon to find some have been left in. These dates make splendid fruit purées.

Figs are high in calcium and potassium as well as sugar. They can be stuffed: soak them first to reconstitute them and use a cottage cheese stuffing or one based on almonds—figs and almonds are a traditional combination.

Peaches and **nectarines,** usually available halved, are used in the same way as apricots.

Pears keep their distinctive slightly gritty texture when dried, and are a good addition to compotes.

Prunes (dried plums) are lower in sugar and calories than dates or figs. Ready-made prune purée can also be bought; this is popular in France, where it is used in confectionery, pastries and cakes.

Raisins and currants are all dried grapes, widely used for fruit cakes and mincemeats. Some golden raisins are unsulfured and are sprayed with vegetable rather than mineral oil, so it is worth trying to find them. Lexia raisins from Australia are large, sticky and very sweet and are sold with the seeds removed. Another sweet variety, the Muscatel from Spain, is not chemically treated.

SEASONINGS AND FLAVORINGS

Any well-stocked vegetarian pantry should contain a wide range of flavorings and seasonings, from spices and vinegars, seaweeds and syrups, to flavorings made from nuts and vegetables and the indispensable soybean products.

Soybean products

The soybean, difficult to digest when whole, is easily assimilated when fermented and provides nutrients as well as flavorings. The best known fermented products are **shoyu, tamari** and **miso.** The soy sauce familiar to many non-vegetarians is too often a synthetic reproduction.

Miso is a living food rather in the same way that yogurt is, and contains bacteria and enzymes which are destroyed by boiling. It is therefore usually added as a flavoring at the end of cooking, often mixed with a little warm water so it dissolves easily. The most commonly available is mugi miso, a combination of soybean and barley with a warm, mellow flavor. Hatcho miso, made from soybeans alone, is denser and more strongly flavored, while genmai miso, made with rice, is lighter and sweeter.

Tamari, shoyu and miso all keep well but should not undergo sudden changes of temperature. Miso may develop a white mold: this is a natural yeast and can simply be mixed back in.

Rock salt, held by some to have the finest taste, and **sea salt** are preferable to refined table salt, which may have additives. Both can be used for cooking and at the table. **Salt substitutes** often consist of potassium salts. One of the most successful combinations of salt with other flavorings is gomashio, or sesame salt, whose nutty flavor complements many vegetable and grain dishes. It will keep for up to two weeks.

Both the strong **mustard powder** and the gentler, more aromatic prepared **Dijon-type mustard** have their place in the kitchen. With mustard powder, make up only as much as you are going to need at any one time.

Horseradish sauce can be bought, but does not compare in flavor with sauces made from the freshly grated root, as the aroma is very volatile. Dried horseradish is the best substitute.

Nuts and seeds provide useful flavorings, from peanut butter to tahini, a beige paste of similar consistency made from sesame seeds.

Dried mushrooms add rich natural flavoring and are popular in Japan and China. They keep well in an airtight container and are reconstituted by soaking in warm water for at least half an hour.

Bouillon cubes and **yeast extracts** are quick ways of adding flavor. Yeast extracts in particular are rich in nutrients, but also in salt and so should not be used too generously. They are sold in screw-top jars and will keep for at least six months.

Sea vegetables

Sea vegetables are an important source of minerals, particularly iodine, calcium, potassium and iron, and of vitamins, mainly the B group including traces of B_{12}, which is rare in vegetable foods; they are also a good protein source. However, their main culinary use is probably as seasoning, and, in the case of agar and carrageen, as setting agents in place of animal gelatine. Much appreciated in Japan, they also have a long tradition of use in other parts of the world, especially around the North Atlantic.

BUYING AND STORING
It is usually best to buy from a health-food store, where sea vegetables are sold already cleaned, dried and packaged. Unopened, they will keep indefinitely; opened, up to 4 months in an airtight container.

PREPARATION
Dried nori, dulse, kombu, wakame and arame need a preliminary brief soaking for 5 minutes or so to soften them, although this is not necessary if they are to be added directly to a soup or stew.

The exception is dulse, which needs to be rinsed and then soaked again for 10 minutes. Nori need not be softened if it is to be crumbled over a salad. Carrageen may need rinsing before use.

Nori is traditionally toasted and wrapped around small rice balls, which are then dipped in shoyu. After its preliminary soaking, it can be used to flavor soups or as a salad ingredient, when it should be rinsed and boiled for about 15 minutes.

Dulse can be eaten raw, or, if dried, simmered for 30 minutes after being soaked. It is a dark, leafy vegetable with a sweet, tangy taste and is particularly good with cooked cabbage.

Kombu can also be eaten raw as well as cooked. It has a sweet flavor and is good for stocks and soups.

Wakame should have the central vein cut out after soaking. It is then simmered for 10 minutes or cut into small pieces and served as salad. Of all the sea vegetables, it is the one that comes closest in taste to green land vegetables.

Arame has a broad leaf and is usually shredded into hair-like threads. (Another sea vegetable, hijiki, looks similar but more matchstick-like. It can be used in the same way.) Arame can be lightly steamed, sautéed or eaten cold.

Agar is a vegetable gelatine, available in powder or flake form. The powder is easier to use and ensures better results. The main point to watch for when using it is to make sure that it is thoroughly dissolved in boiling water or liquid before use, otherwise it will not set. Use 2 teaspoons agar powder to 2½ cups liquid for a delicate jelly.

Carrageen is most often used to make carrageen aspic, or blancmange. Soak ½ ounce dried carrageen in water for 15 minutes. Drain, rinse and cover with 2½ cups milk; bring to the boil and simmer, covered, for 20-30 minutes. Strain, cool slightly, sweeten to taste, pour into a wet mold and leave to set. This basic method can be adapted to fruit puddings or savory molds.

Sweeteners

Rather than substituting one kind of sugar for another, it is important to monitor your intake of sugar and cut down on the total. There is little difference nutritionally between white and brown sugar, but **brown sugar** does contain a little fiber.

A product of cane sugar, **molasses** especially blackstrap molasses, contains small amounts of minerals, including calcium and iron, and some B vitamins. Its strong flavor makes it suitable for fruit breads and ginger cakes. It will keep up to 6 months in an airtight jar.

Honey is twice as sweet as sugar, so you need to use only half the amount of sugar given in a recipe (reduce the liquid elsewhere to allow for the water content of honey). Look for the word "pure" on the label: this indicates that the product has not been tampered with. Blended honey may contain sugars, syrups and possibly additives. A jar of clear honey may sometimes crystallize if stored at a low temperature. Simply warm gently and the honey will become clear again.

Maple syrup is not as sweet as honey but it does contain some minerals, especially calcium. Other syrups available include corn syrup, rice syrup, sorghum syrup and barley syrup, also known as malt extract.

Fruit juice concentrates are very useful flavorings and can be combined with other sweeteners, such as honey, to reduce the total amount of sweetener needed in cakes and pastries—on their own the taste is too strong. Add them to fruit salads, sauces and cereals. Once opened, store the bottle in the refrigerator for up to 3 weeks. Dried fruits, especially dates, are also good for sweetening.

Carob powder, or carob flour, made from the seeds of the Mediterranean carob tree, tastes very much like chocolate. It is naturally sweeter than cocoa and has no caffeine, a lower fat content and also contains some vitamins. When substituting carob for cocoa, use about half the quantity suggested. It makes cakes and biscuits a very dark brown.

Herbs

BUYING AND STORING
Most herbs should be bought and used fresh whenever possible, although a few (principally oregano, marjoram, sage, bay leaf and dill) keep their aroma well when dried. Buy small amounts or dried herbs, if possible from a whole-food store where there is a large turnover.

To dry your own herbs, pick them when the leaves are dry, preferably just before flowering. Tie in bunches and hang upside down in a cool dark place.

HERB CHART

HERB	SOUPS	STEWS	SAUCES	SALADS	GARNISH	OTHER REMARKS
Basil	yes	—	yes	yes	yes	Goes particularly well with tomatoes; an essential ingredient of pesto (see p.115).
Bay leaf	yes	yes	yes	—	—	A bay leaf, combined with a sprig of thyme and some parsley, makes a *bouquet garni*.
Chervil	yes	yes	yes	yes	yes	The mixture known as *fines herbes* is made of finely chopped chervil, parsley, tarragon and chives.
Chives	—	—	yes	yes	yes	Particularly good with potato salad.
Coriander leaves	yes	yes	yes	yes	yes	Use like parsley.
Dill weed	—	—	yes	yes	yes	Good with potatoes and green vegetables.
Garlic	yes	yes	yes	—	—	Extremely versatile and enhances other flavors.
Lemon balm	yes	yes	—	—	—	Use to flavor summer drinks and herb teas.
Sweet marjoram	yes	yes	—	—	—	Goes well with nuts, eggs and tomatoes.
Mint	—	—	yes	yes	yes	Use to flavor young vegetables, especially peas and new potatoes, or add to yogurt or bean dishes. Also good with fruit and summer drinks.
Oregano	yes	yes	yes	—	—	Indispensable to many Greek and Italian dishes.
Parsley	yes	yes	yes	yes	yes	Use generously both as flavoring and as garnish. Combines well with other herbs.
Rosemary	yes	yes	—	—	—	Good with oily foods. Strong camphor-like flavor.
Sage	—	yes	—	—	—	Use sparingly; very pungent.
Savory	yes	yes	—	yes	yes	Use like thyme or marjoram; good with beans.
Tarragon	yes	yes	yes	—	yes	Particularly good with cheese, cream, eggs, sauces and mild-flavored vegetables.
Thyme	yes	yes	—	—	—	Good with most vegetables, such as tomatoes, zucchini, eggplants and peppers.

When dry, crumble them and put in small jars.

Some herbs can also be frozen for use as flavoring rather than as a garnish: parsley, coriander leaves, chives, dill, tarragon and chervil are all suitable. Blanch in boiling water for a few seconds (otherwise they will lose their color and look unappetizing). Blanching also helps to retain flavor and aroma. Drain them, leave in sprigs and open-freeze. Place in plastic bags and keep for not more than 3-4 months. Keep dried herbs away from light or heat, in airtight containers.

USING

To get the best flavor from fresh herbs, tear or snip them rather than chop them, except parsley. Dried herbs are more pungent than fresh, so use only one teaspoon of the dried herb where you would use 2-3 teaspoons of the fresh one.

Spices

Even a small amount of spice, judiciously used, alters the whole character of a dish. The term generally refers to the dried roots, bark, pods, berries or seeds of aromatic plants. Most spices come from the East, but allspice, chili peppers and vanilla originated in the New World.

BUYING AND STORING

Buy spices whole whenever possible since they keep their flavor and freshness much better. Turmeric and chili peppers (including cayenne and paprika) are generally sold ready-ground. Keep in airtight containers, in a cool dark place.

PREPARATION

Some spices can be crushed using a pestle and mortar: they include allspice, cardamom, cloves, coriander, cumin, dill and fennel seed, juniper, black peppercorns and saffron. Poppy seeds are tough and need a proper nut mill, which can of course also be used for other spices. Aniseeds, capers, caraway, celery, dill and fennel seeds are generally used whole. Green peppercorns are not strictly speaking a spice, as they are not dried. They are easily crushed or mashed. Nutmeg needs grating: a cheese grater does perfectly well. Ginger can also be grated, especially when fresh, or it can be sliced thinly or chopped. Always prepare spices just before they are to be cooked.

Chili peppers can be chopped (remove the seeds unless you are quite sure you like the chili hot),

or kept in a jar of oil to impart their flavor. Keep adding more oil as you use it—you will need only a few drops at a time. This is an excellent standby for the spaghetti with oil, garlic and chili on page 113. Saffron threads are often mixed with a little warm water, when they will expand and give out their color and flavoring more easily. They may also be lightly crushed and put in a warm oven for a few minutes.

Chili peppers in oil

Saffron threads

USING

Many spices benefit from being lightly fried in a little oil before being added to the dish they are to flavor. This seems to bring out and reinforce their aroma, removing any suspicion of rankness or coarseness, and applies particularly to coriander, cumin, cardamom, ginger and fenugreek.

Cinnamon and mace, being difficult to grind, are often used whole to flavor liquids—sauces or drinks—from which they can be easily removed once they have yielded their aroma. In the same way, a vanilla bean can be used to flavor drinks, syrups or custards.

Coriander, cumin, cardamom, peppercorns, turmeric, cloves, ginger and chili peppers are the most important spices for curry. Some recipes call for garam masala, a combination of spices. This can be bought, or you can make your own: there is no standard recipe (the name means "hot mixture"). It is a starting mixture rather than a complete curry powder. A possible mixture might be 4 parts coriander, 1 part cumin, 1 part chili, all lightly roasted or fried and added to 1 part ground black peppercorns.

VEGETABLES

Organically grown vegetables (a phrase used to describe produce that has been grown without the aid of artificial fertilizers, pesticides or other sprays) are usually more expensive than intensively farmed vegetables, because it costs more to produce them. They tend to be smaller and more irregularly shaped than supermarket produce grown for eye appeal. Still, many people consider this is a small price to pay for vegetables that are uncontaminated by chemicals and that have a finer flavor and better keeping qualities. They contain minerals and fiber and are excellent sources of vitamins, particularly vitamin C. Root vegetables supply starch and natural sugars for energy. They complement beans, grains and nuts, providing taste and color, palatability and texture, as well as the vitamins and minerals we need.

BUYING

Freshness is all-important, and being wrapped in plastic does nothing for a vegetable's flavor, so wherever possible buy from a reputable greengrocer. Look for plumpness and fresh, bright color: avoid damaged, shrunken or wrinkled, faded or limp vegetables.

STORING

The following should be eaten as soon as possible: salad greens and vegetables to be eaten raw; green vegetables; pods; fruit vegetables such as zucchini, peppers and eggplants (but tomatoes are often picked unripe and allowed to ripen); sprouts; mushrooms; and above all sweet corn. If any of these vegetables do have to wait, remove any plastic wrappings and keep them in a cool, dark place since light and heat destroy crispness and nutrients, particularly vitamins B_2 and C. Greens can lose up to 50 percent of their vitamin C in one day if kept at room temperature.

If kept in a cool, well-ventilated place, carrots and onions will keep longer—several weeks—and potatoes will keep for several months but will lose much of their vitamin C content.

Some fresh vegetables are suitable for freezing and this causes very little loss of nutrients. Sweet corn, spinach, Swiss chard, broccoli, carrots, peas and beans (snap and broad) are all good.

To freeze, prepare the vegetables as directed below and blanch them by plunging into boiling water for a minute; do about a pound at a time, so that the water does not cool down too much. This destroys the enzyme that causes deterioration. Drain them and plunge immediately into cold water to prevent further cooking. Drain again, using a salad spinner. Freeze on a tray in a single layer, covered with a plastic bag. Pack in plastic containers or bags. They will keep for up to a year. Use straight from the freezer and do not thaw first, or the vitamin content will be reduced.

PREPARATION

Many vegetables are best eaten raw, for both flavour and nutrition. If you have any suspicion that your vegetables may have been contaminated by chemicals, it is advisable to wash or scrub them.

Raw salad greens should be rinsed thoroughly and put in a plastic bag in the refrigerator until just before use, when they should be prepared, dressed and eaten immediately. **Root vegetables** and **tubers** should be scrubbed and cooked in their skins. In general, do not peel first: scrubbing removes most pesticides, and much of the goodness of root vegetables is contained in or near the skin. Potatoes can lose up to 25 percent of their protein if peeled too thickly.

Celeriac is the exception that does need peeling before cooking. Peel others (except potatoes) after cooking and chop, slice or dice them. Jerusalem artichokes, small rutabagas, especially the young white ones, and small kohlrabi can also be left whole, and all can be mashed or puréed.

Some vegetables (Jerusalem artichokes, celeriac, potatoes) turn brown when cut: to prevent this, drop them in water, preferably lightly acidulated by the addition of 3-4 teaspoons of lemon juice or vinegar to each 5 cups of water, or rub with lemon juice. **Eggplants** also go brown, but this does not matter since when cooked it will not show. I do not find it necessary to salt them to draw out their bitter liquid.

With **okra,** cut off the conical cap at the stalk end, salt them and leave for an hour, then rinse carefully and dry. Cut **fennel** in thin slices across, discarding the stems and, if tough, the bottom.

Spinach and **other leafy vegetables** should be well washed and drained before cooking. Do not discard the outer leaves: they are often the most nutritious, but must of course be well washed to remove any pesticides.

COOKING

When choosing vegetables for a meal, calculate about ½ pound per person for a main dish, less for a side dish (see also page 78).

Of the many different ways of cooking vegetables, boiling is one of the most popular. It is also one of the least desirable, as up to 45 percent of the minerals and 50 percent of the vitamin C may be lost. If you must boil vegetables, use the minimum amount of water and make sure it is boiling when you add the vegetables. Never add baking soda: it may keep the color in, but it destroys vitamin C. For green vegetables, ½-inch water should be enough. If spinach has been thoroughly rinsed and not too well drained, it will need no further liquid. Root vegetables should be barely covered. Keep the pan tightly covered—this will help prevent vitamin loss—and cook as shown opposite.

Steaming is good, since vitamins are not lost in the cooking liquid. Put the vegetables in a basket over a pan of rapidly boiling water. Don't pack them too tightly, and cover with a well-fitting lid.

Baking or braising is particularly suited to root vegetables and potatoes. Prick the skins first to prevent them from bursting. I have also successfully baked green vegetables, particularly Brussels sprouts, first brushing both the sprouts and the dish with a little oil. This produces a crisp cooked vegetable, the leaves on the outside well cooked and the inside tender.

To braise vegetables, brown them lightly in a little oil and bake in the oven, adding a little hot liquid, in a covered dish.

Asparagus is best cooked with the stems in boiling water but the tops out of it, so that the tender tips cook in the steam.

Sprouts

Easy and quick to grow at home, sprouts provide fresh, uncontaminated green vegetables of outstanding nutritional value: they contain valuable amounts of protein, as well as vitamins A, B complex, C and E, minerals and enzymes.

The changes that take place as the seed grows are incredible. The total vitamin content can increase by up to 800 percent within a few days.

BUYING

Buy untreated seeds from a heath-food store or a firm specializing in organically grown produce, as almost all seeds sold for planting will have been treated with fungicides and pesticides. Split beans or seeds will not sprout.

GROWING

If you don't have proper tiered sprouting trays, fine sieves or mesh trays, or a wide-necked jar with a cover of muslin or other porous substance, will do very well. Pick over the seeds carefully, removing any tiny stems and stones.

Put 2 tablespoons of seeds in a jar and soak them in plenty of lukewarm water overnight, to encourage them to germinate more quickly. Next day, drain off the water. Put the seeds on a suitable tray or leave them in the jar. Put in a warm place but not in direct sun. They need good ventilation and a constant temperature of 55 to 70°F. Remember to allow enough space in the container for growth—they will increase in volume by 4 to 6 times.

Every night and morning pour warm water over the seeds. Turn the jar, if you are using one, upside down so the water can drain away completely. If not properly drained, the sprouts can go moldy, but be careful not to rinse them so vigorously that you damage the delicate shoots. Grain sprouts take 2-3 days, beans and lentils 5-7 days, to be at their best. When ready, give them a final rinse.

STORING

Sprouts keep in the refrigerator for up to 4 days. Use an airtight container with a double layer of wax paper or muslin at the bottom to absorb excess moisture and retard deterioration.

USING

All sprouts can be eaten raw in salads. The delicate green leaves of mustard, garden cress and alfalfa look particularly pretty and can also be used as garnish. Aduki bean sprouts have a distinct flavor of peanuts; mung beans taste a little like delicate peapods, but if grown for too long, they will develop too intense a flavor and lose some of their nutritive value. Fenugreek sprouts taste spicy.

The best known and easiest to sprout are mustard and garden cress, mung beans and alfalfa; aduki beans are also easy, and so are whole lentils.

Sprouts are good as an addition to bread: use wheat sprouts, or alfalfa sprouts grown to only ¼ inch.

COOKING TIMES AND METHODS FOR DIFFERENT VEGETABLES

VEGETABLE	STEAM	BOIL	BAKE (WHOLE)	BRAISE	STIR-FRY
Potatoes	25-30 minutes	20 minutes	1-1½ hours	15-20 minutes	
Carrots	20 minutes	10-15 minutes	45-60 minutes	15-20 minutes	yes
Turnips, white	25-30 minutes	10-15 minutes		15-20 minutes	yes
Rutabagas	25-30 minutes	20 minutes		15-20 minutes	yes
Parsnips		15-20 minutes	45-60 minutes	15-20 minutes	
Celeriac & kohlrabi	20 minutes	10-15 minutes		15-20 minutes	yes
Salsify	30-40 minutes	20-30 minutes			
Sweet potatoes	25-30 minutes	20 minutes	1-1½ hours		
Jerusalem artichokes		15-20 minutes			
Radish/daikon					yes
Beets		40-60 minutes			
Asparagus		10-15 minutes			
Fennel	12-15 minutes	10-12 minutes		15-20 minutes	yes
Onions			45-60 minutes		
Leeks	15-20 minutes	10-15 minutes		8-10 minutes	
Celery	12-15 minutes	8-10 minutes		10-12 minutes	yes
Globe artichokes		30-40 minutes			
Snap beans	4-8 minutes				yes
Broad beans		10-15 minutes			
Peas		8-12 minutes			yes
Sugar Peas	6-8 minutes				yes
Okra		15-20 minutes			
Mushrooms					yes
Sweet corn		8-15 minutes			yes
White cabbage	4-6 minutes				yes
Red cabbage				45-60 minutes	
Brussels sprouts	6-10 minutes		25-30 minutes		yes
Cauliflower	4-8 minutes				
Broccoli	4-8 minutes				yes
Spinach*		6-8 minutes			
Bok choy	4-8 minutes				yes
Spinach beet	10-12 minutes				
Swiss chard	10-12 minutes				
Belgian endive				10-12 minutes	
Chicory, batavian or curly					yes
Chinese leaves	4 minutes				yes
Zucchini	4-8 minutes				yes
Squash	10-20 minutes		45-60 minutes		yes
Peppers					yes
Cucumbers	5-10 minutes				

All the above times give *very lightly cooked* vegetables, many with a crisp, crunchy texture. If you prefer vegetables softer, you will need to increase the cooking time.
*Spinach is not strictly speaking boiled, but cooked in the water still adhering to it after a final rinsing.

Eggplants are usually sautéed and/or baked, often with a stuffing: see specific recipes for directions.
Tomatoes can be broiled for 3-4 minutes. No times have been given for frying or sautéing, as these will be found in specific recipes.

FRUIT

Fresh fruit, preferably eaten raw, is part of any healthy diet. Most fruits contain vitamin C (which cannot be stored in the body). They also contain a high proportion of natural sugars (fructose), carbohydrates and fiber as well as minerals and other vitamins.

BUYING

Buy fresh, firm, plump fruit that is not shrunken or damaged. Fruit with pits, such as peaches, plums and cherries, should be firm, neither rock-hard nor too squashy. Melons should be heavy, slightly softened at the stalk end and smell ripe. Pineapples too should smell ripe and the leaves should come away without too much effort.

Kiwi fruit can be bought when still hard and will ripen at home. Papayas will also go on ripening at home until soft enough to eat. Mangoes should be slightly soft, figs soft but not squashy—the skin should feel as if it is just at bursting point but not beyond it. When buying persimmons, check with your greengrocer: some can be eaten immediately, while some are far too bitter and must be kept until squashy. Passion fruit have wrinkled skins when ripe. Guavas turn light yellow and are very fragrant and soft. Lychees turn to a vivid rosy red.

STORING

Pears in particular have only a day or so when they are at their best, and strawberries, raspberries and other soft fruits are best eaten as soon as possible after picking. Ripe figs and persimmons should also be eaten quickly. Melons, pineapples, mangoes, papayas and guavas should all be eaten within a few days of ripening; so should grapes and fruit with pips.

Apples, however, store well, especially if kept without touching one another in a cool, dry, well-ventilated place. Other fruits that keep well are all the citrus family, kiwi fruit and bananas. Lychees keep up to three months in the refrigerator.

PREPARATION

Scrub fruit if you think it needs it, but try not to peel unnecessarily. Citrus fruits are often sprayed to give them a healthy shine. This should not affect the fruit inside, but if you are going to use the peel (or eat the fruit whole, as you can tiny kumquats) they will need washing.

If making a fruit salad, slice or section the fruit well ahead of time and leave the salad in a cool place for the flavors to develop and mingle. Brush sliced apples and pears with lemon juice so that they will not discolor. Apricots and peaches (and tomatoes) are easy to peel if you pour boiling water over them and leave for 1 minute.

Section oranges and grapefruit by cutting down on either side of the membranes to get skinless segments. For zesting, use a special zester if you have one; otherwise use a potato peeler or a small sharp knife, but since the strips of peel will be a little thicker than true zest, they can be simmered in water for 5-6 minutes to soften them.

Grapes can be halved and the seeds hooked out with a hairpin or paperclip. (See also page 223.)

Melons are usually halved or cut into segments, and pineapples can be halved lengthwise, when the flesh can be removed easily. You can also slice pineapples across and remove the peel and core.

Kiwi fruit look prettiest when sliced across. Figs can be halved or sliced. Lychees should be peeled. Persimmons look attractive when sliced across, or (if the kind that must be allowed to ripen) they can have their tops sliced off and the insides scooped out; passion fruit can have the same treatment.

Soft fruit need to be picked over carefully and any moldy specimens removed; hull, or trim them as necessary. This can be done a few hours in advance and they should then be kept cool.

SLICING FRUIT

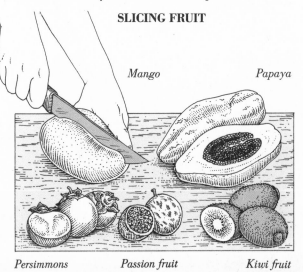

Mango *Papaya*

Persimmons *Passion fruit* *Kiwi fruit*

Papayas can be eaten like melons. They are particularly good with a sprinkling of lime juice. Guavas are usually peeled and the seeds discarded.

Mangoes are not the most accommodating of fruit to prepare. Remember that the pit is flat and oblong, and examine the fruit to ascertain how the pit is positioned. Cut down on either side and close to it: you will have two shallow "cheeks," which are easy to deal with—the flesh can be scooped out and chopped or diced; the flesh round the pit will also yield a few more cubes.

USING
It is hard to improve on the refreshing flavor of raw fruit, and most of the best ways of cooking it are simple so as to keep as much of the taste and goodness as possible. Apple crumble is a basic recipe, and can be varied by using different fruit. Stew peeled, sliced apples in a little water for 5 minutes, or until soft, with sugar, honey or dried dates to taste. Sprinkle with one of the crumble toppings suggested on page 206 and bake at 350°F for 40 minutes.

OILS, FATS, DAIRY PRODUCTS AND ALTERNATIVES

Oils

Oils are used mainly as a cooking medium for frying and sautéing, as a condiment and also sometimes as shortening in baking bread, cakes or biscuits. Fats are fundamentally the same as oils, but are solid at room temperature (see also page 229). They are a principal source of energy and, when unrefined, of nutrients since they contain vitamins and minerals, especially vitamin E. There are three main types of oil obtained from seeds, beans and nuts.

Cold-pressed oil is still extracted using the ancient method of hydraulic pressing. Much of the oil remains in the pulp, but that which is extracted is of high quality and full of flavor. Unfortunately true cold-pressed oil is very expensive.

Semi-refined oil requires greater pressure and higher temperatures. The extraction rate is higher, but the vitamin content suffers.

Refined oil, confusingly labeled "pure," is produced by a method called solvent extraction, which removes most of the goodness as well as bleaches and deodorizes the oil. Many of the vitamins are then added back artificially along with preservatives to prevent the oil from going rancid. This is generally the cheapest type available.

BUYING
It depends what you want your oil for: dressing salads, frying vegetables and grains, or baking. For eating raw, as a salad dressing, use cold-pressed or unrefined oil: it is tastier and is nutritionally the most valuable.

Olive oil has a rich flavor, but one that varies widely depending on the country of origin. "Virgin oil" means oil from the first pressing, the best quality of oil and recommended for salad dressings.

Safflower oil is pale in color, with a delicate flavor, and is high in linoleic acid and low in cholesterol (see page 229), which justifies its high price.

Sunflower oil is perhaps the best all-purpose oil. It is high in linoleic acid, second only to safflower oil but slightly cheaper.

Sesame oil does not go rancid quickly, and food containing it will not go stale, which makes it a good oil for baking.

Corn oil is cheap to produce; almost tasteless, it is popular as a cooking oil. It is also widely used as an ingredient in margarine.

Peanut oil is another very popular oil. It is particularly good for frying since it can be heated to very high temperatures without burning.

Soybean oil is also cheap and popular.

Walnut oil has a strong, nutty taste and is very expensive, so it is used chiefly for dressing salads.

STORING
Cold-pressed oils, apart from sesame oil, do not keep well. They are not heat-treated or otherwise stabilized and may go rancid, so buy comparatively small quantities (enough for a month or two) and keep in a cool, dark place. If it is too cold and the oil congeals, do not worry—the oil will liquefy very quickly when brought to room temperature. Semi-refined oils will keep up to three months.

Fats

Butter is high in saturated animal fats (see page 229) and as such should not be overindulged in, but current medical thinking is that animal fats do not have an adverse effect on cholesterol levels if eaten in conjunction with twice the amount of polyunsaturated fats (see page 229). Since most of us could do with reducing our total fat intake, this leaves a comparatively small amount of butter available, but still an appreciable one, and for its addicts there is no real substitute, either for taste or quality. So unless you need to keep to a low-cholesterol diet, use butter (preferably unsalted) for cooking whenever it will make a difference.

Margarine is often presented as the healthy alternative to butter. In fact many margarines are highly refined and contain additives. Soft margarines contain about 30 percent polyunsaturated fat. In hard margarines the original polyunsaturated fats have been hydrogenated, so they are not much better for you than butter from the point of view of fat content. If you do not eat any animal products, then you will want a vegetable-based margarine; if you do eat butter but want to cut down on cholesterol, an excellent compromise is to mix equal parts of butter and good-quality oil (safflower or sunflower). This will keep for several days in a covered container in the refrigerator.

Ghee is clarified butter, popular in cooking because any impurities have been removed and it can be heated to a much higher temperature than ordinary butter without burning. To make your own, simply melt butter and filter it through muslin. Vegetable ghee is also available. This is oil that has been hydrogenated to make it solid at room temperature. So has **vegetable shortening,** which is hard enough to grate. Neither will do anything to lower your cholesterol level, but they should not contain unwelcome additives.

Milk products

Milk provides protein, vitamins and minerals, particularly calcium and phosphorus, as well as the essential B_{12}, which is lacking in a strictly non-animal diet. However, it also contains saturated fat. Skim milk has had most of the fat content removed and in the process has also lost vitamins A, D and E (but not B). Goat's milk is often tolerated by those who cannot drink cow's milk.

Yogurt is a living food in which bacteria act on the milk sugars to produce lactic acid, a job normally done by our digestive juices. It is easy to assimilate, being in a sense predigested, and eating it regularly helps the digestion. Many commercial yogurts contain additives, preservatives and coloring agents, so it is worth making your own. Yogurt-makers are available, which maintain the milk at exactly the right temperature while it ferments, thus cutting out the guesswork and giving a consistent product.

MAKING YOGURT IN A VACUUM BOTTLE OR BOWL
Bring 2½ cups of milk to the boil, then let it cool to approximately 98.6°F, or until you can keep your finger in it comfortably for a count of ten. Add a generous tablespoon of good live plain yogurt, mix thoroughly, pour into a vacuum bottle and stopper tightly. If you have no vacuum bottle, pour the mixture into a bowl, cover it with a plate or plastic wrap, wrap it well in a towel or blanket and leave in a warm place, free of drafts. It will be ready after 8-12 hours (do not leave it too long or it may turn sour). Store in the refrigerator, where it will keep for up to a week. Save a tablespoon or so for a starter for your next batch. If your batches of yogurt become progressively weaker, you may need to buy fresh starter.

Buttermilk If properly made, this is another easily digestible milk product. It has a protein and mineral content similar to that of whole milk but has less vitamin A and hardly any fat.

Soybean products

Over more than a thousand years, the Chinese have evolved many ways of preparing the soybean. One is **soy milk,** an easily digested substitute for dairy milk and recommended to sufferers from allergies. To make it, soak soybeans in water overnight (one cup of beans will produce about 8 cups soy milk). In the morning, strain them and grind them to a meal with the same volume of water (each cup will have roughly doubled in size, so add two cups of water for each original cup of beans). Put this in a large pan and add the same quantity of water (another four cups for each original cup). Bring to the boil and boil for 20 minutes, uncovered. It should be at a fairly rapid boil to ensure that all toxins are destroyed;

you'll find that the water froths up considerably —sprinkling cold water on top will help to settle it. Strain before use. It makes an excellent substitute for milk in custards, puddings and milk shakes.

Tofu is soybean curd, another way of utilizing the soybean. Its high protein content (it is also rich in iron, calcium and B vitamins while containing few calories and saturated fats and no cholesterol) makes it a nutritious substitute not only for meat and fish but also for dairy products —the Chinese hardly use milk. In Chinese and Japanese cooking it is a most versatile ingredient, whether marinated, stir-fried or deep-fried, beaten into dressings and sauces, or added to soups, croquette mixes, even puddings. Surprisingly, this easily digested "miracle" food is taking time (rather as yogurt did) to become popular in the West. Perhaps our taste buds needs a while to get used to its consistency and flavor, or lack of it. It is bland, with a hint of an aftertaste that some might find sickly, others dry, due to the low-fat content —this can be counteracted by adding a little oil. It blends beautifully with other flavors, for example, in mixed vegetable dishes, binding them together and adding texture and consistency.

It is available in various forms. Silken tofu is the softest, a mixture of some curds and whey, with a consistency like firm gelatine. It is best for mashing or blending for dips, dressings and sauces. It is usually sold in cartons or packs, which will keep until the date stamped on them. Once opened, it should be used within two days.

Firm tofu is a heavily pressed version, with a dense texture like firm cheese; it can be cubed, sliced and marinated. When sold loose, you will usually find it refrigerated, submerged in deep buckets of water. It will keep fresh for a week, in water in the refrigerator, with the water changed daily. It is also sold in vacuum-sealed packages, which keep unopened for 3-4 weeks. Once opened, keep it under water and treat it just like loose tofu, otherwise it will develop a fresh skin. Soft tofu, with a texture between firm and silken, can be treated like firm tofu.

Tofu can be frozen, which drastically changes its look and texture. Squeeze out thawed tofu to get rid of excess water. It will then resemble a spongy latticework, with a chewy texture that soaks up sauces and marinades with ease.

Cheese

Strict vegetarians eat only cheese made with non-animal rennet. These can be found in health-food stores and include Cheddar and other hard cheeses, as well as the soft cheeses, such as cottage cheese, ricotta and feta, some varieties of which do not use rennet anyway. Although a good source of protein, cheese made from whole milk is high in fat and cholesterol, so use it sparingly and substitute low-fat cheese wherever possible.

Eggs

It is hard to ignore the horrors of battery farming. Vegetarians will prefer to buy humanely produced free-range eggs, which are generally considered to have a superior taste, although nutritionally there is little difference.

Eggs, particularly the yolks, are an excellent source of protein and contain all the essential amino acids. They are also high in fat and cholesterol, which is why many people are advised to limit their consumption of eggs.

STORAGE

Store eggs in a cool place. There is no need to keep them in the refrigerator. If the shell is soiled, wipe it with a dry cloth; washing removes the protective film. Avoid shiny shells since this is an indication of age. When cracked open, the yolk of a fresh egg remains firm and round.

SUBSTITUTES FOR EGGS

Eggs in cooking can be replaced in a number of ways. All the following variations will alter the texture and flavor to a certain extent but it's certainly worth experimenting if you want to cut down on cholesterol or have allergy problems.

Where eggs are used to enrich a dish such as pastry or bread dough, use soy flour instead. One to two tablespoons mixed with 2 cups flour give a richer pastry; ½ cup soy flour in 4 cups flour gives a rich bread dough. Soy flour mixed to a creamy consistency with water can be used instead of glaze. One to two tablespoons of soy flour can be added to savory bakes as a substitute for an egg, but will not bind the mixture in the same way. Tahini (see page 19) can be used instead of an egg as a binding agent. In a nut roast, for example, instead of 2 eggs, use 2 tablespoons tahini and add extra stock or water.

GARNISHES

Whether you're preparing everyday meals for yourself or your family or giving a dinner party, spend a little extra time ensuring that the food looks good. Even a sprinkling of chopped herbs or nuts makes such a difference to the look of the dish and takes only a moment to do. Carefully arranged julienne strips of carrot, fluted mushroom caps or melon balls, for example, take a little longer but are well worth the extra effort.

A garnish should contrast visually or in taste or texture—a sprinkling of bright color, crunchy seeds or nuts, or spicy poppy or sesame seeds. It should not overpower the dish or mask its flavor at all. Here are some suggestions.

Chopped herbs: in addition to parsley and chives, use mint, coriander, chervil, dill, fennel leaves, lemon balm, savory and tarragon. Basil leaves are traditionally torn rather than cut, since this is supposed to retain the flavor better. Watercress leaves are usually left whole.

Spices: pepper of all kinds—coarsely ground black peppercorns, crushed green peppercorns, chili powder, cayenne, paprika (you can be generous with this since it is so mild); capers; ground cinnamon—this goes particularly well with chocolate-flavored dishes.

Seeds: anise, caraway, celery, dill, fennel, mustard, poppy and sesame.

Nuts: almonds, walnuts, cashews and hazelnuts can be blanched (see page 209), chopped or left whole. Use the tip of a sharp knife to split almonds in half or flake them thinly. Put pistachios in boiling water for a minute with a pinch of baking soda to enhance their bright green color.

Chopped hard-boiled egg: use both yolk and white.

Vegetables and fruit: these offer a lot of scope for decoration. Some —onions, kiwi fruit, pineapple—can be simply sliced across, while others lend themselves to more elaborate treatment (see illustrations). Apples, mushrooms and celeriac discolor on peeling and need to be kept in water to which a little lemon juice or vinegar has been added, or else brushed with lemon juice.

CARROT

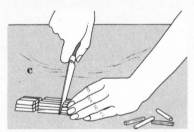

Carrots can be grated, diced or cut into julienne strips. For julienne strips, first trim off the top, base and sides to get a neat squared-off shape. Cut this into thin slices (*a*) and cut the slices lengthwise into matchstick-sized strips (*b*). These can then be cut across into short lengths (*c*) or diced. Other root vegetables—celeriac, kohlrabi, swedes, rutabagas—as well as peppers, zucchini, mushrooms, cucumber and celery, are also suitable for cutting into julienne strips or dicing.

CELERY

To make tassels from celery or scallions, cut into short pieces and slice these down into thin strips almost but not quite as far as the end (*top*). Put in cold water to open out. For celery crescents (*above*), cut slices across or on the diagonal.

CUCUMBER

A ridged effect with contrasting colors is achieved by scoring cucumber peel lengthwise with a fork.

GRAPES

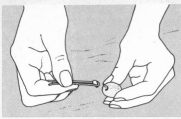

Using the rounded end of a hairpin makes it easy to remove grape pips.

LEMON

Grate the rind of lemon or oranges, or use a zester for professional-looking fine strips (*above*). Lemon quarters or wedges can be dusted with paprika.

For lemon or orange twists, make a cut to the center with a sharp knife (*a*). Hold the slice on either side of the cut and twist in opposite directions (*b*). Cucumber slices can be treated in the same way.

MELON

A special scoop is used to produce small balls of melon or cucumber.

MUSHROOMS

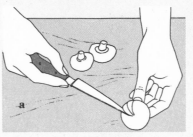

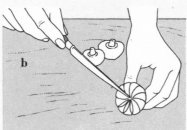

To flute mushroom caps, use the tip of a sharp knife, held at an angle to make a series of curved cuts from the center outward (*a*). Reversing the angle, make another series of cuts in the other direction (*b*). Remove the skin from between the cuts (*c*).

PEPPERS

Cut peppers downward or across into thin rings.

RADISHES

For radish roses, slice downward from the base almost to the stalk. Put them in cold water and they will open up.

TOMATOES

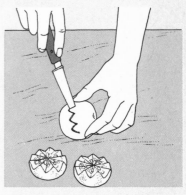

To cut tomato halves in a zigzag pattern, insert the point of a sharp knife into the center and make a series of V-shaped cuts all around the tomato until you can pull the halves apart. Leave cherry tomatoes whole.

EQUIPMENT

Vegetarian cookery doesn't really call for any special equipment, so don't feel you have to buy a whole new battery of cooking utensils. Here are a few suggestions and guidelines for buying and using a selection of the most useful kitchen tools.

Knives
Choose knives carefully, as they are going to be in constant use. An 8-inch chef's knife is a good all-purpose knife. With a long blade you can chop more ingredients at the same time, and, because of the depth of the blade, it is less likely to slip. A small serrated knife is ideal for slicing citrus fruits or tomatoes and a short-bladed paring knife is useful for peeling vegetables and fruits. Work with the ingredients close to the handle where the blade is

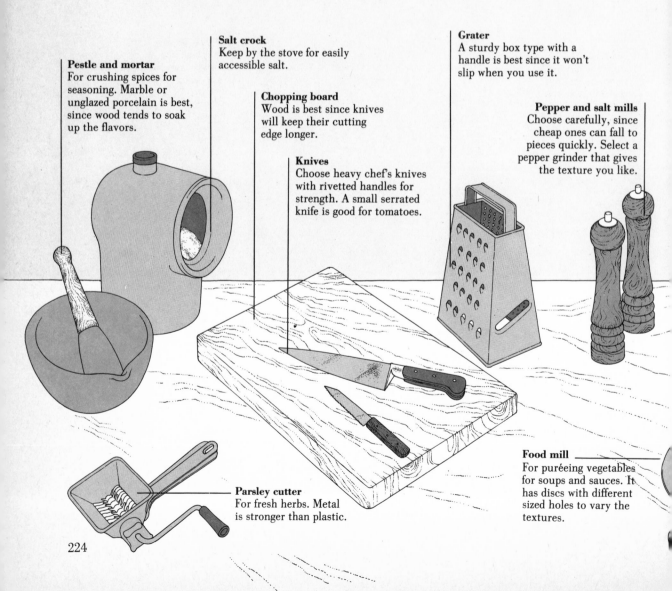

Pestle and mortar
For crushing spices for seasoning. Marble or unglazed porcelain is best, since wood tends to soak up the flavors.

Salt crock
Keep by the stove for easily accessible salt.

Chopping board
Wood is best since knives will keep their cutting edge longer.

Knives
Choose heavy chef's knives with rivetted handles for strength. A small serrated knife is good for tomatoes.

Grater
A sturdy box type with a handle is best since it won't slip when you use it.

Pepper and salt mills
Choose carefully, since cheap ones can fall to pieces quickly. Select a pepper grinder that gives the texture you like.

Parsley cutter
For fresh herbs. Metal is stronger than plastic.

Food mill
For puréeing vegetables for soups and sauces. It has discs with different sized holes to vary the textures.

deepest. Carbon steel knives sharpen more easily than stainless steel knives but the latter tend to keep their edges longer. Carbon steel also reacts with the acids in certain foods, especially fruits. It is very important to keep your knives sharp. If a blade is dull, it is more likely to slip and you will have to expend more effort.

Pans

A good pan should have a close-fitting lid and strong secure handles. Ideally both the handles and the knob on the lid should be made of a heat-resistant material.

I prefer a good-quality stainless steel pan and look for not only a thick, heavy bottom but thickness round the sides as well. Try not to scratch stainless steel, as small amounts of metallic compounds then dissolve into the food. If you burn a pan, cover the burn with plenty of salt and a little water, leave overnight and it should clean easily the next day. Enameled cast iron pans are also excellent. Glass, ceramic and thin enamel cookware can heat unevenly, causing

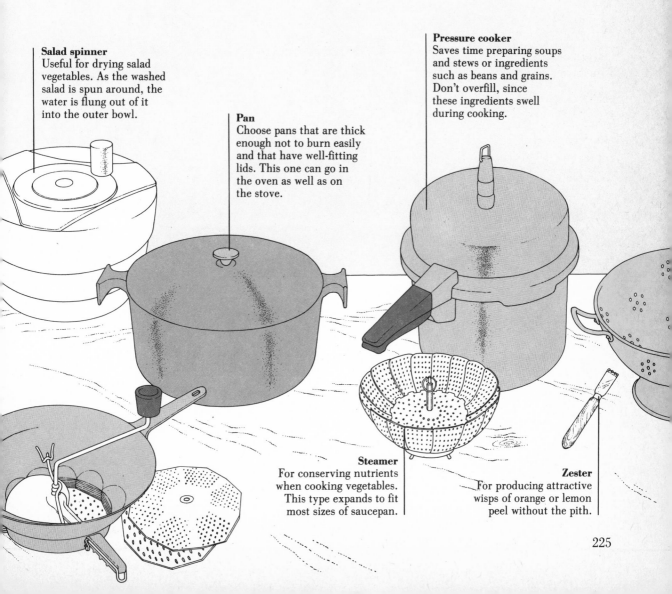

Salad spinner
Useful for drying salad vegetables. As the washed salad is spun around, the water is flung out of it into the outer bowl.

Pan
Choose pans that are thick enough not to burn easily and that have well-fitting lids. This one can go in the oven as well as on the stove.

Pressure cooker
Saves time preparing soups and stews or ingredients such as beans and grains. Don't overfill, since these ingredients swell during cooking.

Steamer
For conserving nutrients when cooking vegetables. This type expands to fit most sizes of saucepan.

Zester
For producing attractive wisps of orange or lemon peel without the pith.

225

foods to stick or burn. Aluminum oxides will dissolve into food cooked in aluminum utensils, and certain foods, such as eggs, will discolor. For cooking foods with the minimum of water or oil, it is advisable to use non-stick pans.

Other useful pans are a pressure cooker and a slow cooker. By trapping the steam and increasing the pressure, a pressure cooker raises the temperature to above the boiling point of water, so the food cooks more quickly. A slow cooker is excellent for casseroles, soups, dried fruit and grains.

Electrical equipment

A blender is essential if you want to avoid hours of chopping and sieving. It blends liquids better and faster than a food processor. In addition it is very useful to have a food processor or mixer. Both are available with a variety of attachments for mincing, grating, shredding, making pastry or dough. One advantage of the shredding gadgets on a mixer is that you can continue shredding until you have enough without having to stop from time to time to empty the container.

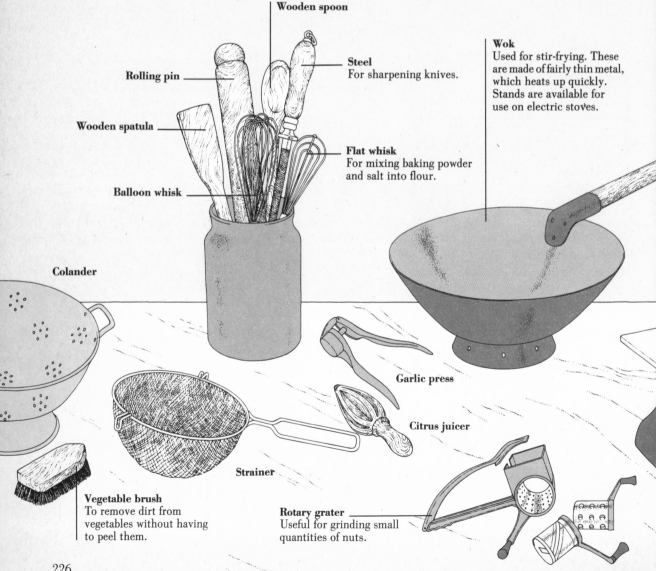

Wooden spoon

Rolling pin

Wooden spatula

Balloon whisk

Steel
For sharpening knives.

Flat whisk
For mixing baking powder and salt into flour.

Wok
Used for stir-frying. These are made of fairly thin metal, which heats up quickly. Stands are available for use on electric stoves.

Colander

Garlic press

Citrus juicer

Strainer

Vegetable brush
To remove dirt from vegetables without having to peel them.

Rotary grater
Useful for grinding small quantities of nuts.

With a food processor, choose one that grates, shreds and slices as well as mixes and purées. Don't rely on it to chop everything for you though, because it is just as important to have a variety of shapes and sizes in a dish as it is to vary texture. Processors cannot grind small quantities as finely as a nut grinder.

Other useful items
There are many other tools that are useful to have in your kitchen, for example a pestle and mortar for grinding spices (see pages 224), a nut mill or small rotary grater for grinding small quantities of nuts or cheese finely, a garlic press and a citrus juicer.

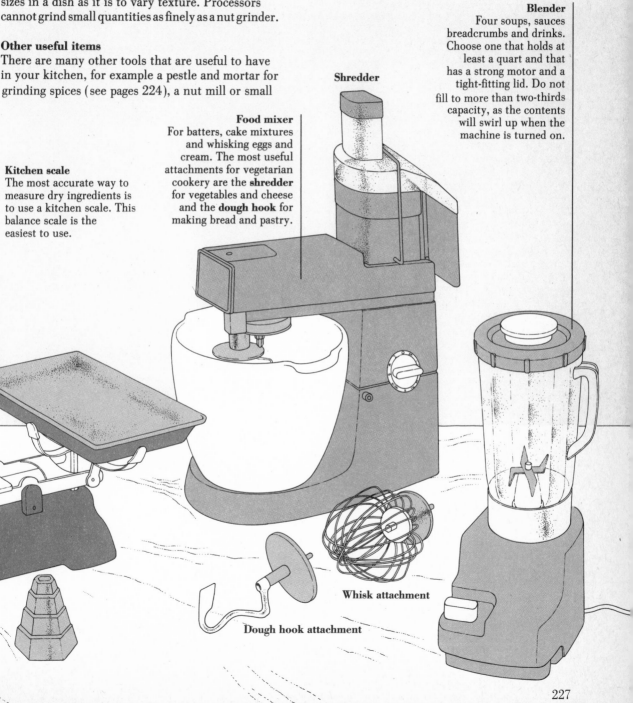

Shredder

Food mixer
For batters, cake mixtures and whisking eggs and cream. The most useful attachments for vegetarian cookery are the **shredder** for vegetables and cheese and the **dough hook** for making bread and pastry.

Kitchen scale
The most accurate way to measure dry ingredients is to use a kitchen scale. This balance scale is the easiest to use.

Blender
Four soups, sauces breadcrumbs and drinks. Choose one that holds at least a quart and that has a strong motor and a tight-fitting lid. Do not fill to more than two-thirds capacity, as the contents will swirl up when the machine is turned on.

Whisk attachment

Dough hook attachment

227

DAILY NUTRITIONAL REQUIREMENTS

Proteins, fats, carbohydrates, vitamins and minerals are all essential to life. This part of the book explains why they are so necessary, which foods supply them (including complementary proteins) and which are the best sources, and provides the recommended daily allowance of each one. Also included is a section describing the nutritional profiles of some of the commoner foods.

A common fear about giving up meat and fish it that it will lead to an unbalanced diet, particularly with regard to protein. In fact, a vegetarian diet is likely to supply more than adequate amounts of protein, for both adults and children, even if dairy products are not eaten.

A whole-food diet is of course not necessarily the same as a vegetarian one, but the two are often combined. Unrefined cereals, unprocessed beans and lentils and untreated dried fruits and nuts are far better than canned, bottled and packaged foods with their hidden salt, sugar and additive content. A balanced whole-food vegetarian diet embodies the principles of healthy eating: plenty of protein, fiber, vitamins and minerals while cutting down on fat, sugar and salt.

What we need for health are the nutrients (proteins, fats, carbohydrates, vitamins and minerals), as well as water and fiber —these are not nutrients as such, but without them metabolism cannot take place, nutrients are not digested and absorbed, and waste matter is not eliminated.

Protein

We needs protein to build new cells and repair damaged tissues. The importance of the protein in the food we eat is determined by the percentage of that protein that can be used by the body. This in turn depends on the pattern of amino acids present. Amino acids are the constituents of protein: about half of them must be supplied in our food, while the rest can be synthesized from these basic nine, which are known as essential amino acids. They

can be fully utilized only if present in a particular pattern or proportion, and if one of them is in short supply, the others are affected proportionately. The three most likely to be in short supply, especially in a vegetarian diet, are lysine, methionine and tryptophan. It is important therefore to try to ensure that the intake of these three is well balanced.

Some foods have a natural amino acid pattern close to the ideal, and their protein is therefore almost fully used by the body. Milk, eggs, fish, cheese and meat are good examples. Such foods are known as complete proteins and, in the past, misleadingly, as first class proteins. Since, apart from soybeans; most plant proteins are incomplete, the implication has been that a vegetarian diet must be inferior.

This might be so if we were to get our vegetable protein from a single source. Our natural instinct, however, is to vary our diet, which both makes it more palatable and is more likely to provide a complete range of protein. In India, for example, rice and lentils are generally eaten together. Since rice, like most grains, is low in lysine but high in methionine, while lentils, like most legumes, are the other way round, they complement each other to provide a complete protein, which can be superior to protein from a single source, such as meat. The diagram (right) shows which foods can be eaten together to provide high-quality protein. Many are popular combinations such as beans on toast, cereal with milk, tortillas with refried beans, pasta with beans, hummus (chick peas with sesame seeds), corn and lima beans, or bread and cheese.

COMPLEMENTARY PROTEINS

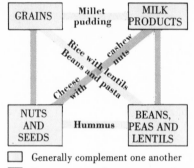

☐ Generally complement one another
▨ Sometimes complement one another

GOOD SOURCES OF PROTEIN	
U.S. recommended daily allowance: 56 g (men); 46 g (women)	
	g per 100 g
Yeast extract	39.7
*Soy flour	36.8
*Parmesan	35.1
Wheat-germ	26.5
*Cheddar & similar cheeses	26.0
Peanuts	24.3
*Brie & similar cheeses	22.8
Black walnuts	20.5
Pistachio nuts	19.3
Almonds	16.9
Bran	14.1
*Cottage cheese	13.6
Whole-wheat flour	13.2
Oatmeal	12.4
*Eggs	12.3
Brazil nuts	12.0
Rye flour	8.2
Chick peas (cooked)	8.0
Lentils (cooked)	7.6
*Complete proteins.	

Fats

Although fats are necessary to health, we need only small amounts and are far more likely to eat more than we need, especially in a diet rich in hidden fats in meat, cheese, milk and many convenience foods. On a vegetarian diet the staple foods of grains, beans, peas and lentils are all low in fat.

Fats may be saturated or unsaturated. The former are found mainly in animal products, including butter, cream and cheese, which also contain cholesterol, a fatlike substance that (although necessary for health) can, if present to excess in the blood, build up a deposit on the artery walls and eventually clog them. Although research has not yet supplied the details, it is generally agreed that a high level of blood cholesterol is linked with susceptibility to heart disease, and saturated fats should therefore be eaten in moderation.

Monounsaturated fats, found in olive oil and other vegetable oils, seem not to affect the blood cholesterol level, while polyunsaturated fats, such as linoleic acid, also found in vegetable oils, appear to lower it. In the Mediterranean, where oil consumption is high, incidence of heart disease is low.

Remember, though, that when oils or liquid fats are hydrogenated in order to make them solid (for example vegetable shortening, vegetable ghee), the oils have been artificially saturated and behave just like saturated fats.

Carbohydrates

Our main source of energy is provided by carbohydrates occurring as sugars and starches (in fruits, milk, grains, legumes and vegetables, as well as the more obvious sugar, honey and syrup). Refined carbohydrates, for example, cakes and biscuits containing white flour and sugar, provide a lot of calories but few nutrients, and their consumption has been linked with not only tooth decay but also heart disease, high blood pressure and diabetes. Again, a whole-food and vegetarian diet will help to guard against these diseases and is also rich in fiber, another form of carbohydrate, which, although indigestible is important to our diet, since it is essential for the elimination of toxins.

FATTY ACIDS
g per 100 g

VEGETABLE OILS	SATURATED	MONO-UNSATURATED	POLY-UNSATURATED
Corn	17.2	30.7	51.6
Olive	14.7	73.0	11.7
Peanut	19.7	50.1	29.8
Safflower	10.7	13.2	75.5
Soybean	14.7	25.4	59.4
Sunflower	13.7	33.3	52.3

NUTS	SATURATED	MONO-UNSATURATED	POLY-UNSATURATED
Almonds	8.3	71.6	19.6
Brazil nuts	26.7	34.3	39.0
Chestnuts	18.2	39.2	41.9
Hazelnuts	7.5	81.1	10.9
Coconut	83.0	7.0	1.8
Peanuts	15.2	50.1	29.8
Walnuts, English	11.4	16.3	71.4

GOOD SOURCES OF FIBER

	g per 100 g
Bran	44.0
Dried apricots	24.0
Desiccated coconut	23.5
Dried figs	18.5
Prunes	16.1
Dried peaches	14.3
Almonds	14.3
Soy flour	11.9
Whole-wheat flour	9.6
Parsley	9.1
Brazil nuts	9.0
Dates	8.7
Whole-wheat bread	8.5
Peanuts	8.1
Haricot beans (cooked)	7.4
Raspberries	7.4
Oatmeal	7.0

Vitamins

Essential for growth, tissue repair and regulation of the metabolism, most vitamins cannot be made in the body, so it is important to ensure that we get enough in our food.

VITAMIN A (retinol) Needed for healthy skin and mucous membranes, and for vision in dim light. Found as such only in animal products, but can be made in the body from a substance called carotene, present in many brightly colored orange or green vegetables ($6\mu g$ carotene $= 1\ \mu g$ retinol or retinol equivalent). If massive doses are taken over a period, excess can build up to toxic levels, but this is unlikely.

Deficiency Can cause eye fatigue or irritation and night blindness in the early stages, but quickly corrected by prompt treatment.

GOOD SOURCES OF VITAMIN A U.S. recommended daily allowance: 5,000 International units	retinol equivalents in μg per 100 g
Dandelion greens	2,333
Sorrel	2,150
Carrots	2,000
Parsley	1,166
Spinach (cooked)	1,000
*Butter	985
Sweet potatoes (cooked)	667
Dried apricots	600
Watercress	500
Broccoli (cooked)	417
*Cheddar & similar cheeses	410
Chicory and escarole	334
Melon (cantaloupe)	334
Mango	200
*Eggs	140
*Milk	40
*Contains retinol	

B VITAMINS Usually treated as a group, since tend to occur together. Main functions: to convert food into energy and ensure proper formation of red blood cells. Work best when all present in a balanced ratio; excess of one can create deficiency of others. If taking a supplement of one in particular, ensure adequate supplies of the others. Try to take as food rather than tablets.

VITAMIN B$_1$ (thiamine) Needed chiefly to metabolize carbohydrates: the more carbohydrates you eat, the more B$_1$ you need. Easily lost through cooking and storage.

Deficiency If other B vitamins in short supply and carbohydrate intake high, results in beri-beri.

VITAMIN B$_2$ (riboflavin) Easily destroyed by light. Milk, a primary source, can lose up to 70 percent of B$_2$ content if left in direct sunlight for two hours.

Deficiency Common, especially in people who do not drink milk. Can show itself as bloodshot eyes and sore or cracked lips.

VITAMIN B$_3$ (niacin or nicotinic acid) Can be converted in the body from the amino acid tryptophan, found chiefly in milk and eggs.

Deficiency Can cause irritability, nervousness and eventually severe depression and pellagra, a potentially fatal skin disease associated with mental problems.

VITAMIN B$_6$ (pryidoxine) Needed in particular by women who are pregnant, on oral contraceptives or suffering from pre-menstrual tension. High alcohol consumption also increases need. Works best in conjunction with B$_2$ and magnesium. Easily destroyed by heat and during food processing.

Deficiency Symptoms include anemia, fatigue, depression, nervous disorders and migraine.

VITAMIN B$_{12}$ Found mainly in animal products, although sea vegetables contain traces. Unless eggs and dairy products are eaten, a supplement must be taken. Easily destroyed by light and heat.

Deficiency Can lead to paralysis; deficiency of both B$_{12}$ and folic acid (see below) results in pernicious anemia.

FOLIC ACID Another B vitamin, found, as name suggests, in leaves. If plenty of raw green leafy salads are eaten, deficiency unlikely. Vegetables lose much of their folic acid in cooking.

Deficiency Found in some women who are pregnant or on oral contraceptives; leads to large-cell anemia, involving exhaustion and depression. May lead to neural tube defects, such as spina bifida in fetus.

VITAMIN C (ascorbic acid) Needed to maintain connective tissue protecting and supporting all body cells, and for proper absorption of iron. Important in preventing disease and aiding recovery from illness, especially after an operation. Large amounts required by people under stress or taking drugs, including antibiotics, tranquilizers, alcohol, nicotine and coffee. Not known to be toxic even in massive doses, since excess will be eliminated in urine.

Quickly and easily lost in cooking, whenever cut surfaces are exposed to air, and destroyed by heat.

Deficiency and consequent weakening of connective tissue leads to bleeding, especially in gums, lowers resistance to infection and slows down healing. Deficiency likely unless a fair amount of fruits and vegetables is eaten raw and those that are cooked are treated carefully.

GOOD SOURCES OF VITAMIN B₁

U.S. recommended daily allowance: 1.5 mg

	mg per 100 g
Yeast extract	3.10
Wheat germ	1.45
Brazil nuts	1.00
Peanuts	0.90
Bran	0.89
Soy flour	0.75
Millet	0.73
Oatmeal	0.50
Whole-wheat flour	0.46
Rye flour	0.40
Hazelnuts	0.40
English walnuts	0.30
Whole-wheat bread	0.26
Peas (cooked)	0.25

GOOD SOURCES OF VITAMIN B₃

U.S. recommended daily allowance: 20 mg

	mg per 100 g
Yeast extract	58.0
Bran	29.6
Peanuts	16.0
Yeast	11.0
Wheat germ	5.8
Whole-wheat flour	5.6
Dried peaches	5.3
Mushrooms	4.0
Wholewheat bread	3.9
Dried apricots	3.0
Fava beans (cooked)	3.0
Millet	2.3
Soy flour	2.0
Dates	2.0

GOOD SOURCES OF VITAMIN B₁₂

U.S. recommended daily allowance: 6 μg

	μg per 100 g
Egg yolk	4.9
Eggs	1.7
Cheddar & similar cheeses	1.5
Parmesan	1.5
Brie & similar cheeses	1.2
Yeast extract	0.5
Cottage cheese	0.5
Milk	0.3
Light cream	0.2
Heavy cream	0.1
Yogurt	trace
Butter	trace
Sea vegetables	trace

GOOD SOURCES OF VITAMIN B₂

U.S. recommended daily allowance: 1.7 mg

	mg per 100 g
Almonds	0.92
Wheat germ	0.61
Brie & similar cheeses	0.60
Cheddar & similar cheeses	0.50
Parmesan	0.50
Eggs	0.47
Mushrooms	0.40
Millet	0.38
Bran	0.36
Soy flour	0.31
Parsley	0.30
Yogurt	0.26
Dandelion greens	0.26
Rye flour	0.22
Milk	0.20
Broccoli (cooked)	0.20

GOOD SOURCES OF VITAMIN B₆

U.S. recommended daily allowance: 2.0 mg

	mg per 100 g
Bran	1.38
Yeast extract	1.30
Wheat germ	0.93
English walnuts	0.73
Soy flour	0.57
Hazelnuts	0.55
Bananas	0.51
Whole-wheat flour	0.50
Peanuts	0.50
Avocado pear	0.42
Rye flour	0.35
Currants, etc.	0.30
Brussels sprouts (raw)	0.28
Prunes	0.24
Cauliflower (raw)	0.20
Brie & similar cheeses	0.20

GOOD SOURCES OF FOLIC ACID

U.S. recommended daily allowance: 0.04 mg

	mg per 100 g
Yeast	1,250
Yeast extract	1,010
Wheat germ	330
Chicory and escarole	330
Bran	260
Spinach (cooked)	140
Sweet potatoes (cooked)	140
Broccoli (cooked)	110
Peanuts	110
Brussels sprouts (raw)	110
Almonds	96
Cabbage (raw)	90
Rye flour	78
Peas (cooked)	78
Hazelnuts	72
Avocado pear	66

GOOD SOURCES OF VITAMIN C
U.S. recommended daily allowance: 60 mg

	mg per 100 g
Red pepper	204
Black currants	200
Parsley	150
Sorrel	119
Green pepper	100
Lemons	80
Watercress	60
Cabbage (raw)	60
Strawberries	60
Cauliflower (raw)	60
Oranges	50
Grapefruit	40
Lychees	40
Broccoli (cooked)	34
Mangoes	30
Radishes	25
Raspberries	25
Spinach (cooked)	25

VITAMIN D Needed for absorption of calcium and phosphorus. Formed by action of sunlight on oils in skin: most people who get a reasonable amount of sun need little, if any, extra in their diet, except for children and pregnant or lactating women.

Best dietary sources are dairy products. Free-range eggs provide a little and margarine is often fortified with it. Can be stored in liver, so excess possible but most unlikely when the vitamin has been produced by natural means.

Deficiency Can cause rickets and weakened or porous bones.

VITAMIN E Needed for formation and maintenance of body cells; helps wounds to heal without formation of scar tissue; thought to have rejuvenating effect. Widely available

in foods, chiefly cold-pressed vegetable oils, cereal products (wheat germ and bread made from stone-ground whole-wheat flour), eggs and nuts.

Deficiency Rare, but can cause fatigue and anemia.

VITAMIN K Helps blood to clot. Can by synthesized in body. Widely available in food (in vegetables, cereals, sea vegetables).

Deficiency Unlikely.

Minerals

Like vitamins, needed to ensure that the body functions properly and for growth and repair of cells. Some (chiefly calcium, iron, potassium and magnesium) needed in appreciable quantities; others (zinc and iodine the most important) needed only in very small amounts and are known as trace elements.

CALCIUM Needed for healthy bones, teeth and nerves. Vitamin D must also be present.

Deficiency Can lead to nervous exhaustion, irritability, leg cramps and insomnia (hence efficacy of hot milk nightcap). In children can mean stunted growth and rickets.

IRON Needed to carry oxygen around body and for formation of red blood corpuscles. Absorption greatly helped by vitamin C.

Deficiency Leads to fatigue and anemia; can arise after loss of blood and iron supplements may be necessary—since these tend to destroy vitamin E, take supplement of this too.

GOOD SOURCES OF CALCIUM
U.S. recommended daily allowance: 1 g

	mg per 100 g
Parmesan	1,220
Cheddar & similar cheeses	800
Spinach (cooked)	600
Brie & similar cheeses	380
Parsley	330
Dried figs	280
Almonds	250
Watercress	220
Soy flour	210
Brazil nuts	180
Yogurt	180
Egg yolk	130
Skim milk	130
Goat's milk	130
Cow's milk	120
Lemons	110

GOOD SOURCES OF IRON
U.S. recommended daily allowance: 18 mg

	mg per 100 g
Blackstrap molasses	16.1
Bran	12.9
Wheat germ	10.0
Parsley	8.0
Soy flour	6.9
Dried peaches	6.8
Millet	6.8
Egg yolk	6.1
Yeast	5.0
Dried figs	4.2
Oatmeal	4.1
Dried apricots	4.1
Spinach (cooked)	4.0
Whole-wheat flour	4.0
Yeast extract	3.7

SODIUM and **POTASSIUM** Often treated together, since balance between them is important. Act together to regulate body fluids and amount of water retained.

Sodium deficiency Rarely seen except in cases involving salt loss through perspiration, such as heatstroke. For most people sodium is adequately supplied even without table salt. Excess more common, leading to high blood pressure with attendant risk of stroke and heart attack; also prevents absorption of potassium in the body.

Potassium deficiency Serious, can lead to heart attack. Associated with high sodium levels and hypoglycemia (low blood sugar). Although potassium found in wide range of foods, deficiency can occur easily when vegetables overcooked, little raw fruit eaten and diet high in salt and refined foods.

GOOD SOURCES OF POTASSIUM

U.S. recommended daily allowance: not established (suggested, 3,000 mg)

	mg per 100 g
Blackstrap molasses	2,927
Yeast extract	2,600
Dried apricots	1,880
Soy flour	1,660
Bran	1,160
Dried peaches	1,100
Parsley	1,080
Dried figs	1,010
Wheat germ	1,000
Golden raisins	860
Prunes	860
Almonds	860
Dark raisins	860
Brazil nuts	760

MAGNESIUM Needed to retain potassium in cells and for proper functioning of vitamin B_6. Should be taken in proportion to calcium (about half as much magnesium as calcium).

Deficiency Common in diets rich in refined foods, soft drinks, alcohol and confectioneries. Symptoms can be muscle cramps (often causing insomnia), nervous depression and convulsions. Excess, causing lethargy, less common but can occur if too many indigestion remedies containing magnesium taken.

GOOD SOURCES OF MAGNESIUM

U.S. recommended daily allowance: 400 mg

	mg per 100 g
Bran	520
Brazil nuts	410
Wheat germ	300
Almonds	260
Soy flour	240
Black walnuts	190
Peanuts	180
Millet	162
Whole-wheat flour	140
English walnuts	130
Oatmeal	110
Whole-wheat bread	93
Chick peas (cooked)	67
Haricot beans (cooked)	65
Dried apricots	65
Spinach (cooked)	59

PHOSPHORUS Vital for bones and teeth. If more than twice as much phosphorus as calcium taken, calcium and zinc deficiency can arise.

Deficiency Virtually unknown as phosphorus widely available. Excess more dangerous.

ZINC Exact role not yet fully understood. Although present in many foods, not always fully absorbed, especially if phytic acid present (as in whole grains). Zinc content of crops depends largely on soil—chemical fertilizers can neutralize zinc in soil. As far as is known, even the prolonged ingestion of supplements is non-toxic.

Deficiency Can cause infertility and stunting and slow down healing of wounds.

GOOD SOURCES OF ZINC

U.S. recommended daily allowance: 15 mg

	mg per 100 g
Bran	16.2
Brazil nuts	4.2
Parmesan	4.0
Cheddar & similar cheeses	4.0
Almonds	3.1
Peanuts	3.0
English walnuts	3.0
Whole-wheat flour	3.0
Oatmeal	3.0
Brie & similar cheeses	3.0
Rye flour	2.8
Hazelnuts	2.4
Whole-wheat bread	2.0

IODINE Essential for correct functioning of thyroid. Only minute quantities needed. Most reliable sources are sea vegetables. Land vegetables (particularly onions and watercress) will contain iodine if present in soil. Nuts and unrefined oils also contain iodine.

Deficiency Even slight deficiency can lead to thyroid disease and high level of blood cholesterol and affect mental and physical development.

FOOD PROFILES

Listed below are some of the most common ingredients of the vegetarian kitchen pantry. Their protein, carbohydrate, fiber and fat contents are given in grams per 100 grams. Vitamins and minerals are listed where significant quantities occur.

SYMBOLS

Fo : Folic acid
Fe : Iron
Ca : Calcium
Na : Sodium
K : Potassium

Mg : Magnesium
P : Phosphorus
Zn : Zinc
Tr : Trace only
— : No data

Grains

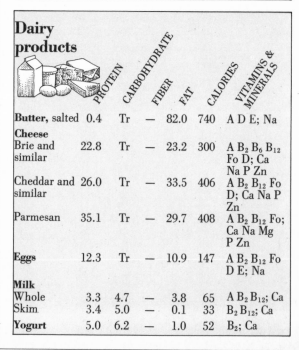

	PROTEIN	CARBOHYDRATE	FIBER	FAT	CALORIES	VITAMINS & MINERALS
Bran	14.1	26.8	44.0	5.5	206	$B_1 B_2 B_3 B_6$ Fo E; Ca Fe K Mg P Zn
Whole-wheat bread	8.8	41.8	8.5	2.7	216	$B_1 B_3$ Fo; Fe Na Mg P Zn
Whole-wheat flour	13.2	65.8	9.6	2.0	318	$B_1 B_3 B_6$ Fo E; Fe Mg P Zn
Millet	9.9	72.9	3.2	2.9	327	$B_1 B_2 B_3$; Fe K Mg P
Oatmeal	12.4	72.8	7.0	8.7	401	$B_1 B_3$ Fo; Fe Mg P Zn
Brown rice (cooked)	2.5	25.5	0.3	0.6	119	B_3; Na
Rye flour	8.2	75.9	—	2.0	335	$B_1 B_2 B_3 B_6$ Fo; Fe K Mg P Zn
Wheat germ	26.5	44.7	—	8.1	347	$B_1 B_2 B_3 B_6$ Fo E; Fe K Mg P

Beans and lentils

	PROTEIN	CARBOHYDRATE	FIBER	FAT	CALORIES	VITAMINS & MINERALS
Broad beans	4.1	7.1	4.2	0.6	48	B_3
Butter beans	7.1	17.1	5.1	0.3	95	K Zn
Haricot beans	6.6	16.6	7.4	0.5	93	Fe Mg Zn
Red kidney beans	7.8	21.4	—	0.5	118	Fe
Lentils	7.6	17.0	3.7	0.5	99	B_6; Fe
Soy flour	36.8	23.5	11.9	23.5	447	$B_1 B_2 B_3 B_6$; Ca Fe K Mg P

Nuts

	PROTEIN	CARBOHYDRATE	FIBER	FAT	CALORIES	VITAMINS & MINERALS
Almonds	16.9	4.3	14.3	53.5	565	$B_1 B_2 B_3$ Fo E; Ca Fe K Mg P Zn
Brazil nuts	12.0	4.1	9.0	61.5	619	$B_1 B_3 B_6$ E; Ca Fe K Mg P Zn
Hazelnuts	7.6	6.8	6.1	36.0	380	$B_1 B_6$ Fo E; Mg P Zn
Peanuts	24.3	8.6	8.1	49.0	570	$B_1 B_3 B_6$ Fo E; K Mg P Zn
Walnuts, English	10.6	5.0	5.2	51.5	525	$B_1 B_3 B_6$ Fo; Fe K Mg P Zn

Dairy products

	PROTEIN	CARBOHYDRATE	FIBER	FAT	CALORIES	VITAMINS & MINERALS
Butter, salted	0.4	Tr	—	82.0	740	A D E; Na
Cheese						
Brie and similar	22.8	Tr	—	23.2	300	$A B_2 B_6 B_{12}$ Fo D; Ca Na P Zn
Cheddar and similar	26.0	Tr	—	33.5	406	$A B_2 B_{12}$ Fo D; Ca Na P Zn
Parmesan	35.1	Tr	—	29.7	408	$A B_2 B_{12}$ Fo; Ca Na Mg P Zn
Eggs	12.3	Tr	—	10.9	147	$A B_2 B_{12}$ Fo D E; Na
Milk						
Whole	3.3	4.7	—	3.8	65	$A B_2 B_{12}$; Ca
Skim	3.4	5.0	—	0.1	33	$B_2 B_{12}$; Ca
Yogurt	5.0	6.2	—	1.0	52	B_2; Ca

Vegetables

	PROTEIN	CARBOHYDRATE	FIBER	FAT	CALORIES	VITAMINS & MINERALS
Artichoke, globe (cooked)	1.1	2.7	—	Tr	15	Fo
Asparagus (cooked)	3.4	1.1	1.5	Tr	18	A Fo E
Avocado pear	4.2	1.8	2.0	22.2	223	B_6 Fo E
Beet (cooked)	1.8	9.9	2.5	Tr	44	Fo; Na
Broccoli (cooked)	3.1	1.6	4.1	Tr	18	A B_2 Fo C
Brussels sprouts (cooked)	2.8	1.7	2.9	Tr	18	A B_6 Fo C
Cabbage, Savoy (raw)	3.3	3.3	3.1	Tr	26	A B_6 Fo C
Carrots (raw)	0.7	5.4	2.9	Tr	23	A B_6; Na
Cauliflower	1.6	0.8	1.8	Tr	9	B_3 Fo C
Celery	0.9	1.3	4.9	Tr	8	Na
Cucumber	0.6	1.8	0.4	0.1	10	
Leeks (cooked)	1.8	4.6	3.9	Tr	24	B_6; Fe
Lettuce	1.0	1.2	1.5	0.4	12	A Fo
Mushrooms	1.8	0	2.5	0.6	13	B_2 B_3 Fo; K
Mustard & Cress	1.6	0.9	3.7	Tr	10	A C
Onions	0.9	5.2	1.3	Tr	23	
Parsley	5.2	Tr	9.1	Tr	21	A B_2 B_6 C; Ca Fe K
Peas (cooked)	5.0	7.7	5.2	0.4	52	A B_1 B_3 Fo
Peppers, green	0.9	2.2	0.9	0.4	15	A B_6 C
Potatoes (baked)	2.6	25.0	2.5	0.1	105	B_3 B_6
Potatoes (boiled)	1.4	19.7	1.0	0.1	80	B_6
Snap beans (cooked)	0.8	1.1	3.2	Tr	7	A Fo
Spinach (cooked)	5.1	1.4	6.3	0.5	30	A B_2 B_6 Fo C E; Ca Fe Na K Mg
Sweet Potatoes (cooked)	1.1	20.1	2.3	0.6	85	A B_6 Fo E
Tomatoes	0.9	2.8	1.5	Tr	14	Fo C
Watercress	2.9	0.7	3.3	Tr	14	A Fo C; Ca Na
Zucchini (cooked)	1.0	2.5	0.6	0.1	12	

Fruit

	PROTEIN	CARBOHYDRATE	FIBER	FAT	CALORIES	VITAMINS & MINERALS
Apples	0.3	11.9	2.0	Tr	46	
Bananas	1.1	19.2	3.4	0.3	79	B_6 Fo
Cherries	0.6	11.9	1.7	Tr	47	
Figs	1.3	9.5	2.5	Tr	41	A
Grapes, black	0.6	15.5	0.4	Tr	61	
Grapefruit	0.6	5.3	0.6	Tr	22	C
Lemons	0.8	3.2	5.2	Tr	15	C; Ca
Mangoes	0.5	15.3	1.5	Tr	59	A C
Melon, cantaloupe	1.0	5.3	1.0	Tr	24	A Fo
Oranges	0.8	8.5	2.0	Tr	35	C Fo
Peaches	0.6	9.1	1.4	Tr	37	A B_3
Pears	0.3	10.6	2.3	Tr	41	
Plums	0.6	9.6	2.1	Tr	38	B_3
Pineapple	0.5	11.6	1.2	Tr	46	C
Raspberries	0.9	5.6	7.4	Tr	25	C
Strawberries	0.6	6.2	2.2	Tr	26	Fo C
Watermelon	0.4	5.3	—	Tr	21	

Dried fruit

	PROTEIN	CARBOHYDRATE	FIBER	FAT	CALORIES	VITAMINS & MINERALS
Apricots	4.8	43.4	24.0	Tr	182	A B_2 B_3 B_6; Ca Fe Na K Mg
Currants	1.7	63.1	6.5	Tr	243	B_6; K
Dates	2.0	63.9	8.7	Tr	248	B_3 B_6 Fo; Mg
Figs	3.6	52.9	18.5	Tr	213	B_3 B_6; Ca Fe Na K Mg
Peaches	3.4	53.0	14.3	Tr	212	A B_2 B_3; Fe K
Prunes	2.4	40.3	16.1	Tr	161	A B_2 B_3 B_6; K
Raisins, dark	1.1	64.4	6.8	Tr	246	B_6; Na K Mg
Raisins, golden	1.8	64.7	7.0	Tr	250	B_6; Na K

ACKNOWLEDGMENTS

Author's acknowledgment
I would like to thank my friends and staff at both "Sarah Brown's," Scarborough, England, and the Vegetarian Society U.K. for all their help with this book. Grateful thanks too to Jill Dunwoody for additional information and research on foods and nutrients; Jane O'Brien for preparing and testing recipes; Sue Buckley for typing the original draft; Joanne Edmonds of Show Space, York; and Pauline Ashley, Chris Glazebrook, Barry Hampshire, David Sulkin and Fiona Elliott for their encouragement and support.
Sarah Brown

Dorling Kindersley would like to thank the following for their cooperation and help in the production of this book: Rachel Grenfell, Jemima Dunne and Joanna Godfrey Wood for their editorial assistance; Fred and Kathie Gill for proof reading; Anne Fisher for her design assistance; Sloane Square Tiles, The Cocktail Shop, The Reject China Shop, The Craftsmen Potters Association, Covent Garden Kitchen Supplies, David Mellor, The Copper Shop, Divertimenti and The Swiss Centre for supplying photographic props; Cornucopia of Ealing and Petty Wood and Co for supplying ingredients and for their helpful

advice; Andy Butler, assistant to Philip Dowell; Hilary and Richard Bird for the index; and Roger Hillier, Jean Coombes and Anne Burnham.

Photography
Philip Dowell
Peter Myers (pages 112, 113, 117, 119, 121, 162, 165 and 171)

Food for photography prepared by Valerie Barrett (except page 119)

Designer
Carolyn Russell (except pages 119, 162, 165 and 171)

Illustrators
Rodney Shackell
Russell Barnett
Lindsay Blow

Typesetting
Modern Text Typesetting

Reproduction
A. Mondadori, Verona

The information in the nutritional tables is taken from **The Composition of Foods** (4th edition), McCance and Widdowson, H.M.S.O., London 1978, and **Composition of Foods**, Watt and Merrill, United States Department of Agriculture, 1963.